American Public Opinion and the Modern Supreme Court, 1930–2020

American Public Opinion and the Modern Supreme Court, 1930–2020

A Representative Institution

Thomas R. Marshall

LEXINGTON BOOKS
Lanham • Boulder • New York • London

Published by Lexington Books
An imprint of The Rowman & Littlefield Publishing Group, Inc.
4501 Forbes Boulevard, Suite 200, Lanham, Maryland 20706
www.rowman.com

86-90 Paul Street, London EC2A 4NE, United Kingdom

British Library Cataloguing in Publication Information Available

Library of Congress Cataloging-in-Publication Data Available

ISBN 978-1-7936-2330-0 (cloth)
ISBN 978-1-7936-2332-4 (pbk.)
ISBN 978-1-7936-2331-7 (electronic)

Contents

List of Figures and Tables

FIGURES

TABLES

Preface

I first began to compare Supreme Court decisions with nationwide public opinion poll questions during the 1980s. At that time, viewing the courts from the perspective of public opinion was a relatively new idea. Far fewer poll questions and far less scholarly research were then available. Since that time, a large and sophisticated academic literature has linked the courts with American attitudes using many perspectives and research methods. Pollsters continue to query Americans' attitudes toward the courts, often focusing on the Supreme Court.

I thank the many authors and pollsters upon whose work this book draws. Their efforts broaden our understanding of how public opinion and judicial decision-making interact. I hope that I accurately describe their work. Any omissions or errors of interpretation are my own. I gratefully acknowledge all those who provided data, answered questions, or commented on this book or on my past articles, books, and papers. I thank my colleagues and the library staff at the University of Texas at Arlington, and my editors and reviewers at Lexington Books.

This book aims at two goals. I update, expand, and reconsider research on whether, when, and why Supreme Court decisions represent American attitudes. The evidence herein relies chiefly on secondary survey research, including several thousand poll questions asked by American pollsters since the 1930s. The appendix lists the poll-to-decision matches so that other authors may reexamine or extend this research.

I also examine Americans' changing perceptions and evaluate current criticisms of the Supreme Court. Many Americans now view the Court as a representative, ideological, and partisan decision-maker, not solely as a legalistic institution. I refer to this widely held view in this book's title. Very likely, this perception will become more widespread in the years ahead. Under these conditions, not surprisingly, the Supreme Court faces rising criticism. Whether changing public perceptions and current criticisms are a good or bad thing for the Court merits careful consideration. I hope this book will encourage that important conversation.

List of Abbreviations

FDA: Food and Drug Administration
GfK: Growth from Knowledge
NORC: National Opinion Research Center
SCOTUS: Supreme Court of the United States
NPR: National Public Radio

Introduction

On June 26, 2015, a large contingent of spectators, demonstrators, and reporters converged at the U.S. Supreme Court building. Most Supreme Court decisions attract few spectators, no demonstrators, and little media attention. That day was different. The Court was to announce a high-profile decision on marriage equality and, as if to heighten the suspense, doing so on the term's final day.

The justices' five-to-four decision in *Obergefell v. Hodges* is indisputably a landmark, but to most Court watchers, the *Obergefell* ruling did not come as a surprise. Two years earlier, the Court, also by a five-to-four vote, struck down that part of the Defense of Marriage Act, a 1996 Congressional law signed by the then-president Bill Clinton, that barred married same-sex couples from receiving a wide range of federal benefits available to heterosexual couples. Justice Anthony Kennedy's majority opinion in the 2013 *U.S. v. Windsor* ruling made it clear that he believed such legislation violated the constitution. Justices Ginsburg, Breyer, Sotomayor, and Kagan joined Justice Kennedy's opinion in *Windsor*, and all five justices still sat on the Court in 2015. The four dissenters in *Windsor*—Chief Justice Roberts and Justices Scalia, Thomas, and Alito—remained on the Court, and their dissents in *Windsor* left little doubt as to their views on the matter. Predictably, all four justices dissented in *Obergefell*.

Obergefell and *Windsor* illustrate four enduring political realities. First, Americans routinely turn their political and economic disputes into lawsuits. This is not new. As long ago as 1835, Alexis de Tocqueville wrote that "there is hardly a political question in the United States which does not sooner or later turn into a judicial one." During the early 1800s, many prominent political disputes reached the Supreme Court, including *Marbury v. Madison*

(1803), *Dartmouth College v. Woodward* (1819), *McCulloch v. Maryland* (1819), *Gibbons v. Ogden* (1824), and *Barron v. Baltimore* (1833).

In recent decades, the proliferation of litigation-oriented interest groups and growing activism from state attorneys general ensured that many hotly contested disputes would become federal-level lawsuits that would eventually reach the Supreme Court. The disputes over marriage equality are not unique.[1] Among the better-known examples from the past two decades are *Kelo v. City of New London* (2005), *Citizens United v. Federal Election Commission* (2010), *National Federation of Independent Business v. Sebelius* (2012), *Shelby County v. Holder* (2013), *Trump v. Hawaii* (2018), *Trump v. Sierra Club* (2019), and *Department of Commerce v. New York* (2019).

Second, as these disputes reach the Supreme Court, the justices will in time make one or more decisions. In *Windsor*, a five-to-four majority of justices overturned an IRS tax policy under the 1996 federal Defense of Marriage Act that barred same-sex married couples from receiving federal state tax exemptions otherwise available to the surviving spouses of heterosexual couples. In *Obergefell*, the same five-to-four majority of justices overturned a two-to-one split decision from a federal appeals court that had upheld state laws in Ohio, Kentucky, Michigan, and Tennessee, limiting marriage to heterosexual couples. True, the justices explain their decisions by offering written opinions couched primarily in legal arguments. Even so, the *Windsor* and *Obergefell* rulings are by any ordinary standard policy decisions. The Supreme Court decides on policies enacted by Congress, the White House, the agencies, state legislatures, state courts, local governments, and sometimes those enacted by popular votes in the states and localities. That Supreme Court justices, like other federal judges, are nominated by the president, confirmed by the U.S. Senate for life ("during good behavior"), never directly elected or reelected, and once confirmed, typically serve for decades until old age or death does not make a Court ruling any the less a policy decision. This is not a new argument. Judicial scholars have taken this position for many years (Pacelle 2002: 12–30; Baum 1988, 1989, 2019; O'Brien 2020: 234–45).

Third, most Supreme Court decisions prevail, if not necessarily indefinitely, typically at least for many years. Some decisions are overturned—rarely by constitutional amendment, more often by statutory changes or by the justices themselves in later years. Particularly likely to endure are rulings that enjoy widespread and growing public opinion support, that are based on constitutional law and so are difficult to overturn, and that can be easily enforced by the lower courts (Hall 2013, 2014). Predictably, *Windsor* and *Obergefell* quickly won compliance. The IRS complied with the *Windsor* decision. Lower federal judges ordered compliance with *Obergefell* where scattered incidents of resistance occurred. Events following *Windsor* and *Obergefell* make it likely that these two decisions will be enduring. Pollsters soon ceased to ask questions about the *Windsor* decision but on *Obergefell* polls showed growing public support for marriage equality.[2] With few exceptions, states and localities quickly fell into line with *Obergefell*. By the year 2020, nearly 600,000 such marriages had occurred. Under these conditions, it seems likely that the *Windsor* and *Obergefell* decision will prevail.

Windsor and *Obergefell* illustrate a fourth important point: Supreme Court decisions better represent some interests than others. Both the *Windsor* and *Obergefell* decisions favored the gay and lesbian litigants and their supportive interest groups who sued the federal government and several states. This view of representation is easy to see. Court watchers often point out which litigants, economic interests, social movements, interest groups, or government interests fare best at the Supreme Court. Nor is this view new. During the 1950s and 1960s, the Warren Court, led by Chief Justice Earl Warren, was very friendly to civil rights litigants and interest groups but not particularly friendly to business. Later, beginning in the 1980s, the Rehnquist and Roberts Courts were much more business friendly (Bednar 2010: 1185; Coyle 2013: 307–24; Epstein, Landes, and Posner 2013a, 2017).

This book looks beyond the litigants and interest groups that are directly involved in a lawsuit; instead it examines how well the Court or the justices represent Americans' views at the grass roots. This view of representative role is also simple and straightforward. Supreme Court decisions and the individual justices' votes often do, but sometimes do not, agree with the preferences of the American public nationwide. Similarly, Supreme Court decisions and the justices' votes may or may not agree with the attitudes of specific demographic or partisan groups of Americans. This concept of representative role can best be measured by turning to modern public opinion polls. This book uses nationwide poll questions since the mid-1930s to move beyond how well litigants, economic interests, social movements, organized interest groups, or units of governments fare at the Court. Instead, the focus is on how well the Court represents nationwide American public opinion or important parts thereof. Chapter 1 describes Americans' changing perceptions of the Court's representative role.

The controversy over marriage equality resonated throughout the nation for over three decades. Not surprisingly, pollsters asked many questions tapping Americans' opinions on the issue. Just six weeks before the *Obergefell* decision was announced, a Pew Research Center survey conducted by Princeton Survey Research Associates reported that a 56-to-39% majority of American adults nationwide favored "allowing gays and lesbians to marry legally."[3] Several other polls conducted at that time used different wording and reported similar results.[4] Thus, the five-to-four *Obergefell* ruling represented—that is, agreed with—majority public opinion. Accordingly, the five-member *Obergefell* majority—Justices Kennedy, Ginsburg, Breyer, Sotomayor, and

Kagan—agreed with a nationwide poll majority. The four *Obergefell* dissenters—Chief Justice Roberts and Justices Scalia, Thomas, and Alito—disagreed with the polls.

Examining representation can be extended further. Modern surveys typically report both nationwide results and results by gender, age, race, education, partisanship, and other demographics. Attitude differences between social and demographic groups are one of three ways in which pollsters seek to "explain" poll results, as are important events and the well-recognized artifacts of survey research such as question wording or the sequence of questions. This book examines both nationwide public opinion and the attitudes of four groups by race, gender, education, and party affiliation.[5] Breaking down nationwide poll results by key subgroups better describes exactly whom Supreme Court decisions and the justices' individual votes best represent.

An example may clarify this point. In the Pew Research Center poll question cited earlier, a nationwide 56-to-39% poll majority favored the *Obergefell* decision. So did majorities of most demographic and political groups. Most self-identified Democrats favored the *Obergefell* ruling (by 65-to-29%). So did a 65-to-31% majority of Independents. Women favored the decision by 60-to-35%. So did men (by 53-to-42%). White non-Hispanic respondents favored the ruling (59-to-37%) as did Hispanics (56-to-38%). By 69-to-26%, those with a college education or more favored the ruling, as did those with some college (56-to-39%). Those with a high school education or less split about evenly (49-to-47% in favor). Only among Republicans and Blacks were majorities opposed. Among Republicans, only 34% favored, while 63% opposed the *Obergefell* ruling. Among Blacks, only 41% were in favor versus 51% opposed. Accordingly, the five majority justices in *Obergefell* represented—that is, their votes agreed with—nationwide public opinion and Democrats, Independents, women, men, whites, Hispanics, and those with some college education or more. The four *Obergefell* dissenters represented Republicans and Blacks. Chapters 3–5 return to the question of how well the modern Supreme Court and its justices represent nationwide polls and key population groups, reporting results from the mid-1930s through the Court's 2020–2021 term.

Many Supreme Court decisions closely match, in substance, one or more timely nationwide poll questions. This book reports on 531 poll matches from the 1930s through the Court's 2019–2020 term. The appendix also lists several additional matches that either occurred or were identified after this book was written. *Obergefell* and *Windsor* illustrate the most frequent result. Most of the Court's full, written decisions agree with nationwide public opinion majorities or pluralities. So do most denials of certiorari, that is, Supreme Court decisions not to hear an appeal from a lower court. Other decisions clearly disagree with public opinion majorities, and in a few instances, the polls are closely divided or yield conflicting results. Chapter 2 describes the poll-matching methods used herein.

THE PLAN OF THIS BOOK

Chapter 1 reviews three questions. The first is historical evidence on the Supreme Court's role as representative institution. The second is recent American views on whether the Court does or should follow public opinion. The third is the wide-reaching normative debate about the Court's representative role. The first and third questions long predate modern public opinion. The second question relies heavily on recent polling evidence. As chapter 1 suggests, the Supreme Court often represents some political, social, or economic interests better than others. The debate over whether the Court does or should represent public opinion, however, remains contentious and unresolved.

Chapter 2 compares six different measurement strategies and outlines this book's approach to studying how well the Supreme Court represents grassroots Americans. The poll-matching method compares specific Supreme Court decisions to timely poll questions on the issue in question. This chapter also describes coding rules, weighting measures, and a simple schema to classify Supreme Court decisions and the justices' votes as either consistent or as inconsistent with public opinion. This book uses poll matching to compare 531 Supreme Court decisions with American public opinion from the 1930s through the Court's 2019–2020 term. This approach is wholly empirical rather than normative.

Chapter 3 turns to the Supreme Court's record of representing public opinion since the mid-1930s. Three-fifths to two-thirds of the Court's full, written decisions agree with public opinion. Denials of certiorari equally often agree with the polls. This record is relatively consistent across time and Courts. Decisions on nearly all issues agree with the polls at least half of the time. On some issues, the Court agrees with public opinion nearly four-fifths of the time. The Court's record of representing public opinion equals or exceeds that of Congress, the White House, the federal agencies, state and local governments, and the lower state and federal courts. As a representative policy maker, the Supreme Court is fully a coequal branch.

Chapter 4 shifts the focus to the justices who served on the modern Court. Some justices much better represent public opinion than do others. This chapter examines representation by the justices' background, ideology, tenure, and partisanship. Chapter 4 names 5 "great" and 10 "near-great" justices on representative role—a new measure of judicial role unrelated to other measures of judicial greatness.

Chapter 5 takes a deeper dive by asking how well the Court and the justices represent Americans by gender, race, education, and partisanship. The modern Court has mostly represented major groups in an even-handed fashion. All 10 groups considered here "win" at least half the time, and, at times, some groups fare much better than that. Not all the justices are so even-handed. This chapter offers each group's purely hypothetical best-case and worst-case Court. The chapter also discusses symbolic representation.

The final chapter summarizes this book's findings and considers the Supreme Court's future as a representative institution. The modern Court's record of representation is relatively positive compared to the lower courts, state and local governments, and the federal government. Public support for the Court remains relatively high compared to Congress and the president. Even so, the dwindling number of ideologically flexible justices, the prospects of an ideologically unbalanced Court, the justices' lengthening tenure, and the justices' increasingly partisan voting patterns raise questions about whether this even-handed pattern of representation will continue. The Court now faces growing criticism. Many proposed reforms would not greatly affect how well the Court represents American public opinion, but some would likely reduce the level of representation.

This book evaluates the modern Supreme Court as a representative institution by asking how well the Court's decisions and the justices' votes represent American attitudes. This is not to argue that the U.S. Supreme Court is unique in this way. Other countries' high courts make important policy decisions that can be compared to public opinion. So do American state and local courts. Many accounts so view American presidents and the Congress. Unelected institutions such as the Federal Reserve Board, the Food and Drug Administration, the Census Bureau, the Centers for Disease Control, and the Securities and Exchange Commission also make important public policy decisions on which poll questions are available. A book can aim for only so much, however, and this book focuses on the modern Supreme Court.

NOTES

1. For a discussion of recent LGBTQ disputes see Bishin, Freebourn, and Teten (2021). For a discussion of media coverage see Colistra and Johnson (2021).
2. Between May 2015 and March 2019, Pew Research Center reported that support for marriage equality rose from 56% to 61% and that opposition fell from 39% to 31%, continuing a pattern of slowly growing support. In 2001, Pew reported 35% in favor and 57% opposed. Gallup polling with different wording and between 1996 and 2021 shows a similar trend. A January 2021 Ipsos/PRRI survey using the wording

"allowing gay and lesbian couples to marry legally" put the numbers at 71-to-28% in favor.

3. The complete poll question is, "Do you strongly favor, favor, oppose, or strongly oppose allowing gays and lesbians to marry legally?" with interview dates of May 12–18, 2015, and based on 2,002 landline and cell phone telephone interviews. All results reported in this book rely on nationwide samples of all American adults unless specified otherwise. These results may be found at https://www.people-press .org/2015/06/08/support-for-same-sex-marriage-at-record-high-but-key-segments -remain-opposed/

4. A June 2015, 10–14 CBS/*New York Times* poll reported a 57-to-35% majority in favor using the question wording, "Do you think it should be legal or not legal for same sex couples to marry?" A Public Religion Research Institute survey, June 17–21, 2015, conducted by Social Science Research Solutions, reported 54-to-38% in favor using the question wording, "Now, we would like to get your views on some issues that are being discussed in the country today. Do you strongly favor, favor, oppose or strongly oppose . . . allowing gay and lesbian couples to marry legally?" Other surveys archived in the iPoll archive reported similar estimates.

5. American pollsters often ask other demographics such as household income; employment status; urban, suburban, or rural residence; or region. Practices vary widely. The four groups reported here are among the most often asked and most consistently coded. Some accounts include income, but consistently coding income since the mid-1930s is exceedingly difficult because some surveys do not ask about income or only do so in broad categories inconsistently so over time or across polls. Education is more often asked and serves as a rough surrogate for income. For a discussion, see Enns and Wlezien (2011), Gilens (2005, 2012), and Gilens and Page (2014).

Chapter 1

Viewing the Supreme Court as a Representative Institution

Exactly whom the American courts best represent is a long-standing issue. Modern public opinion polling began during the 1930s, but disputes over whom the courts do or should best represent go back much further in time. The earliest disputes arose during the colonial period amid growing conflicts between British-appointed colonial governors, judges, and administrators, on the one side, and colonial juries, merchants, consumers, voters, and assemblies, on the other (Bailyn 1974: 32). To Americans today, colonial-era law and the colonial courts may seem puzzling and even chaotic. Skilled lawyers were in short supply in the American colonies and few judges were well educated in law. Plural office holding was common. Some colonial assemblies themselves heard legal disputes. Nor were the legal foundations of colonial law clearly defined. Lawyers might argue from British legal precedent, colonial charters, assembly actions, parliamentary or Board of Trade decisions, equity, natural law, prior colonial court rulings, or local colonial traditions, whichever best suited their clients' interests (Bailyn 1974: 54–63; Friedman 2010: 20–37; Hoffer, Hoffer, and Hull 2018: 15–19).

Disputes over whom the colonial courts best represented played an important role in events leading to the American Revolution. Except in home rule or proprietary colonies, royal governors mostly appointed high-level judges, sometimes bringing in judges from other colonies or from England. In turn, colonial assemblies sometimes used their power to set and pay the salaries of royal governors and judges to gain advantage over judges or to force unpopular judges to resign (Putnam 1997: 23–24). Colonial juries sometimes simply ignored a judge's instructions. In 1734, New York grand juries refused to indict the printer John Peter Zenger; a year later, a trial jury acquitted Zenger in a celebrated libel case, a judge's instructions notwithstanding (Buranelli 1957: 35–49; Putnam 1997: 59–62). Similar cases occurred elsewhere

(Bailyn 1974: 119–20; Middlekauf 1982: 79, 196–198). Many colonial juries and some local judges refused to convict local merchants accused of smuggling (Bailyn 1974: 48; Fowler 1980: 98–101; Middlekauf 1982: 65, 166; Wolkins 1922). Occasionally, public reactions over land disputes or British tax acts led to mob violence against tax collectors and judges (Nash 2005: 57–59, 103–14). After the early 1760s, the rift between colonial and British interests grew larger as colonial courts became increasingly often involved in tax, smuggling, and libel cases.

British colonial administrators and the colonial assemblies also engaged in a second long-running dispute over the colonial courts. This dispute involved whether colonial judges served only at the pleasure of the Crown, and so faced dismissal for ruling unfavorably, or alternatively whether judges, once appointed, served independently of colonial administrators, a practice then commonly described as during good behavior (Bailyn 1974: 92; Smith 1976). Under Parliament's widely unpopular Townshend Acts in 1767 and 1768, the newly anticipated tax revenues would pay the salaries of colonial governors and judges, thus eliminating the colonial assemblies' financial control over governors and judges. The last of the five Townshend Acts in 1768 allowed for trials without juries for accused smugglers in royal naval courts by British-appointed judges (who could collect 5% of penalties imposed).[1] Colonial protests were widespread, sustained, and sometimes violent, just as were earlier colonial protests over the 1764 Sugar Act and the 1765 Stamp Act. A decade later in 1776, the Declaration of Independence listed these disputes among the justifications for rebellion and independence: "[The king] has made Judges dependent on his Will alone, for the tenure of their offices, and the amount and payment of their salaries." After the American Revolution, the debate began anew over the courts' policymaking role and independence. Now free of royal appointees and with the colonial assemblies in full political control, most newly enacted state constitutions gave judges fixed terms of office and barred them from holding other offices such as in the state legislatures (Gerber 2011).

These long-ago disputes illustrate a similar point as do the *Windsor* or *Obergefell* decisions. Judicial decisions are policy choices that inevitably better represent some interests than others. Certainly, there are important differences in studying how well early American courts compare with modern-day courts as a representative institution. The first difference is obvious. One may study whom judicial decisions best represent in a limited way even before or without relying on public opinion polls. Yet studying the courts' representative role without relying on poll questions can only focus on the parties and interests directly involved. During the late colonial period, the increasingly frequent conflicts over judges' appointments, salaries, retention, and rulings pitted colonial litigants, juries, and assemblies against British administrators.

It is impossible to measure precisely how colonial public opinion played into these quarrels. No polls existed during colonial times. One might roughly estimate colonial public opinion by examining jury decisions; town hall meetings, special committees, conventions, and colonial assembly speeches and actions; or speeches, letters, or writings by influential people. Other possibilities include organized group actions, election results, boycotts, petitions, public rallies and protests, newspaper coverage, pamphlets, or assaults and mob violence (Bailyn 1974; Kramer 2004: 24–29, 168; Middlekauf 1982: 57–64, 89–107). Yet absent modern polls, mass public opinion cannot be determined with any great precision.

During these early times, the term "public opinion" meant two very different things. Sometimes the term meant the attitudes of well-educated and influential people (Forbath 2010: 1195–96). Alternatively, the term meant the attitudes of ordinary people, those mostly without much influence or full citizenship, and when so used, the term was often pejorative (Bailyn 1974: 70–74; Forbath 2010; Middlekauf 1982: 171; Nash 2005: 57–59). Either way, early descriptions of public opinion are often exceedingly vague and imprecise and do not reflect the modern-day concept that public opinion includes all adults.

Further, early American society had a limited concept of citizenship. Most adults, including women, the poor, and slaves, could not vote, serve on juries, or hold public office, and their attitudes went unmeasured and largely ignored. This is no small issue. During colonial times, less than a tenth of American adults held suffrage rights (Allan 1948: 95–96). Even by the 1780s, only 160,000 adult white men in a population of nearly four million held enough property to vote in constitutional ratification elections (Randall 2003: 76). Colonial-era judges and juries may have acted in a decidedly representative role, often favoring local colonial interests rather than British administrators. Yet both the measure and the meaning of public opinion were very different from what they are today. This book takes advantage of many social, political, and polling changes in focusing on the Supreme Court's representative role since the mid-1930s.

From early times, normative debates raged over what *should* be the Supreme Court's representative role. Many early American politicians did not view the Court's proper role as representative, at least not in following current public opinion. Alexander Hamilton's essay, *Federalist 78*, set out the consensus view among the constitution's supporters. The federal judiciary would be indirectly constrained by popular opinion since the president would nominate and the Senate would confirm federal judges. Even so, Hamilton saw the federal courts as an effective check on mass public opinion. In Hamilton's view, the federal judiciary would be "an excellent barrier" against the "encroachments and oppressions of the representative body" and "an essential safeguard against the effects of occasional ill humors in the society." A well-educated and learned set of federal judges who enjoyed irreducible salaries and life tenure could resist "dangerous innovations" and "serious oppressions of the minor party in the community." *Federalist 78* laid out an argument for the Supreme Court's power of judicial review, a then-controversial position never explicitly written into the constitution itself (Miller 1959: 200–205; Gerber 2011: 329–43).

Antifederalist opponents of the constitution suspected that Hamilton would be correct and that the federal courts would act as a check on popular opinion, state legislatures, and state courts (Cooke 1982: 54). In almost all the state debates over ratification, antifederalists raised fears that the federal courts would overturn the decisions of state legislatures, state courts, and local juries (Cooke 1982: 54–64; Friedman 2010: 37–41; Gerber 2011: 34–37; Main 1961: 124–60; Mason 1964: 4–13, 104–10). Notwithstanding their complaints, enough states ratified the constitution that it took effect.

Hamilton's largely negative views of mass public opinion were conventional, at least among Federalists, and did not solely reflect Hamilton's own experiences during those tumultuous times. During the 1600s, 1700s, and early 1800s, the so-called classical view viewed mass public opinion as emotional rather than well-reasoned; as easily, often, and quickly changeable; and as violent, coercive, and contrary to more principled views of individual rights (Neumann 1977; Spier 1950; Palmer 1936; Kramer 2012). A more positive view of mass public opinion did not fully emerge until the Jacksonian era of American politics (Forbath 2010: 1196).

Hamilton's support for judicial independence, specifically life tenure during good behavior and irreducible salaries for federal judges, was not entirely theoretical. His views likely reflected his assumptions about who exactly would sit on the newly constituted Supreme Court. From the federal courts' earliest days, a president's impressions of a nominee's political loyalties and what interests a nominee would best represent were important in making nominations (Epstein and Segal 2005: 2–3, 18–27; Shapiro 2020: 12–17). President George Washington made 13 nominations to the Supreme Court, 10 of whom served, and all of them loyal federalists.[2] The second president, John Adams, made four more nominations, three of whom served, each a federalist. All these justices reliably voted to support federalist goals on important rulings, including disputes over judicial review, the federal government, and contracts, discussed next. Several less well-known admiralty and jurisdiction questions similarly favored federal authority (Hoffer, Hoffer, and Hull 2018: 34–50).[3] Presidents Jefferson, Madison, and Monroe, the next three Democratic-Republican presidents, predictably picked Supreme Court nominees whom they thought would support their own policy goals. Together, these three presidents made nine nominations, all Democratic-Republicans, six of whom served; several, however, disappointed their appointing presidents (Abraham 2008: 57–75). In short, from early times, presidents regarded the justices as policy and partisan representatives.

Although the early Supreme Court heard relatively few appeals, many of its key decisions favored the federal government and businesses rather than the states with the Court striking down about six state laws per decade (Whittington 2005: 865). *Hylton v. United States* (1796), an early example, upheld a 1794 federal tax on carriages. More such decisions followed (Rossiter 1964: 93–98). Several key rulings favored the federal government, contracts, and commercial interests over the states, including *Dartmouth College v. Woodward* (1819), extending Contract Clause protections to private businesses; *McCulloch v. Maryland* (1819), upholding the National Bank under the implied powers doctrine; and *Gibbons v. Ogden* (1824), interpreting the interstate commerce clause to favor the federal government rather than the states. These rulings were bold steps for a Court still finding its way (Levinson 1988; Friedman 1998).

These early landmark rulings presaged a long albeit somewhat inconsistent line of such decisions. Over the next century, *Swift v. Tyson* (1842), *Santa Clara v. South Pacific Railway Co.* (1886), and *United States v. E.C. Knight Co.* (1895) were all business-friendly decisions. In *Adkins v. Children's Hospital of the District of Columbia* (1923), the Court went further, striking down a federal minimum wage law for women and children. In *Lochner v. New York* (1905), by five to four, the Court struck down a state maximum-hours law, limiting working hours in bakeries to 60 a week. The majority opinion in *Lochner* outlined a freedom (or "liberty") of contract view of the Fourteenth Amendment that made it difficult for states to regulate wages and working conditions. For three more decades, the Court sometimes followed the *Lochner* doctrine, although the record is inconsistent (Phillips 2000). By the mid-1930s, the Court declared nearly 200 state laws unconstitutional, sometimes under the *Lochner* precedent (Chemerinsky 2014: 98) and sometimes on other grounds (Phillips 2000: 58). Very likely, several of these pro-business decisions were widely unpopular (Powell 1924: 572–73), but lacking modern polls, it is impossible to be certain of any numbers.

Early Supreme Court decisions that better represented some litigants than others were not limited to federalism and commerce cases. Until the Civil War, the Court usually favored slaveholding interests, including disputes over fugitive slaves such as *Groves v. Slaughter* (1841), *Prigg v. Pennsylvania* (1842), *Smith v. Turner* (1849), *Strader v. Graham* (1851), and *Abelman v. Booth* (1859). The 1857 *Dred Scott v. Sandford* decision was the most infamous of these decisions. In Chief Justice Taney's version of that badly divided decision, slaves could not become citizens and owners could bring slaves into the Western territories.[4] Smith (1997: 271) and Graber (2006:

30–32) review the historical evidence, suggesting that a hypothetical public opinion poll at the time—at least a poll conducted among white males but excluding women and Blacks—would likely show that on the question of full Black citizenship, the *Dred Scott* ruling not only favored slaveholding interests but had a popular majority in favor. That the Court regularly favored slaveholders is clear but, of course, no such poll existed.

More questions about whom Supreme Court decisions best represented followed. Shortly after the Civil War, the Reconstruction-era Court faced highly controversial appeals over loyalty oaths, lawsuits brought by prisoners tried under martial law, and appeals over paper money. The Court's initial rulings were seemingly against Northern public opinion and certainly against a decidedly hostile Congress. Soon following were newly passed Congressional acts, jurisdiction-stripping laws, changes in the numbers of justices, and new appointees who promptly voted differently than their predecessors. Friedman (2002a) cites the Reconstruction era as the last in which Congress successfully used Court curbing as a political weapon against the justices.

As this brief review suggests, legal scholars, historians, politicians, and journalists have long viewed the Supreme Court as a political and representative policymaker with some litigants faring much better than others. Until the 1930s, though, it was impossible to show what grassroots Americans thought about specific Court decisions. Not until even later was it possible to tell whether most Americans viewed the Supreme Court as a representative versus a legalistic policymaker. Over time, this changed. Recent polling, described later in this chapter, shows that many, perhaps most Americans now view the Court as primarily a political and representative, not as a legalistic institution. Polling also best shows how the Supreme Court acts as a representative institution in making decisions. This chapter now turns to describing how these views emerged. Chapter 2 outlines this book's methodology. Chapters 3 asks how well the modern Supreme Court represents nationwide public opinion. Chapters 4 and 5 ask whom the modern Court and the justices best represent. Chapter 6 asks how the perception and reality that Court is a representative institution may affect the Court's future.

VIEWING THE COURT AS A
REPRESENTATIVE INSTITUTION

Since its earliest years, Supreme Court decisions better represented some interests than others.[5] How well the Court represents Americans at the grassroots level remained unclear until the mid-1930s. Nor, until recent decades, was polling available on how Americans viewed the Court's decisions. To preview this section, many perhaps most Americans now view the Supreme

Court as a representative, not a legalistic institution. This view occurred in part due to modern public opinion polling and in part due to four other important changes. This section describes each of these changes.

The first change involves the rise of modern public opinion polling beginning during the mid-1930s. During the 1820s, American journalists first conducted so-called straw polls based on a show-of-hands by local voters (Smith 1990). Straw polls usefully forecast which candidates would likely win upcoming elections but suffered from many flaws. Straw polls were often conducted weeks or months before the election and used haphazard and nonrandom sampling methods. Local voters who supported unpopular candidates faced social pressure to remain silent. Many straw polls had large forecasting errors (Robinson 1932).[6] By the early 1900s, some straw polls relied on much larger samples of voters, often interviewing tens of thousands of voters or more, sometimes statewide or nationally, and using mail-back postcards, quick one-on-one interviews conducted on street corners, ballots left at stores, or newspaper inserts. Pre-election straw polls were widely conducted—at least until *The Literary Digest*'s spectacularly incorrect forecast that Alf Landon, the Republican nominee, would win the 1936 presidential election. A few straw polls asked about issues such as Prohibition, veterans' bonuses, and tax cut plans, but none apparently asked questions about lawsuits reaching the Supreme Court (Karol 2007; Robinson 1932, 1937).

During the 1930s, innovative pollsters, including George Gallup, Elmo Roper, and Archibald Crossley, employed better if still flawed quota sampling methods, longer questionnaires, and more frequent surveys (Converse 1987). Their reports gave nationwide results and reported attitudes by respondents' demographics and partisanship. These early pollsters often worked for the media and, not surprisingly, asked about legal controversies that reached the Supreme Court or about the Court itself. Early Gallup polls asked questions on minimum wage laws, the Tennessee Valley Authority, the Agricultural Adjustment Act, foreign war debts, Social Security, the Wagner Act, poll taxes, and other disputes that resulted in Supreme Court rulings. Additionally, during the mid-to-late 1930s, Gallup polls asked over 50 questions about the Court itself and about President Franklin Roosevelt's so-called court-packing plan (Caldeira 1987).[7]

The widespread switch to telephone-based polling during the 1960s and more recently to online polling, advances in computer-assisted interviewing, improved sampling methods, and a growing number of pollsters led to more and better surveys (Berinsky 2006; Berinsky et al. 2011; Converse 1987). By the early 1970s, American pollsters increasingly often asked identically worded poll questions over time, thereby better measuring overtime poll shifts. Since the early 1990s, web availability and online archives, particularly the iPoll archive, made it easier to identify Supreme Court–focused poll questions. The growing popularity of advanced statistical methods and of poll experiments improved the evidence. Chapter 2 returns to these questions.

Since the 1930s, American pollsters have asked well over five thousand nationwide poll questions on the Supreme Court. These poll questions mostly fall into a few categories. About a third of poll questions tap Americans' preferences toward an issue raised in a specific Supreme Court decision. Some such questions explicitly mention the Supreme Court, but most do not. Sometimes pollsters ask the same question repeatedly over time, making it possible to measure attitude shifts. Gallup poll questions on the death penalty, abortion restrictions, or marriage equality are well-known examples. More often, though, pollsters ask only one or two questions tapping attitudes toward a dispute that reaches the Court. From the 1930s through the 1960s, on average, about four Supreme Court decisions annually could be poll-matched with one or more timely poll questions. That figure rose to about eight thereafter. Through the Supreme Court's 2019–2020 term, some 531 Supreme Court decisions can be poll-matched with one or more poll questions. Most such poll questions ask about issues raised in the Court's full, written (merits) decisions; fewer poll questions ask about denials of certiorari. These poll matches provide the evidence on the Court's record as a representative institution and are listed in the appendix.

Many other poll questions ask about Americans' attitudes toward nominees to the Court or toward the justices themselves. Pollsters' interest in the Supreme Court typically spikes whenever a controversial nomination occurs. As a recent example, the iPoll archive lists well over 100 questions on awareness of or support for Justice Brett Kavanaugh's confirmation in 2018. Some questions measure awareness of specific decisions, of the Court as an institution, or of the individual justices. Several series of questions tap confidence in or approval of the Court. Still other poll questions tap Americans' images and beliefs about how the Court should or does reach decisions. These poll questions are discussed later in this chapter. Together, these poll questions help to explain how fully the Court is a representative institution. Without using these poll questions, one could still describe which litigants or interests win at the Court, but one could say little with certainty on how well the Court represents Americans at the grassroots level or how Americans view the Court.

A second change began during the 1930s and 1940s when the justices routinely began to write dissenting and concurring opinions. As early as during the Marshall Court, the justices often disagreed in private conference but seldom wrote dissents or concurrences (Brookhiser 2018: 108, 196–97, 217–19, 236; Henderson 2007). A few dissents or concurrences became famous such as Justice Harlan's dissent in *Plessy v. Ferguson* (1896). Yet dissents remained relatively rare, usually appearing in under 10% of written decisions, notwithstanding disagreements during conference (Cushman 2015; Post 2001). During the late 1930s and 1940s, dissents and concurring opinions became a norm. Well over half of written decisions, per term, now include one or more dissents or concurrences (Bennett, et al. 2018; Corley 2010; Corley et al. 2019; Corley, Steigerwalt, and Ward 2013; Epstein, Segal, and Spaeth 2001; Epstein, Landes, and Posner 2013a: 68; Friedman 2018; Kelsh 1999; Hendershot, et al. 2012; Walker, Epstein, and Dixon 1988). Dissents and concurrences allow the media and the public to see that the justices disagree on how to decide cases and to assess each justice's votes and reasoning. Media coverage on rulings now routinely reports the justices' vote splits. Dissents lead to more media attention but to less positive coverage and to more ideological or political framing in news stories (Zilis 2015, 2017; Salamone 2018). Dissents may also lower public support (Zilis 2015; cf. Salamone 2018; Gibson, Caldeira, and Spence 2005).

A third change involves scholarly thinking. A growing number of studies over many years sought to explain Supreme Court decisions and the justices' votes in terms other than legal tradition. As the number of dissents and concurrences grew, some political scientists tied the justices' voting patterns to their liberal-versus-conservative values (Pritchett 1941, 1948; Truman 1951; Peltason 1955; Murphy 1964; Rosenblum 1955). By the 1960s and the 1970s, this approach became a mainstay of judicial analysis, both for the Supreme Court and for lower federal and state courts. Several accounts considered public opinion. One study asked whether judges are "nothing more than black-robed representatives, responsive to the wishes of their 'constituents'?" (Gibson 1980: 345). Professors Jeffrey Segal and Harold Spaeth's well-known attitudinal model (1993, 1996, 2002) argued that the justices routinely vote their own liberal-versus-conservative values in liberal-versus-conservative disputes (see also Segal, Spaeth, and Benesh 2005). Further, Professors Segal and Spaeth argued that these values are mostly apparent when a justice joins the Court and remains relatively stable over his or her Court tenure.

Some of this work does not view nationwide public opinion as greatly influencing the justices' decision-making (Segal and Spaeth 1993: 239–40; Solomine and Walker 1994; Devins and Baum 2019), but many accounts do. Some accounts do so even for times before reliable public opinion polls existed (Braden 1948; Dahl 1957; Casper 1976; Friedman 1998, 2001, 2002a, 2010; Funston 1975; Lain 2016; Lofgren 1987). By most accounts, the Court occasionally defies but mostly follows popular majorities, as best as current public opinion can be determined. Several accounts compare specific decisions to timely public opinion polls, and report that most Supreme Court and lower federal court decisions agree with poll majorities or at least with poll trends (Barnum 1985; Franklin and Kosaki 1989; Hoekstra 1995; Jessee and

Malhotra 2013; Malhotra and Jessee 2014; Marshall 1989, 2008; Persily, Citrin, and Egan 2008; Cook 1975; Hall 2013; Kritzer 1979; Pildes 2011a; Silverstein and Hanley 2010).

Poll questions can still explore other questions, including legitimacy and representation. Many accounts beginning with Caldeira and Gibson (1992) focus on legitimacy and diffuse support—that is, Americans' support for and willingness to protect the Court from serious threats to its independence. Chapter 6 returns to this question. Questions about representation are common. Page and Shapiro (1983); Johnson and Martin (1998); Clawson, Kegler, and Waltenberg (2001); Epstein and Martin (2010); Burstein (2003); Marshall (1989, 2008); and Shapiro (2011), among others, examine how closely public opinion is tied to Supreme Court decisions. By the public mood measure, discussed further in chapter 2, the Court often but not always responds to Americans' shifting liberal-conservative attitudes (Stimson 1991, 1999; McGuire and Stimson 2004; cf. Johnson and Strother 2021). In some accounts, this results from new appointments (Norpoth and Segal 1994; Cottrell, Shipan, and Anderson 2019), or by other accounts from vote shifts by sitting justices (Casillas, Enns, and Wohlfarth 2011; Flemming and Wood 1997; Giles, Blackstone, and Vining 2008; Mischler and Sheehan 1993, 1994). Justices may be most responsive to public opinion when public support for the Court is low or when a decision is especially salient (Bryan and Kromphardt 2016; Marshall 1989: 82–88; 2008: 48; Strother 2019).

Public opinion has still other links to the Court. When the Court is popular, Congress more favorably treats the Court's requests (Ura and Wohlfarth 2010) and less often engages in Court curbing (Clark 2011). When the Court is popular, the justices strike down more Congressional laws (Clark 2011). Justices write opinions more clearly and use less harsh language if a decision is likely to be unpopular (Black et al. 2016a, 2016b; Wedeking and Zillis 2018). Justices more often attend the annual State of the Union address when the Court's poll ratings are low (Williams and Smith 2018). State-level public opinion, particularly copartisans' opinions, influences Senators' support for Supreme Court nominees (Kastellec, Lax, and Phillips 2010; Kastellec et al. 2015). A nominee's refusal to answer Senators' questions can increase his or her poll support (Chen and Bryan 2018), just as can a nominee's race, ethnicity, or gender (Badas and Stauffer 2017).[8] Several accounts (Brace and Boyea 2008; Hall 1992, 1995, 2014a; Cann and Wilhelm 2011; Cardarone, Canes-Wrone and Clark 2009; Canes-Wrone, Clark, and Semet 2018) expand this discussion from federal to state courts, arguing that judicial elections tie state judges to state public opinion on high-profile issues and sometimes on other issues (Canes-Wrone, Clark, and Semet 2018).

This now-extensive body of work yields several conclusions. Comparing Supreme Court decisions to specific poll questions, three-fifths to two-thirds of decisions reflect timely public opinion or at least poll trends. Whether nationwide public opinion directly influences federal judges, including the justices, independent of what the judge would have otherwise decided, remains much debated (Burnstein 2003; Epstein and Martin 2010). By some accounts, public opinion mostly influences low-salience decisions (Casillas, Enns, and Wohlfarth 2011; Giles, Blackstone, and Vining 2008; Unah, Rosano, and Milam 2015). By other accounts, public opinion mostly influences highly salient decisions and decisions that require enforcement outside the court system (Hall 2014b; Strother 2019). Collins and Cooper (2016) argue that public opinion more greatly influences either extremely high- or low-salience decisions than decisions of middling salience.

Several accounts ask whether Supreme Court decisions themselves influence public opinion on the issues arising in the decision. The evidence is mixed. Decisions that receive one-sided, positive news coverage and commentary may favorably influence public opinion. Other decisions only polarize attitudes. Some decisions lead to at least short-term drops in poll support for the Court's decisions. Overall, very few decisions greatly lead public opinion on the issue in question, at least not so in the short term. Very likely this is because few decisions receive much media attention, because post-decision news analysis and commentary are often mixed or critical, and because many Americans pay little attention to the Court's rulings. Such studies include Franklin and Kosaki (1989); Hanley, Salomone, and Wright (2012); Hoekstra (1995); Engel (2013); Linos and Twist (2016); Malhotra and Jessee (2014); Marshall (1989, 2008); Christenson and Glick (2015a, 2015b); Ura (2014); Kugler and Strahilevitz (2016, 2017); Rosenberg (1991); and Unger (2008). Whether respondents accept a decision may depend on how respondents perceive that the Court reaches its decision and whether a respondent agrees with the ruling (Woodson 2015).

Vigorous debates, often normative and by law school professors, occur over exactly how representative the Supreme Court is. Alexander Bickel's influential book *The Least Dangerous Branch* (1962) renewed a spirited historical debate as to whether it violates democratic norms for life-tenured federal judges to make important policy decisions despite being, once confirmed, largely insulated from the ebb and flow of elective politics. Some of the ensuing, wide-ranging normative debate focuses on early American political thought versus modern interpretations of American democracy (Friedman 1993, 1998, 2002b). Other works, again chiefly by law professors, argue that when both elite and nationwide public opinion are carefully considered, the Supreme Court is rarely counter-majoritarian (Devins and Fisher 2004; Klarman 1995, 1996, 1998; Lain 2004, 2015; Winter 1991). At times, the Court even seems more responsive to public opinion than are the elected branches (Lain 2012; Whittington 2005).

Bruce Ackerman's *We the People: Foundations* (1991), Mark Tushnet's *Taking the Constitution Away from the Courts* (1999), and Larry Kramer's *The People Themselves* (2004) sparked the modern debate over judicial supremacy and popular constitutionalism. A large outpouring of work that followed reevaluated the ties between Supreme Court decision-making and popular views. Such work describes judicial policymaking as much more often consistent with public opinion than not; questions whether judges are particularly good at reading the finer points of public opinion; and argues that few Court decisions greatly influence public opinion (Rosen 2006).[9] Still other work suggests that elected officials sometimes willingly pass thorny issues to the courts and questions whether the Supreme Court can make unpopular policies that are long-lasting.[10]

Nearly all political scientists and many law school professors now agree that the justices mostly vote their own partisan and ideological values in a results-oriented fashion, at least in cases with liberal-conservative meaning.[11] As Lerner and Lund (2010: 1257) write, "In the legal academy, this traditional ideal (that justices will decide disputes based on original intent and precedent) is considered laughable at best and pernicious at worst." Chemerinsky (2014: 342) puts the point bluntly: "liberal and conservative justices alike defer to the legislature when they agree with it and are willing to overrule it when they disagree. Let's stop pretending it is any other way." Writes Barry Friedman (2016: 997): "Poll numbers and public commentary suggest people are seeing (the justices) as ideological and results-oriented rather than reasoned lawgivers." By these views, the Supreme Court is chiefly a partisan, ideological, and (sometimes) representative institution.

In time, these scholarly debates among law school professors and political scientists reached broader audiences. By the 1950s, most introductory college-level American government textbooks described the Supreme Court as a political and policymaking entity, rather than solely as a legalistic institution (Wells 1957: 38). By this author's count, nearly all college-level introductory American government textbooks now describe the justices as voting their partisan and liberal-versus-conservative views on important cases. Two-thirds of introductory American government textbooks compare Court decisions to public opinion. College-level judicial politics textbooks typically include a chapter or two on popular influences on the courts such as interest groups and public opinion. These accounts foster a widespread public perception, described further in this chapter, that the Court is in some way a representative institution (Sherry 2016: 915–16).

The news media routinely attribute Supreme Court decisions to the justices' partisanship and liberal-versus-conservative leanings. As an example, consider the five-to-four decision in *Trump v. Sierra Club* (2019), staying federal district and appeals court injunctions and allowing the Trump administration to divert military funding to continue building the so-called border wall along the U.S.-Mexico border. The *New York Times* described the vote as falling along liberal versus conservative lines (Liptak 2019). So did other major news outlets, including NPR, the *Los Angeles Times*, the *Washington Post*, RealClearPolitics, Fox News, CBS News, the *Wall Street Journal*, the *Boston Globe*, and *USA Today*. *Politico* described the justices' vote as falling along Republican versus Democratic lines. Such media coverage is now common. During the Court's 2019–2020 term, most news stories on major Supreme Court decisions from Associated Press, Reuters, or major outlets such as the *New York Times*, the *Washington Post, USA Today*, and the *Wall Street Journal* described the justices' votes from a partisan or ideological frame. Typically, the media refer to the justices' ideology and partisanship during the first few paragraphs immediately after the headline and after the first paragraph that describes a decision's winners and losers.[12]

A fourth change occurred as American politics grew steadily more polarized along partisan lines and as each president's nominees to the Court more clearly divided along liberal versus conservative lines (Devins and Baum 2019; Pildes 2011b).[13] By today's standards, earlier presidents, including Hoover, Truman, Eisenhower, Kennedy, and Ford, did not focus on a Supreme Court nominee's ideology (Epstein and Segal 2005: 121–39). More recent Republican presidents only nominated quite conservative justices and Democratic presidents only nominated quite liberal justices (Clark 2009). By the early 1990s, this pattern was well established. In turn, Senators, the media, and interest groups made Supreme Court nominations steadily more divisive and partisan.

Throughout American history, many Supreme Court nominations failed. Some failed on a nominee's policy views; others failed on a nominee's weak credentials, disinterest, or personal shortcomings; still others failed on a president's weak standing with the U.S. Senate (Abraham 2008; Gerhardt 2002; Hemel 2021). Recently failed nominations reflected a mix of these reasons, as illustrated by the failed nominations by Presidents Lyndon Johnson, Richard Nixon, Ronald Reagan, George W. Bush, and Barack Obama. From the 1890s until the 1960s, nearly all justices won overwhelming Senate approval, until the 1950s without formal hearings, and even later often on a bipartisan basis notwithstanding a nominee's relatively one-sided policy views (Stone 2010). One-sided Senate confirmations for well-credentialed nominees continued through the early 1990s. In 1986, Antonin Scalia, a very conservative justice, was confirmed 98 to 0. In 1993, Ruth Bader Ginsburg, a very liberal justice, was confirmed 96 to 3. This pattern of bipartisan confirmations thereafter changed as Senate confirmation votes grew steadily more divisive and more partisan. More recently, Justice Sotomayor was confirmed 68 to 31, Justice Kagan 63 to 37, Justice Gorsuch 54 to 45, Justice Kavanaugh 50 to 48, and

Justice Barrett 52 to 48. High-profile, highly polarized nomination battles with nearly all the Senators voting along party lines likely make the justices' policy and partisan views readily apparent to the public (Hulse 2019; Devins and Baum 2017; Whittington 2006).[14]

Partisan battles over Supreme Court nominees now begin well before Senate hearings and roll-call votes. During the run-up to the 2016 presidential election, Senate Republicans refused to allow hearings or a vote on President Obama's nominee, Merrick Garland, then a federal appeals court judge. During the 2020 election season, President Trump nominated and Republican Senators confirmed Justice Barrett to the Court over Democratic Senators' unanimous objections. In turn, some liberal activists aligned with the Democratic Party urged Democratic presidential nominee Joe Biden, if elected, to "pack the Court" by adding extra justices. Even casual followers of national politics are unlikely to miss the point.

Fifth, as older justices retired or died, the vote splits on high-profile, non-unanimous cases grew more partisan and polarized. This pattern is surprisingly recent. Even the controversial decisions from the New Deal era and contentious decisions such as *Bush v. Gore* (2000) did not neatly divide Democratic justices from Republican justices. Only as Democratic presidents picked only liberal justices and Republican presidents picked only conservative justices, did a clear pattern of partisan vote splits on the Court emerge (Devins and Baum 2017). As Epstein and Posner (2018) wrote, "For the first time in living memory, the court will be seen by the public as a party-dominated institution, one whose votes on controversial issues are essentially determined by the party affiliation of recent presidents." As they further note, several major decisions each term fit this pattern. Chapter 5 finds support for the growing perception that the justices vote as partisan figures. Not surprisingly, many Americans view the Court as a partisan and representative body (see Clark 2009; Epps and Sitaraman 2019).

Elected politicians' criticism may also foster growing awareness that the courts are partisan, ideological, and representative. President Trump pointedly criticized federal judges, some by name, including Supreme Court justices.[15] In a well-known exchange from November 2018, President Trump criticized a California federal district judge as "an Obama judge." Replied Chief Justice Roberts: "We do not have Obama judges or Trump judges, Bush judges or Clinton judges. What we have is an extraordinary group of dedicated judges doing their level best to do equal right to those appearing before them. That independent judiciary is something we should all be thankful for." None daunted, President Trump tweeted in response: "Sorry Chief Justice John Roberts, but you do indeed have 'Obama judges,' and they have a much different point of view than the people who are charged with the safety of our country." In February 2020, President Trump tweeted that both

Justices Ginsburg (during a 2016 interview) and Sotomayor (in a written dissent) demonstrated a bias against him and should recuse themselves from upcoming hearings on Trump's tax returns and financial records. Neither did.

Republicans are not alone in their criticisms. In March 2020, Senate Minority Leader Chuck Schumer speaking at a pro-choice rally outside the Supreme Court building said "I want to tell you, Gorsuch. I want to tell you, Kavanaugh. You have released the whirlwind and you will pay the price!" adding that "you won't know what hit you if you go forward with these awful decisions." Schumer's many critics interpreted those remarks as a political or even a physical threat. Chief Justice Roberts complained that the attack was "inappropriate" and "dangerous." Schumer later clarified his words, if not exactly apologized, saying that "they didn't come out the way I intended to" but added that "I'm from Brooklyn. We speak in strong language."

Sometimes a justice's speeches and appearances can reinforce perceptions that the justice favors some groups over others. The justices now make many more public appearances than in decades past (Hasen 2016; Posner 2013; Schmidt 2013; Lerner and Lund 2010). A few justices even become minor celebrities. Media interviews, book tours, and appearances at political groups' meetings can spark complaints that a justice has a liberal or conservative bias or a bias against a particular individual.[16] Within recent years, such complaints have been levied against Justices Ginsburg, Scalia, Alito, Kagan, Thomas, and Sotomayor (Coyle 2013: 253–56, 341–42; Friedman 2016; Sherry 2020; Hasen 2016). Many of the justices' public appearances are not at all controversial. Even the best-traveled justice can avoid controversy in speeches by emphasizing the importance of principled legal reasoning.[17] Doing so may increase the Court's and the justice's own popularity (Krewson 2019; Strother 2019; see also Black, Owens, and Armaly 2016; Glennon and Strother 2019; Strother and Glennon 2021). On balance, though, the justices' appearances are increasingly often controversial compared to past years.

Taken individually, it is difficult to unscramble the impact of these changes and probably futile to try to do so. Taken together, the impact on American public opinion is easier to see. Since the year 2000, American pollsters wrote at least two dozen poll questions asking how Americans perceive that the justices should or do make decisions (Marshall and Connolly 2021). These poll questions provide strong evidence that many, and by some questions most Americans now view the Supreme Court as a representative institution. By large margins, Americans believe that the justices usually cast votes based on their liberal-conservative and partisan loyalties, their personal experiences, or the views of their appointing president, not on law or legal analysis. The next section describes this evidence.

PUBLIC OPINION ON THE COURT'S
REPRESENTATIVE ROLE

Since the mid-1980s, pollsters have often asked Americans how they believe that the justices do or should decide cases.[18] Poll question wording varies greatly, and opinions may differ as to which wording best captures the concept of representation. Pollsters asked most of these questions since 2000 when the *Bush v. Gore* decision greatly raised awareness that the Court sometimes ventures into highly partisan disputes (Biskupic 2019: 127–28). These poll questions provide evidence that many, and by some questions most Americans do not believe that the justices decide cases on legalistic grounds, but rather on partisan and ideological grounds. Americans rank representing public opinion highly on questions that ask how the Court *should* decide cases, but not on questions about how the Court *does* decide.

These poll questions fall primarily into three types. The first asks how the Court *should* make decisions. A second group of poll questions asks how the Court *does* decide cases. Third are several indirect poll questions that ask whether the Court should behave like other representative institutions by being more transparent or having term limits. Other poll questions track the Court's approval ratings before versus after events such as presidential elections or nominations to the Court. By the polling evidence, many Americans no longer view the Supreme Court as a legalistic institution, but rather as one more akin to directly elected policymakers. Academic studies buttress these findings.[19]

The first group of poll questions asks how the Court *should* make decisions. Roughly half of Americans believe that Supreme Court decisions *should* consider majority public opinion, although far fewer think that the Court's decisions *do*. A September 2020 survey for Marquette Law School by National Opinion Research Center (NORC) reported that 44% of Americans said that the Supreme Court should consider public opinion when deciding a case, while 55% said the Court should ignore public opinion. In a July 2015 Pew survey, most (56%) American adults said that when the justices decide cases, they should consider what most Americans think, while 39% said that what most Americans think should not influence the justices. Two Quinnipiac surveys, one in 2003 and the other in 2005, asked national registered voters "How much influence do you think the views of the majority of Americans should have on the decisions by the Supreme Court? A great deal, some, only a little, or none at all?" In 2005, half (50%) of the respondents said a great deal, while 29% said some, 9% said only a little, and 11% said none. The responses in 2003 were 38%, 38%, 10% and 12%, respectively.

Other poll questions report roughly similar results (Sinozich 2016). Between 1987 and 2015, CBS or CBS/*New York Times* nationwide surveys five times asked, "When the Supreme Court decides an important constitutional case, should it only consider the legal issues, or should it also consider what the majority of the public thinks about that subject?" Between 40 and 60% said that the Court should consider what "the majority of the public" thinks.[20]

By several other poll questions, Americans split about equally on whether representative role *should* play a role in Supreme Court confirmation battles. In 2005 and 2018, Gallup asked: "Suppose a nominee for the U.S. (United States) Supreme Court is qualified and has no ethical problems. Do you think U.S. Senators would be justified—or unjustified—in voting against that nominee if they disagree with the nominee's stance on current issues such as abortion, gun control, or affirmative action?" Half of the respondents said that voting against the nominee would be justified—51% did so in 2005 during George W. Bush's presidency and 49% did so in 2018 during Donald Trump's presidency. Nearly as many Americans said it would not be justified—46% in both 2005 and 2018. Perhaps not surprisingly, since both Presidents Bush and Trump were Republicans, Democrats, liberals, low-income, and younger respondents more often supported considering a nominee's policy views.[21]

Similarly, about half of Americans now believe that a nominee to the Court *should* answer policy questions before being confirmed. In a September 2020 Marquette Law School survey conducted by NORC, half (51%) of Americans said that a nominee "should . . . be required to publicly declare how they would vote on controversial cases such as gun rights or abortion rights before they are confirmed to the Court." Nearly as many (48%) disagreed.

Although many, sometimes most Americans believe the justices *should* consider what most Americans think, fewer Americans believe that the justices *do* so. In an April 2012 Kaiser Health Poll about an upcoming decision on the Affordable Care Act, only 7% said that "the views of average Americans" would play the most important role in the justices' decision. Thirty percent said that "the justices' analysis and interpretation of the law" would play the most important role, followed by "whether the justices themselves hold liberal or conservative views" (at 21%), "whether a justice was appointed by a Republican or a Democratic president" (at 16%), "national politics" (at 12%), and the justices' past personal experiences (at 4%). Recombining the answers, 30% said that legalist reasons matter most but 49% said partisan or ideological reasons. Representing the views of average Americans trailed far behind at only 7%.

A July 2014 Kaiser Health Poll asked about a recent ruling on birth control coverage. Only 8% of Americans said that "the views of average Americans" played "the most important role in the justices' decision"—ranking behind four other options: the justices' analysis and interpretation of the law (at 22%), the justices' personal liberal or conservative views (at

17%), the justices' own religious views (at 13%), and whether a justice was appointed by a Republican or Democratic president (at 12%), and ahead only of the justices' gender (at 6%).[22] In short, most Americans believe that the justices decide based on their partisan, ideological, or personal views. Fewer Americans give legalistic reasons, with public opinion trailing far behind.

Still other polling evidence is available. Indirect evidence that Americans view the Court as a representative institution appears in large poll shifts, by partisanship, in the Court's approval ratings following a presidential election (Bartels and Kramon 2021). Since 2000 Gallup polls have regularly asked "Do you approve or disapprove of the way the Supreme Court is handling its job?" Self-identified Republicans' approval for the Court rose by an average of 30% from before until after the 2000 and 2016 presidential elections, both elections that produced a new Republican president, George W. Bush and Donald Trump, respectively. Republicans' approval of the Court dropped by 16% when Barack Obama, a Democrat, won the presidency in 2008. By contrast, self-identified Democrats' approval for the Court rose by 37% from before until after the 2008 presidential election, when a Democrat won the White House, but dropped by an average of 28% for the 2000 and 2016 elections when Democrats lost the White House. By these large and consistent short-term poll shifts, grassroots party identifiers react strongly to partisan switches at the White House. Approval for the Court thereafter typically remains higher among the president's partisan supporters throughout that president's term in office (Zilis 2021). The pattern is typical but not inevitable. Between Gallup's September 2020 and September 2021 polling, President Biden (a Democrat) replaced President Trump (a Republican); nonetheless, grassroots approval of the Supreme Court dropped by 13%, 12%, and 12%, respectively, among Democrats, Independents, and Republicans.

Further evidence that Americans view the Supreme Court from a partisan and ideological frame appears in short-term poll shifts before versus after high-profile rulings tapping a highly partisan issue. For instance, the 2012 *NFIB v. Sebelius*, five-to-four decision upheld nearly all the Affordable Care Act, commonly known as Obamacare. At the grassroots level, the partisan divide between Republicans and Democrats on the Affordable Care Act was the largest in health care history, and in magnitude, nearly as large as the split between Republicans and Democrats in presidential elections (Marshall 2015: 317–22). Predictably, after *NFIB v. Sebelius*, the Court's approval ratings dropped by 14% among Republicans but rose by 11% among Democrats.

Another indirect polling indicator is the growing percentage of Americans who believe that the Supreme Court should base its rulings on what the constitution "means in current times," rather than on what it "meant as originally written." Pew Research Center put the percentage of adults who prefer "current times" as rising from 50% to 55% between 2005 and 2020 with the percentage saying "as originally written" dropping slightly from 46% to 43%. The responses are highly partisan; by 2020, among Democrats, 76% said "current times" but only 32% of Republicans did so.

Not surprisingly, Supreme Court appointments can become a major issue in presidential elections, particularly so if a nomination arises during a presidential year, as happened in 2016 and 2020. In a June 2016 Pew survey, two-thirds (65%) of registered voters named Supreme Court appointments as "very important" in their presidential vote choice, a mid-ranking figure among 15 choices. In an October 2020 Pew Research Center survey, most (64%) of registered voters said that Supreme Court appointments were "very important" when "making your decision about who to vote for in the 2020 presidential election"—a figure lower only than for the economy (at 74%) and health care (65%) but higher than for the coronavirus outbreak (55%), foreign policy (51%), or abortion (44%). Interest in the Court was widespread and bipartisan. In the 2020 Pew survey, 61% of Trump voters and 66% of Biden supporters cited Supreme Court appointments as very important.

At the extreme, when the Court makes a highly partisan decision and when party control shifts at the White House, the Court's approval ratings can change very dramatically. The 2000 presidential election offers an extreme instance. The *Bush v. Gore* (2000) decision, narrowly decided five to four, stopped the Florida vote recount, effectively sending George W. Bush, the Republican, to the White House. From August 2000 to January 2001, Republicans' approval of the Court rose from 60% to 80%, but Democrats' approval dropped from 70% to 42%. Journalists sometimes overlook these large poll shifts by partisanship since large, but offsetting partisan shifts can balance out to only a small net poll shift. In magnitude, these large poll shifts often fade over a year or two.

Grassroots partisan splits over Supreme Court nominations are large and steadily growing over time as Americans increasingly sort themselves into Republicans and Democrats according to their conservative versus liberal values (Downs 2021; Levendusky 2010; Sen 2017).[23] The best evidence comes from a frequently asked Gallup poll question: "Would you like to see the Senate vote in favor of (name) serving on the Supreme Court, or not?" Most recently, for President Trump's three nominees (Gorsuch, Kavanaugh, and Barrett), grassroots Republicans' support exceeded that of grassroots Democrats by an average of 64%. For President Obama's three nominees (Sotomayor, Kagan, and Garland), the partisanship gap averaged 46%. For President George W. Bush's three nominees (Miers, Roberts, and Alito), the partisanship gap averaged 41%. For three earlier nominees polled (Ginsburg, Thomas, and Bork), the partisanship gap averaged only 24%. A president's copartisans are always the more favorable, with a larger gap for each

Chapter 1

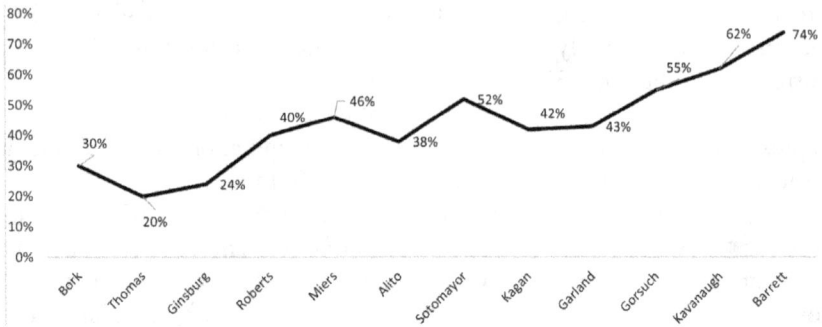

Figure 1.1   Grassroots Partisanship Gaps for Recent Supreme Court Nominees, by President. *Source:* Data collected and analyzed by the author from Gallup polls, 1987 to 2020.

successive president. Americans increasingly view Supreme Court nominees in partisan terms. Figure 1.1 presents these partisanship gaps.[24]

Growing grassroots partisanship gaps should not be surprising. A similar pattern appears, across time, for U.S. Senate confirmation votes on the justices. Historically, highly partisan Senate confirmation votes sometimes occurred, but they did not become a norm until the 2000s. As American politics grew more polarized along partisan lines, a larger number of increasingly diverse interest group became involved, with increasingly early and frequent advertising and grassroots advocacy rather than "inside" lobbying (Cameron et al. 2020; Scherer 2005). Senators use speeches, meetings, and votes to garner support from their home state copartisans (Kastellec et al. 2015; Cameron, Kastellec, and Park 2013; Gelman 2021; Owens 2018; Schoenherr, Lane, and Armaly 2020). Figure 1.2 depicts the partisanship gap in Senate confirmation votes beginning with Justice Thurgood Marshall's confirmation. By the time of President Trump's three nominees, Senate confirmations were very nearly a straight party-line vote (Basinger and Mak 2020).

The polling evidence is consistent. Roughly half and sometimes more of Americans view the Supreme Court as a representative institution and believe that the justices base their votes on partisan and ideological grounds. Depending on the poll question wording, on average, only a quarter to a third of Americans still believe that the justices make decisions on legal grounds.[25] Twice that many Americans believe that the justices make decisions on ideological, partisan, or personal grounds. Fewer than 1 in 10 Americans believe that public opinion is the most important influence on the Court's decisions, although about half of Americans say that public opinion should be very important.

Poll question wording on representative role can vary. These variations usefully show how Americans view the Court's decision-making process. Some

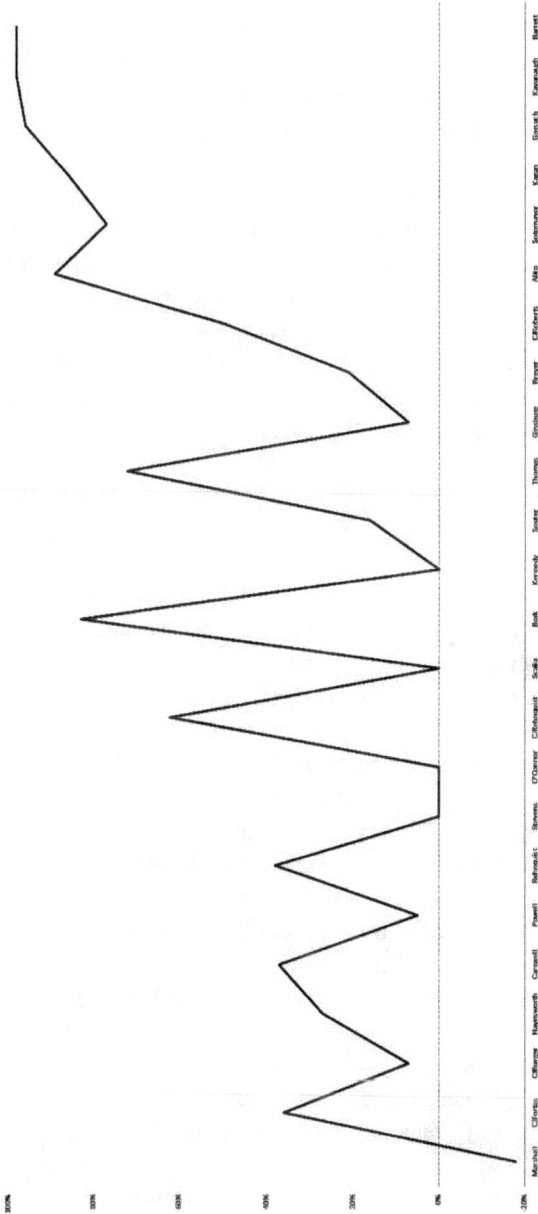

Figure 1.2 Senate Voting Partisanship Gaps for Recent Supreme Court Nominees. *Source:* Data collected and analyzed by the author from U.S. Senate confirmation votes on Supreme Court nominees, 1967 to 2020.

"soft" poll questions ask whether the justices "usually" or "only" or "do" decide cases on legal grounds yet "sometimes" decide on political, partisan, or ideological grounds. On poll questions that use this "soft" question wording, an average of only 17% of Americans say that the justices decide solely on legal grounds, versus 75% who say that political, partisan, or ideological grounds sometimes matter.[26] Other poll questions pose a "harder" choice between how the justices "will" or "did" decide a case, equally describing both the legalistic and non-legalistic options. On these questions, an average of 25% of respondents say that the justices decide on legal grounds, versus 61% who say on partisan, political, or ideological grounds. By either type of question wording, only a quarter or fewer of Americans say that the justices decide on legal grounds, whereas a large majority of Americans say that the justices decide cases on ideological, partisan, and personal grounds.[27] Only if pollsters ask how the Court "mostly" or "mainly" decides cases do as many as half of Americans say that the Court decides on legal grounds as on political grounds. On these questions, an average of 53% say that the Court mostly decides on legal grounds and 47% say on other grounds. Many of the latter questions date back to the early 2000s (Marshall and Connolly 2021).

Breaking down poll results by respondent characteristics is informative. Beliefs that the justices mostly vote along personal, partisan, and ideological grounds are widespread across age, income, race and ethnicity, education, and partisanship. Large poll majorities among all these groups now say that the justices vote on partisanship or ideology, rather than on legal grounds. Where differences between groups appear on poll questions that offer multiple reasons for decision-making, belief in the legal model is the weakest among younger, less well educated, and lower income groups, but higher among Hispanics. However, differences between groups are relatively small and substantively unimportant. No longer do majorities of any large group of Americans believe that the justices decide cases solely on legal grounds.

Although it is speculative to forecast that in future years, even fewer Americans will believe that the justices make their decisions on legal grounds, this seems likely. A little polling evidence is available by comparing poll questions on high-profile issues across time. When *Bush v. Gore* (2000) was decided, several pollsters asked respondents how they believed that the Court would (or soon did) make its decision. Given a choice between legal-based reasons and partisan reasons, on average half (52%) of respondents attributed the decision to legal reasons, versus only 38% who said partisan reasons.

Bush v. Gore is only one of several highly partisan disputes decided by the Supreme Court. About a decade later, a 2012 Kaiser survey asked how the Court would make its decision on the Affordable Care Act's individual mandate provision in *NFIB v. Sebelius* (2012). Only 28% of respondents said that the justices would base their decision on legal analysis without regard to ideology, versus 59% who said the justices' ideological views would influence their decision. In an NBC/*Wall Street Journal* survey, only 35% said the decision was based "mostly on the law" while 55% said "mostly on politics."

Questions that give respondents more options produce lower estimates of legal-based reasons. A 2014 Kaiser survey asked what played the most important role in the justices' recent decision on whether for-profit company health care plans must provide birth control, notwithstanding an employer's religious objections. On *Burwell v. Hobby Lobby* (2014), only 22% of respondents said that the justices' analysis and interpretation of the law were the most important, versus 48% who said the justices' ideological views, religious views, gender, or whether the justice was appointed by a Republican or Democratic president.[28]

Granting the caveat that question wording varies, the percentage of Americans who say that justices decide high-profile, intensely partisan cases on legal grounds may be dropping by an average of 1% or 2% a year. At this rate of change, within a decade, few Americans will still believe that justices decide important cases on traditional legal grounds.[29] Given the changing academic, media, and political trends described earlier in this chapter, this is not surprising.

Still other polling evidence supports these conclusions. Several poll questions ask about transparency and term limits for the Court, both of which are now common features for many other policymakers. A steadily rising percentage of Americans believe that the Court should allow television cameras into their courtroom when hearing arguments in a case. In a mid-December 2000 Gallup/CNN/ *USA Today* poll, half (50%) of Americans said the Court should allow television cameras. In 2013, 61% did—an annual increase of nearly 1%. Support seems likely to grow since younger Americans show the strongest support for televised hearings.

Other polling evidence is available on term limits. Since the mid-1980s, pollsters asked several questions on whether the justices should have term limits, which exist for many but not all popularly elected officials. More Americans favor term limits than life tenure.[30] During the mid-1980s, half to two-thirds of Americans favored term limits for the justices. For poll questions during the 2000s, on average, only 25% of Americans favored life tenure while 69% favored some form of term limits. An October 2021 Grinnell College survey reported that a 62-to-30% majority favored a 15-year term rather than a life appointment. An April 2021 Ipsos/Roper survey reported a 63-to-22% majority in favor of such limits rather than lifetime appointments. As a comparison, a 42-to-38% plurality opposed expanding the Court from 9 to 13 justices. Term limits have broad support across gender and political party affiliation. A little evidence on overtime trends is available. On the most similarly worded questions from CBS/*New York Times* polls, support for term limits slowly grew from 52% in 1987 to 60% in 2012. In short, most Americans prefer that the Supreme Court operate like the way in which many directly elected public officials do.

CRITICISMS OF REPRESENTATIVE ROLE

That so many Americans view the Court as a representative body deeply troubles many Court watchers including some justices. Justice Neil Gorsuch (2019: 6–7) recently wrote:

> Some today perceive a judge to be just like a politician who can and must promise (and then deliver) policy outcomes that favor certain groups. They see the job of a judge as less about following the law and facts wherever they lead and more about doing whatever it takes to "help" this group or "stop" that policy. And it struck me: It's one thing to worry some judges *might* aggrandize their personal preferences over a faithful adherence to the law; but it's another thing to think judges *should* behave like that.

Justice Gorsuch recommends originalism and textualism as the way that justices should decide cases.

Justice Gorsuch is not alone in his criticisms. Many other justices discounted public opinion as a proper influence on how the Court should make decisions (Wilson 1993; Marshall 1989: 36–55).[31] Some justices value the constitution's original meaning over current public opinion (Dorf 2006: 9–20). In *U.S. v. Butler* (1936), Justice Owen Roberts, writing for a six to three majority, outlined the so-called mechanistic jurisprudence argument: "the judicial branch has only one duty, to lay the article of the constitution which is invoked besides the statute which is challenged and to decide whether the latter squares with the former . . . . This court neither approves nor condemns any legislative policy. Its delicate and difficult office is to ascertain and declare whether the legislation is in accordance with or in contradiction of the provisions of the Constitution; and, having done that its duty ends." Justice Sutherland's dissent in *West Coast Hotel v. Parrish* (1937) made the same point: "much of the benefit expected from written constitutions would be lost if their provisions were to be bent to circumstances or modified by public opinion."

In another spin, the Court should at least follow its own past decisions. Many, although not all, precedents presumably conflict with modern-day public opinion, an appointing president's goals, or a justice's own values. The justices often justify decisions on grounds of precedent, although the sentiment is not unanimous. Long ago, legal realists argued that decisions should follow social conditions. Justice Oliver Wendell Holmes summarized the argument: "The life of the law has not been logic; it has been experience" (Holmes 1882). In *Muller v. Oregon* (1908), Louis Brandeis (then an attorney, later a justice himself) filed a legendary legal brief that gave only passing attention to precedent but a lengthy treatment of working conditions. Seven decades ago, Justice William O. Douglas (1949) argued that *stare decisis* was an overrated idea compared to timely public opinion and current circumstances. Later accounts update and expand such arguments (Pohlman 2020; Justice Thomas, concurring in *Gamble v. United States* (2019); Barrett 2003, 2013, 2017). Justices often follow their own past votes on a dispute notwithstanding that their past votes were dissents (Brenner and Spaeth 1995; Hansford and Spriggs 2006; Segal and Spaeth 1996; Schauer 2019; Spriggs and Hansford 2001). Chapter 3 evaluates the link between overturning precedents and public opinion.

Beginning in the late1930s and 1940s, several justices outlined another view in arguing that the Court should protect unpopular groups from majority public opinion. In the well-known language in footnote 4 of the majority opinion in *United States v. Carolene Products Co.* (1938), Justice Stone argued that in future cases, the justices might offer counter-majoritarian protections for unpopular religious, racial, and "discrete and insular minorities." In *Chambers v. Florida* (1940), a coerced confessions case, Chief Justice Hughes, for a unanimous Court, wrote that the federal courts served as "havens of refuge for those who might otherwise suffer because they are helpless, weak, outnumbered, or because they are nonconforming victims of prejudice and public excitement." In *West Virginia Board of Education v. Barnette* (1943), a flag salute case involving Jehovah's Witnesses children, Justice Jackson, for a six to three majority, wrote:

> The very purpose of a Bill of Rights was to withdraw certain subjects from the vicissitudes of political controversy, to place them beyond the reach of majorities and officials and to establish them as legal principles to be applied by the courts. One's right to life, liberty, and property, to free speech, a free press, freedom of worship and assembly, and other fundamental rights may not be submitted to vote; they depend on the outcome of no elections.

Many justices criticized the idea that the Court should act in a representative and majoritarian manner. A classic statement is Justice Black's dissent in *Dennis v. United States* (1951), a case about Communist Party organizers during the Cold War era. In dissenting against the defendants' convictions, Justice Black wrote: "Public opinion being what it now is, few will protest the conviction of these Communist petitioners. There is hope, however, that, in calmer times, when present pressures, passions and fears subside, this or some later Court will restore the First Amendment liberties to the high preferred place where they belong in a free society."

Several other justices denied that public opinion should influence Supreme Court decisions. Dissenting in *Planned Parenthood of Southeastern Pennsylvania v. Casey* (1992), Chief Justice Rehnquist wrote that "the Court's duty is to ignore public opinion and criticism on issues that come before it." Rehnquist added:

> Surely even the suggestion (of relying on public opinion to decide controversial cases) is totally at war with the idea of "legitimacy" in whose name it is invoked. The Judicial Branch derives its legitimacy not from following public opinion, but from deciding by its best lights whether legislative enactments of the popular branches of Government comport with the Constitution. The doctrine of *stare decisis* is an adjunct of this duty and should be no more subject to the vagaries of public opinion than is the basic judicial task.

The justices can be inconsistent on the issue (Marshall 1989: 36–54; 2008: 8–14; Wilson 1993). Chief Justice Rehnquist (1986) elsewhere wrote that the justices were not immune to public opinion. So did Chief Justice Warren (1955).[32] So did Justice Scalia (O'Brien 2020: 336–38). Some Court watchers fear that the Court, so popularly viewed, will lose its aura of legal and moral legitimacy (Epps and Sitaraman 2019), although others downplay the risk. Most Court decisions that refer to public opinion are positive in tone with public opinion sometimes used as a standard for interpreting constitutional protections. For example, in *Rakas v. Illinois* (1978) Justice Rehnquist's majority opinion held that "legitimation of expectations of privacy by law must have a source outside of the Fourth Amendment, either by reference to concepts of real or personal property law or to understandings that are recognized and permitted by society."

Outside the Court, many observers have criticized the idea that the justices' decisions should reflect majority opinion. Few critics put the argument more forcefully than Erwin Chemerinsky (2014: 8–10). To Chemerinsky, the Court should, but often fails to, protect unpopular individuals against public officials and popular majorities. Protecting unpopular groups, not representing popular majorities, should be the Court's primary duty: "The primary reason for having a Supreme Court . . . is to enforce the Constitution against the will of the majority. . . . The two preeminent purposes of the Court are to protect the rights of minorities who cannot rely on the political process and to uphold the Constitution in the face of any repressive desires of political majorities" (at 9–10). In reviewing recent decisions involving accused terrorists, Fiss (2015: 92) makes a similar argument: "The Court is expected to protect the values of the Constitution from transient majorities and the officials who serve them."[33]

In criticizing judicial minimalism, described next, Siegel (2005: 2014) argues that "leaving questions to the majoritarian political process is not an inherent good in a democratic society."

Other accounts give at least qualified (sometimes highly qualified) praise for the concept of representative role as a normative theory. One advocate of judicial minimalism reviews several reasons why judges should weigh public opinion, at least at the extremes (Sunstein 2007). Sunstein's reasons range widely and include purely strategic reasons such as avoiding legislation or a constitutional amendment that would undo a decision, perhaps permanently so; the effects of outraged public opinion on upcoming elections; judges' inability to enforce an unpopular decision; and the desire to avoid public hostility. Other reasons include respecting the public's wider experience with an issue, the public's better ability to identify problems with a ruling's consequences, or the belief that judges (including Supreme Court justices) should seldom interfere with elected policymakers' decisions.

Viewing the Court and its justices as representatives of public opinion may be unsettling in still other ways. Representative role is a time-bound concept that compares Supreme Court decisions and the justices' votes to polls conducted at the same time of the decision. Some decisions that are popular in the polls when announced may later become decidedly unpopular. Further, representative role is apparently not a concept much valued by academic and legal scholars. In chapter 4, several justices who rank as "greats" or "near-greats" on representative role only rank as average or below average on other measures of judicial greatness. Furthermore, several justices widely regarded as "great" or "near-great" rank as only average or below average on representative role. Chapter 6 asks, if scholars and the public alike view the Supreme Court as simply another representative policy maker, will the future Court be worse off in terms of its political capital?

This book treats representation as an empirical concept. Taking an empirical approach is very different from taking a normative approach. The normative concerns described in this chapter are undoubtedly of interest. There is a long normative tradition that the justices *should* nearly always defer to the popularly elected branches whose decisions presumably reflect popular opinion (Sunstein 1999; Pildes 2011a; Bickel 1962). Early such views long predate modern public opinion polling (Thayer 1893). Other normative theories take the opposite view. This book looks at public opinion from a different perspective—that is, by using timely public opinion polls as the sole indicator of popular thinking. Chapter 3 examines how closely elected policymakers, versus the justices, represent contemporary public opinion. If anything in this book inadvertently suggests that judicial deference to popular majorities is— or, alternatively, is not—the preferable course that the Court and its justices *should* follow, that is entirely unintended.

CONCLUSION AND DISCUSSION

Many and by some poll questions most Americans now perceive the Supreme Court as a representative institution whose decisions do or should follow public opinion or the justices' partisan, ideological, and policy views. This view is not wholly recent. Historically, the Supreme Court always represented some political, social, or economic interests better than others. Since the 1930s, several changes, including modern polling, made it possible to study the Court's representative role from the grassroots level. Many academics, journalists, interest group advocates, and politicians now so view the justices. The justices' confirmation fights now fall primarily along partisan lines and divided Court rulings often split closely along party lines. That most Americans follow all this is not surprising. Chapter 2 turns to six different approaches by which the Supreme Court's representative role can be measured.

NOTES

1. This practice was not new. Colonial governors had received one-third of smugglers' forfeitures; officials making the seizure received another third; the colony received the remaining third minus costs to informers (Middlekauf 1982: 84–86).

2. Early confirmation practices differed from modern-day practices. Several early nominees were confirmed by the Senate but then declined to serve, and a few nominees withdrew from consideration. Other early nominees lost Senate confirmation votes or had their Senate confirmation votes indefinitely postponed.

3. The Supreme Court never decided the dispute that most clearly divided Federalists and Democratic-Republicans, the 1798 Alien and Sedition Acts.

4. Graber (2006) reviews public reaction to the *Dred Scott* ruling.

5. Abraham (2008) and Shapiro (2020) review early presidents' motives in picking justices.

6. Aside from straw polls, other forecasts of upcoming candidate or issue elections came from newspaper editors, elected officials, party-run canvassing among voters, and early election results (Kernell 2000; Robinson 1936).

7. Frequent polling on the Court's popularity led to a shift in academic, popular, and judicial thinking about how best to measure the Court's legitimacy, substituting popular approval for legal expertise (Bassok 2013, 2016). Arguably, frequent and better polling changed the way Americans think about themselves (Igo 2007) and about public opinion (Forbath 2010).

8. Christenson and Kriner (2017) offer experimental evidence that even the threat of judicial challenge reduces public support for a president's unilateral action.

9. For reviews of this extensive literature, see Knowles and Toia (2014); Ansolabehere and Persily (2008); Lain (2012); Persily and Lammie (2004); Persily, Citrin, and Egan (2008); Rosenberg (1991); and Yamomoto (2018). For earlier work, see Braden (1948).

10. See Devins (2004, 2017); Graber (1993); Kastellec 2016); Rosenberg (1991); Salzberger (1993); and Whittington (2005). Martens (2007) reviews this extensive literature.

11. The justices also weigh jurisprudential issues when making decisions at the certiorari or full-decision (merits) stage, particularly conflicts between circuits or lower court decisions that overturn federal laws or precedent. See Bailey and Maltzman (2008); Black and Owens (2009); Hammond, Bonneau, and Sheehan (2005); Hansford and Spriggs (2006); and Perry (1991).

12. Media coverage seldom refers to the justices' ideology or partisanship when decisions do not follow a liberal-versus-conservative vote split. A recent example is coverage on the June 2020 ruling, 8-1, in *United States Patent and Trademark Office v. Booking.com B.V.* (2020), on trademarking common names as a dot com.

13. Presidents now usually also pick well-vetted, highly ideological judges for the federal appeals and district court appointments. See Devins and Baum (2019); Ruiz et al. (2020).

14. Krewson and Owens (2021) review recent literature and employ a conjoint survey experiment, reporting that a nominee's qualifications and partisanship, and views on originalism, precedent, or the "living Constitution" affect public views.

15. Collins and Eshbaugh-Soha (2019) compare President Trump's comments on federal judges and Supreme Court decisions with comments of other presidents. For experimental evidence on the effect of the Trump tweets, see Kromphardt and Salamone (2021).

16. Growing social media increases the number of such incidents. In October 2019, the president of a conservative advocacy group, the National Organization for Marriage (NOM) tweeted a photo of himself meeting with Justices Brett Kavanaugh and Samuel Alito, claiming to have had a "great day" at the Court. The NOM is often involved in disputes that reach the Court and the group filed amicus briefs in cases then under review. Critics alleged impropriety, asking that those amicus briefs be withdrawn or that the justices recuse themselves; neither, however, occurred. Only a week earlier, Justice Kagan gave a talk at the University of Colorado Law School, notwithstanding other branches of that University having filed amicus briefs in a pending case involving the legal status of noncitizens brought to the United States as children.

17. Describing the Court as making principled, nonpartisan decisions does not necessarily insulate a justice from complaints. In 2021, Justices Breyer and Barrett made highly publicized appearances so describing the Court but failed to quell many of the Court's critics as the Biden Commission began its review of proposed reforms (Howe 2021; Liptak 2021).

18. A few differently worded poll questions from earlier years show closely divided opinions. A Gallup poll question from 1946 asked: "Some people say that the Supreme Court decides many questions largely on the basis of politics. Do you agree or disagree with this?" Of all respondents, 43% agreed, 36% disagreed, and 21% gave no opinion.

19. For similar results, some based on experiments, others based on polling, see Scheb and Lyons (2000); Hansford, Intawan, and Nicholson (2018); Nicholson and

Hansford (2014); Gibson and Caldeira (2011); Bartels, Johnston, and Mark (2015); Bartels and Johnston (2012, 2013); and Gibson and Nelson (2015). Chapter 6 returns to this issue.

20. A 1997 survey (Scheb and Lyons 2000, 2001) reported that 31% of Americans said that "what the majority of the public favors" should have "a large impact" on Supreme Court decisions; 36% said, it should have "some impact"; and 31% said, "no impact." When asked how much impact public opinion does have, the results were 15%, 49%, and 37%, respectively.

21. Using a similar question, a September 2020 Marquette survey conducted by NORC reported that 41% of respondents said that the U.S. Senate would be justified in voting against a nominee "simply because of how they believe the Justice would decide cases on issues such as abortion, gun control, or affirmative action" even if the nominee "is qualified and has no ethical problems." Fifty-eight percent said this would not be justified.

22. Twenty-two percent of respondents said none, don't know, or volunteered another answer.

23. Little polling evidence on partisanship gaps is available for earlier nominees, many of whom were not controversial. Some nominations did spark a grassroots partisan divide. Soon after Justice Hugo Black, the first of FDR's appointees and a U.S. Senator from Alabama, was confirmed, his past membership in the Ku Klux Klan became known. Soon thereafter, a Gallup question asked: "Should Justice Hugo Black resign from the Supreme Court?" Only 36% of Democrats but 61% of Republicans said yes—a moderately large partisanship gap of 25%. Justice Black did not resign.

24. No poll questions are available for Justices Souter and Breyer.

25. Gibson (2012) and Bonneau et al. (2017) support such findings using state-wide, student, or M-Turk samples.

26. Such mixed views are neither recent nor unique to the federal courts (Bybee 2010: 10–22).

27. Some exceptions appear. A September 2019 survey for Marquette Law School asked, "In general, what most often motivates Supreme Court justices' decisions . . . Mainly politics, mainly the law?" and reported 36% (politics) versus 64% (law). Very similar wording by Quinnipiac among national registered voters in 2018 and 2019, however, reported 50% and 55% (politics) versus 42% and 38% (law), respectively. Immediately prior to the 2012 *NFIB v. Sebelius* (2010) ruling, an M-Turk sample reported that 52% of respondents said that legalistic reasons rather than five personal, ideological, or partisan reasons would best explain the Court's upcoming decisions. Immediately after the ruling, those saying a legal reason increased by 4% (Christenson and Glick 2015b: 407–13).

28. In the 2014 Kaiser Poll, conducted by Princeton Survey Research Associates International, only 8% said the views of the average Americans were the most important, and 22% said none, something else, don't know or refused.

29. Less polling evidence is available on low-profile and less highly partisan conflicts. For an example: see Woodson (2015). Experimental evidence would be welcome.

30. Poll support for limiting the justices' length of tenure may long predate the 1980s although early polls did not ask that question. Several poll questions from the 1930s asked about adding new justices or setting mandatory age limits for the justices, but not about term limits, per se. Two-thirds or more of Americans then favored setting a mandatory retirement age for the justices with an age between 70 and 75 as the most common preference (Cushman 2002: 67–74; Caldeira 1987). Hemel (2021: 134–35) reviews arguments for age limits.

31. Even so, since the mid-1930s, three-quarters of Supreme Court opinions that mentioned public opinion are positive in tone. The most common positive mention is that speech or action fosters a better-informed public opinion. This perspective is also frequently debated in legal circles (Meiklejohn 1961; Post 2011; and Tushnet, Chen, and Blocher 2017). Also common are mentions describing contemporary public opinion as an adequate check on government policy or mentions that law and policy should reflect evolving public opinion. Only a fifth of mentions refer to public opinion as a threat to rights (Marshall 2008: 8–14). Breyer (2016) offers an example of a justice's positive mention of public opinion.

32. In a *Fortune* magazine article, Chief Justice Warren wrote: "Our judges are not monks or scientists, but participants in the living stream of our national life steering the law between the dangers of rigidity on the one hand and formlessness on the other. . . ."

33. Court watchers often make such arguments. For a review of decisions on poverty, see Cohen (2020).

Chapter 2

Measuring the Supreme Court's Representative Role

How best can one compare Supreme Court decisions to public opinion? That question has long concerned Court watchers who have devised several methods to do so. This chapter describes six different approaches, each method with its own strengths. The first five methods include the historical method, the case study method, comparative case studies, experiments, and the public mood measure. The sixth method, poll matching, constructs a database from nationally representative poll questions that closely match, in substance, a wide variety of modern Supreme Court decisions. This chapter explains these six strategies, particularly focusing on the poll-matching method used in the remainder of this book.

COMPARING PUBLIC OPINION AND
SUPREME COURT DECISION-MAKING

The Historical Method

This method is the oldest approach to comparing public opinion with Supreme Court decisions. The historical method estimates public opinion without using any poll questions at all.[1] Assessing attitudes before the 1930s requires using indirect measures of public opinion such as public protests, newspaper coverage and editorials, election returns, jury decisions, state laws, or Congressional and White House speeches and actions.

Barry Friedman's influential account, *The Will of the People*, compares Supreme Court decisions with public opinion beginning with early American times.[2] As Professor Friedman describes, the historical method has many strengths and several limits. Describing Supreme Court decisions is relatively straightforward, but measuring public opinion, historically, is more complicated. Elite opinion is easier to measure than is mass public opinion. For legal disputes that primarily affect a single state, it is easier to describe public opinion statewide than nationwide. Accounts that use the historical method typically focus on the Court's best-known, most controversial decision such as, during early times, *Marbury v. Madison* (1803), *McCulloch v. Maryland* (1819), or *Gibbons v. Ogden* (1824). Comparing low-profile decisions with public opinion is more difficult. Even when it is possible to describe mass public opinion, the evidence is often limited, impressionistic, and based on newspaper coverage, speeches or writings by prominent public leaders, election returns, protests, or presidential, congressional, or state legislative actions.

Some historical research takes a different approach. Robert Dahl's often-cited essay (1957) evaluated the Supreme Court's historic role in American democracy. Lacking polls for most of American history, Dahl turned to 78 Supreme Court decisions that held a recently enacted federal law to be unconstitutional. Dahl posited that recently enacted federal laws (a "law-making majority") are the best available measure of contemporary public opinion. Dahl then tracked the fate of these 78 Court rulings. Congress or subsequent Court rulings usually reversed decisions that overturned important, recently enacted federal laws. Dahl concluded that the Court is seldom long out of line with a law-making majority and thus with contemporary American attitudes. As Dahl described it, the Supreme Court is typically a part of the "dominant national alliance." Two decades later, Jonathan Casper (1976) updated the Dahl hypothesis for the years 1958 to 1974. During these times, the Court more often and more successfully overturned federal and state laws, often doing so in defense of unpopular minorities, and despite scant support from elected officials or public opinion (see also Hall 2013; Pildes 2011a, nn. 33, 78). Casper used a historical approach, as had Dahl, rather than using poll questions, although poll questions were, in fact, available for many rulings that Casper considered.

The Case Study Method

A second approach examines poll questions on a particular Supreme Court decision or on several closely related cases. Case studies merit careful attention. Several have attained status as classics.[3] Most case studies focus on landmark decisions, disputes on which pollsters most frequently ask questions. Some case studies focus on a short time frame; others look across longer periods. An early case study by Neil Vidmar and Phoebe Ellsworth (1974) examined Americans' attitudes toward the death penalty, pointing out that poll support for capital punishment greatly depends on the poll question wording, the specific crime in question, the years involved, and respondents' demographics, partisanship, or views on retribution. More recently,

Baumgartner, DeBoef, and Boydstun's (2008) case study on the death penalty examined the relationship between anti-death penalty activists; the media; juries, district attorneys, and judges; Congressional actions; and public opinion. That study concluded that anti-death penalty activists successfully changed media and other elites' views of the death penalty, leading to a sharp decline in the number of executions, and with public opinion slowly following key events.

Case studies have considered many types of decisions. Barry Cushman (2002) reexamined Gallup and Roper polls on several key decisions during the New Deal period, finding poll support for some New Deal policies such as child labor laws, but not other proposals. To Cushman, the Court at the time was not so greatly out of line with public opinion as is sometimes perceived. A study of the 1962 school prayer decision *Engel v. Vitale* reexamined numerous poll questions, the reactions of political elites and activists, and the justices' response (Lain 2015). Such thoughtful case studies provide an in-depth, critical look by comparing different poll questions, different groups of respondents, and different rulings. Well-conducted case studies can challenge misconceptions about public opinion based on an overly casual reading of the polls (Lain 2004: 1422–24; 2015: nn. 378, 385). Some case studies seem intended to give advice to attorneys and political activists. As a general note of caution, one should not carelessly generalize case study results beyond the topic and times covered.

Comparative Case Studies

A third approach compares case studies across several different types of Supreme Court decisions. The rulings so examined usually fall within a relatively short time, although some such studies include longer times. From the earliest examples, most comparative case studies rely on poll questions as evidence of public opinion (Casper 1972; Weissberg 1976; Barnum 1985). The 14 case studies in *Public Opinion and Constitutional Controversy* (Persily, Citrin, and Egan 2008) assess the influence of public opinion and Supreme Court decision-making, each on the other, across topics as diverse as desegregation, abortion, flag burning, criminal due process, government takings of private property, and others. Results from comparative case studies show that most Supreme Court rulings reflect majority public opinion or at least reflect ongoing poll trends. Even so, some rulings clearly disagree with public opinion (Hall 2013: 157; Malhotra and Jessee 2014; Ansolabehere and White 2020). A few rulings favorably influence public opinion in the short term, while a few rulings do so over the long term; many rulings seem not to influence public opinion at all (Kugler and Strahilevitz 2016, 2017; Linos and Twist 2016).

Experiments

A fourth approach includes the growing number of polling experiments that compare attitudes to Supreme Court decisions. Some experiments use nationwide surveys, while others rely on nonrandom samples or convenience samples. Survey experiments divide respondents into at least two randomly divided groups, providing different information to each group. Some experiments include a control group; some do not. Most such accounts consider a single Supreme Court decision; a few consider two or more decisions. Many survey experiments take as a dependent variable respondents' support for the Court or for specific decisions. Independent variables might include the tone of media coverage or interest group commentary, the decision's reasoning, whether the vote was divided or unanimous, or whether the decision upheld or overturned precedent (Farganis 2012; Zink, Spriggs, and Scott 2009; Zilis and Borne 2021). Other independent variables include whom the decision benefits (Zilis 2020) or the decision's or the authoring justice's ideological or partisan direction (Boddery and Yates 2014; Clark and Kastellec 2015; Nicholson and Hansford 2014). Some experiments use counterarguments to test how flexible respondents' attitudes are (Linos and Twist 2016; Kugler and Strahilevitz 2016, 2017). Polling experiments are increasingly popular and usefully provide information on situations, whether hypothetical or real, that poll questions do not cover (Canelo, Hansford, and Nicholson 2018). As a caution, read carelessly, experiments may overstate the real-world strength of relationships, since many Americans misunderstand or pay little attention to Supreme Court decisions.

The Public Mood

A fifth approach is quite different from those just described, most compare specific decisions with poll questions on that topic. Instead, the well-known public mood measure begins by tracking overtime shifts in liberal-versus-conservative American attitudes across a broad array of frequently asked, consistently worded poll questions since the early 1950s (Stimson 1991, 1999, 2012; McGuire and Stimson 2004; Ellis and Stimson 2012). This produces the public mood, a measure approximating a ratio-level measure tapping the nation's liberal-versus-conservative leanings. Sometimes the American public mood is more liberal, at other times, more conservative. The most liberal times fall around 1961, 1973, 1988, 2003, and 2018; the most conservative times fall around 1952, 1968, 1979, and 1994. So, too, the Supreme Court sometimes mostly hands down liberal decisions, but at other times, mostly conservative decisions. Accordingly, one can compare shifts in the public mood to shifts in the Court's decisions or in the individual justices' votes. Most such accounts use nationwide public mood; a few accounts use issue-specific moods (Bryan 2020; Bryan and Kromphardt 2016).

Scholars often use the public mood measure, which allows one to compare how responsive the Supreme Court, Congress, or the President is to public opinion shifts. Often, but not quite always, the Court's liberal-versus-conservative decision-making pattern lags only a few years behind public mood shifts (McGuire and Stimson 2004). As a limitation, many poll questions used to construct the public mood tap issues that seldom arise in Supreme Court decisions. The reverse is also true; the Court's decisions tap many issues not among the public mood's poll questions. The public mood measure uses repeat-item poll questions from both academic surveys and commercial pollsters. Since it relies on frequently asked poll questions, the public mood measure is not especially sensitive to the Court's changing issue agenda.

THE POLL-MATCHING METHOD

All these five methods usefully compare Supreme Court decision-making with American public opinion. This book outlines a sixth approach, the poll-matching method, which compares (or matches) nationwide public opinion to a wide variety of Supreme Court decisions. This method matches each Supreme Court decision with a timely poll question on the issue raised in that decision. In part, poll matching extends the case study approach, described earlier, but differs by seeking to compile, insofar as it is possible, all Supreme Court decisions that match a near-in-time, well-conducted nationwide poll question. Pollsters have often asked questions about controversies that reach the Court, and pollsters continue to do so today. The earliest poll-matched decisions date from the 1930s; the latest decisions examined here are from the 2019–2020 term. The number of poll-to-decision matches has grown steadily over the decades. This book examines 531 poll-to-decision matches listed in the appendix, as well as a few more recently identified matches. Instead of describing the poll matches, one by one, as does the case study method, the poll-matching method constructs a database, and looks for statistical patterns across different types of rulings, different times, and different justices. Classifying so many different decisions as either consistent or inconsistent with public opinion (and occasionally, as unclear) requires several coding rules and reweighting procedures, described below.

Using a database with so many poll-to-decision matches has several advantages. A major advantage is that the term "public opinion" has a clear meaning: it is always and only an estimate of nationwide adult Americans' attitudes as measured through a timely poll question. The evidence is poll-driven, statistical, and based on patterns across time, decisions, votes, and public attitudes. There is thus no need to jump through the hoops and hurdles of interpreting elections, state laws, jury verdicts, Congressional bills, presidential speeches, popular protests, news coverage, or newspaper editorials.[4] Because the number of poll matches is large, the results herein are stable and unlikely to change with a few additional poll matches. Poll matching can examine American attitudes taken as a whole or as the attitudes of populous groups such as men and women; Blacks and whites; high, medium, and low education groups; or Republicans, Democrats, and Independents. The discussion of marriage equality in chapter 1 offers an instance.

Compared to the public mood measure, poll matching directly compares American attitudes with a Supreme Court decision on the specific issue raised in a ruling. One can use poll matching to construct a match even with only a single poll question on a controversy, as often occurs. The poll-matching method draws on a wide variety of poll questions using nationwide adult samples from both commercial and academic pollsters. Once constructed, one can use the database for other scholarly purposes. Further, one can use poll matching to explore purely hypothetical circumstances. For example, how often would Court rulings agree with public opinion *if* there were one additional conservative or alternatively, one additional liberal vote? *What if* the Court more often practiced judicial restraint in favor of federal, state, or local laws and policies? *What if* the Court never overturned its own precedents?

Poll matching has several limitations, some of which must be accepted. Constructing a database necessarily sacrifices the rich in-depth analysis offered by the historical method or by careful case studies. As well, poll matching codes only the result but not the reasoning of a Supreme Court decision or of an individual justice's vote (Knowles 2021: 155–56). Justices may join a majority or plurality decision but write a concurring opinion based on different legal theories or practical stratagems; the same is true of dissents. Even so, if the ruling is popular in the polls, the poll-matching method classifies all the majority and concurring votes as consistent with public opinion. Legal scholars may object to this practice, but there is no obvious alternative. Pollsters do not ordinarily ask about the subtleties of legal reasoning when writing poll questions on pending or recent Supreme Court decisions. For that matter, journalists seldom write headlines or leads that focus on legal reasoning; journalists usually describe a decision's outcome and the winners and losers. If it is a shortcoming at all, poll results entirely define what is public opinion, and the poll-matching method uses no other readings of public attitudes. The 531 poll-to-decision matches analyzed here report only nationwide public opinion or important groups' attitudes, not regional or state results. Some studies estimate survey results for regions or states, but this is often not possible for archived poll data, and this book does not break down nationwide poll results by region or state. Poll matching cannot be used prior to the 1930s, since no scientific polls then existed. Poll matching might be extended to study the justices' votes at the certiorari stage, at least if certiorari votes are available, but this book does not do so.[5]

Reweighting or segmenting the database addresses some of this method's limitations. Fewer poll matches, per term, are available before the 1960s than thereafter, although by the results given here, reweighting by term or issue does not significantly affect the overall results. The database constructed here counts most Supreme Court decisions as one decision per poll match. A few decisions can be better matched by breaking a decision into parts and poll matching with two or more poll questions. In other instances, two or more related decisions may be combined and matched with a single poll question. As a result, the database listed in the appendix differs from other databases. Some Supreme Court rulings receive more media attention and serve as stronger precedents than others. Chapter 3 compares high- versus low-profile decisions but otherwise makes no attempt to reweight by a decision's eventual importance. Nor does the poll-matching method address the question of whether existing poll trends themselves influence Supreme Court decisions. Considerable evidence suggests that decisions often do reflect existing poll trends. Per chapter 1, poll support for marriage equality was steadily rising well before the *Obergefell* decision in 2015. Similarly, poll matching only in a limited way answers the question of whether Supreme Court decisions themselves influence public opinion. For some poll matches one can examine pre-decision poll trends, pre- to post-decision poll shifts, or post-decision poll trends by using identically worded poll questions on surveys with similar sampling methods. Chapter 3 returns to this issue.

Poll matching carries with it several assumptions. Perhaps the most critical is that scientific nationwide poll questions accurately measure American public opinion at that time. There is, of course, no assumption that a poll question can accurately forecast attitudes in years ahead or accurately describes attitudes in years past. If several poll questions are available, the closest-in-time poll question is matched to a ruling.[6]

Poll matching does not necessarily assume that the justices are aware of polls on a dispute, nor that public opinion influences the justices' thinking in a particular way. When many polls are available or when statutes and legal practice suggest a national consensus, as sometimes happens, the justices may in fact know (or surmise) something about public opinion.[7] Occasionally, amicus briefs include poll results. These circumstances often do not occur, and the justices may have no clear understanding of or interest in public opinion. The justices often read public opinion from very indirect sources, such as jury verdicts, state laws, or even by widespread complaints.[8] For most poll-matched rulings, only one or two poll questions are available and sometimes not so until after the Court announces a decision. Not surprisingly, the justices rarely cite specific polls to justify their vote. Justifying a vote in terms of specific poll results might bring withering criticism from other justices, the media, elected officeholders, or the legal community. Still, some tests are available. Chapter 3 asks whether decisions more often agree with public opinion depending on whether the poll question mentions the Court as deciding a case, by the poll's timing, by the issue's importance, or by other possible correlates of representation.

Poll matching does not assume that most Americans know about pending or recent decisions. Americans' awareness of the Court as an institution and of its decisions varies widely but is often limited.[9] In a 2021 Marquette Law School survey, nearly three-quarters (72%) of respondents correctly answered that Republican presidents "definitely" or "probably" appointed a majority of the justices; only 28% of respondents incorrectly said that Democratic presidents appointed most of the justices. In a 2019 Ipsos survey for the Pew Research Center, for example, 63% of Americans correctly named the number of justices. Yet in a 2018 survey by SSRS that asked respondents to name the justices, 61% of respondents could not name any of the justices, and none of the justices were named by as many as a quarter of respondents. In a 2015 Pew Research Center survey, only a third of respondents correctly answered that three of the nine justices were women. According to a 1988 Gallup survey, half (53%) correctly knew that one woman (Sandra Day O'Connor) sat on the Court. In a 2013 GFK/Knowledge Networks survey, only 28% of respondents correctly named Anthony Kennedy as the typical tie-breaking justice when the other choices were Antonin Scalia, Ruth Bader Ginsburg, and Clarence Thomas, none of the three often a tie breaker.

Several poll questions that ask whether Americans correctly understand specific Court rulings yield mixed results even on landmark decisions. On five true/false poll questions from iPoll since 2000, an average of only 40% of respondents correctly described the Court's decision. On eight similar poll questions from the 1980s and 1990s, the average for correct answers was 55%—nearly identical to the 54% figure reported in Ansolabehere and White (2020: 368, 371). These averages are unimpressive when compared to a random-guessing base rate of 50% correct. A 1986 Hearst survey asked respondents to identify the topic of three landmark decisions, *Miranda v. Arizona* (1966), *Brown v. Board of Education* (1954), *and Roe v. Wade* (1973). An average of 43% of respondents correctly identified the answer from a list of three or four choices (criminal rights, racial segregation, and abortion, respectively), versus a random-guessing base rate of 30%. At the extreme, 70% of Americans correctly understood the ruling on the individual mandate provision in *NFIB v. Sebelius* (2012) when queried soon after the ruling. On a moderately well-known immigration dispute, the show-me-your-papers provision in *Arizona v. United States* (2012), about half (46%) of Americans correctly described the decision (Linos and Twist 2016: 236).

That Americans are only modestly well informed about Supreme Court rulings is not surprising. The Court does not allow live television broadcasts during oral arguments or when announcing decisions. The justices often couch their oral arguments and written opinions in obscure legal arguments. The justices seldom grant media interviews or appear on talk shows to persuade Americans that the Court's decisions (or their own dissents) were justified (Chemerinsky 2014: 317–22). Accordingly, poll matching makes no assumptions about how familiar ordinary Americans are about rulings or legal doctrine (Dorf 2006: 281–83).

Further, there is no automatic assumption that Americans react in a particular way to Supreme Court decisions. Chapter 3 offers evidence that few rulings greatly influence public preferences, at least not so in the short term. Nor does the poll-matching method assume that the public has firm, fixed, or well-reasoned attitudes. Respondents' attitudes are taken as stated. Occasionally, pollsters ask so-called counterarguments, which sometimes show that a quarter or a third of respondents will switch their answer after hearing arguments that contradict their original response. On counterargument questions, the original response can be poll matched, but not the follow-up question.[10]

Each poll-to-decision match depends on identifying at least one timely, publicly available question. Pollsters thereby effectively become gatekeepers. As described later in this chapter, it is possible to reweight the database, which is not, per se, a random sample of Supreme Court decisions. Poll matches represent decisions on which there was at least minimal public interest—sometimes considerably so, sometimes only a little so. It may seem doubtful that meaningful public opinion exists on most decisions that do not receive even a single poll question. The resulting database often approximates other measures. For example, the late Hughes Court and the Warren Court appear as the most liberal Courts, while the Vinson and Rehnquist Courts are the least liberal Courts (at 69%, 72%, 35%, and 45% liberal decisions, respectively). Taken individually, the justices fall along a typical liberal-to-conservative spectrum (e.g., Epstein, Landes, and Posner 2015).

Poll matching possibly has another bias worth mentioning. Poll matching may implicitly privilege the views of poll majorities at the expense of those most directly affected by a Court ruling. There are practical limits to examining the attitudes of numerically small groups. Pollsters seldom identify small groups and even if small groups can be identified, the resulting margin of error is large. Measuring representation for small groups such as religious or political dissenters, accused criminals, students, attorneys, law school professors, or supporters of the Federalist Society or the American Constitution Society requires alternative readings of attitudes. Chapter 5 examines representation by gender, race, partisanship, and education.[11]

THE SPECIFICS OF THE POLL-MATCHING METHOD

Data Sources

This book analyzes 531 poll-to-decision matches. The poll questions come from a variety of sources, mostly commercial pollsters. The American polling industry is almost entirely unregulated. Pollsters ask their questions according to their own interests and those of their clients. There is no legal requirement that pollsters ask questions in a consistent format or on a fixed schedule, or publicly release or archive their results. Provided that clients do not require that poll results remain confidential, polling industry norms encourage transparency, and poll questions about Supreme Court decisions are seldom if ever apparently treated as confidential. All the poll-to-decision matches rely on secondary survey research. That is, all the poll questions are from public-release pollsters' work; this study neither carried out nor commissioned any surveys.

Through online access and data archiving, a steadily growing number of poll questions that closely match, in substance, a Supreme Court decision can be identified. Online archives, particularly iPoll, frequently add both recent and older poll questions from academic, commercial, and foundation-based pollsters. Over time, polling practices have varied. During the 1930s, 1940s, and 1950s, most surveys were conducted face-to-face. By the 1960s and 1970s, pollsters more often conducted telephone surveys. More recently, online surveys, panel surveys, and multimode surveys became common. All the poll-matched questions herein are closed-ended, that is, respondents are offered the suggested responses, usually with two choices such as "favor" or "oppose." Poll questions now seldom explicitly offer respondents a "no opinion" option or a "middle position."[12] For some poll matches, identically worded questions are available both before and after a Court decision, further described in chapter 3.

To compile as complete a list of useful poll questions as possible, major nationwide polls were reviewed from online, archived, and print materials. Among the most often used sources are the Gallup poll, the Pew Research Center, the National Opinion Research Center (NORC), the Harris poll, *Public Opinion* magazine, various media surveys, and "The Polls" section of *Public Opinion Quarterly*. The online iPoll archive, searchable by key words, is especially useful. Numerous books, research papers, convention papers, and journal articles yield useful poll questions.

Another useful search strategy involved working through various lists of Supreme Court decisions, casebooks, and landmark decisions to see which could be poll matched. Among the most useful sources, some no longer published, are annual summaries in the *American Political Science Review*, *Western Political Quarterly*, *Congressional Quarterly Weekly Review*, and

Almanac, the *Harvard Law Review,* the *University of Chicago Law Review,* the *New York Times,* SCOTUSblog, the *Supreme Court Compendium,* and various books and news stories. These searches were conducted over many years and as thoroughly as possible but cannot guarantee that every poll-matched Supreme Court decision was identified. Very likely, a few more poll matches from past decision may be identified as additional surveys become publicly available. Even so, the resulting list of poll-matched decisions is diverse and may (to date) be nearly exhaustive.

Coding Rules

Using the poll-matching method for so many decisions across nine decades requires several coding rules. Following past studies (Monroe 1979, 1998; Marshall 1989: 75–77, 2008: 30–35), this study uses only nationwide polls representing all American adults. Poll results from other populations such as registered voters or likely voters, local or statewide residents, community leaders, judges, attorneys, professors, or students are never used even if a poll question clearly matches a specific Court decision. Nor are nationally unrepresentative samples used such as from M-Turk or Survey Monkey. Poll questions must closely match in substance an issue reached in a Court decision. These rules necessitate excluding several otherwise eligible matches such as *Ledbetter v. Goodyear Tire and Rubber Company* (2007) or *Korematsu v. United States* (1944), neither of which generated usable poll questions.

Poll questions can be matched to full, written decisions, per curiam decisions, summary affirmations, denials or certiorari, or denials of habeas corpus or of a stay. Pollsters more often ask questions about full, written (merits) decisions and these matches mostly provide the evidence for chapters 3, 4, and 5. Denials of certiorari, of habeas corpus, or of a stay are less often polled and are generally discussed separately. Whether denials of certiorari should be included is arguable. As many justices have argued, such denials have no precedent value and may only reflect procedural problems with the appeal.[13] Further, the justices seldom explain their views in denials. Even so, such denials can be the Court's "last word" on an issue, as on specific death penalty appeals, and on several issues the Court chiefly makes decisions through denials. Examining denials of certiorari or of habeas corpus or of a stay permits a useful comparison with full, written decisions and with the lower courts. Chapter 3 returns to this issue.

A poll question need not explicitly mention the Supreme Court. Poll questions that explicitly mention the Court typically state that the Court may soon decide an issue or that it has recently done so. Only about one in six poll matches explicitly mentions the Supreme Court. Whether the poll question explicitly mentions that the Court recently decided or will soon decide a dispute does not greatly affect whether the decision agrees with public opinion. Indeed, as chapter 3 describes, post-decision poll questions that explicitly mention that the Court recently handed down a decision show lower levels of agreement with public opinion—implying that Court decisions have little influence on public opinion.

A matching poll question may be asked within five years, either before or after the Court announces its decision. This seemingly generous time frame is seldom reached; for two-thirds of the poll matches, the poll question falls within two years of the decision. The median lag between a poll question and when the matching decision was announced is about 300 days. As chapters 1 and 3 describe, some experiments show that decisions favorably influence fully and recently informed respondents; others show the opposite; still other research shows no consistent short-term or long-term effects. As per chapter 3, recently announced Court decisions little affect American attitudes, and the coding scheme here largely eliminates this potential problem.[14]

Several other coding rules are used. Only one poll match is included for each issue raised in a decision. Typically, this results in one poll match per ruling. A few decisions reach multiple issues; in such instances, two or more poll matches are counted, one apiece for each poll-matched issue. Two well-known examples from the Roberts Court include *NFIB v. Sebelius* (2012) and *Arizona v. United States* (2012). As a result, this database differs from others that count only one case per decision. Closely related decisions, typically decisions announced on the same day, are combined into a single poll match. A decision upholding and applying a specific application of a more general law or policy is counted as upholding the law or policy itself. A decision ordering a lower court to consider or apply a law is counted as upholding that law.

A poll match is not counted until the Court presumably reaches a final decision.[15] A refusal to grant an emergency stay is not counted as a final decision if the effect is to return the case to a lower court for timely considerations. If a poll question shows that most Americans favor a constitutional amendment, it is assumed that most Americans favor a similar law or policy by another means. If an earlier decision is coded, later decisions applying that precedent are not counted as a separate match. However, a later decision overturning an earlier decision is counted as an additional match even if the earlier decision was also poll matched. Although this coding rule may create a bias in the classification schema, fortunately, such instances rarely occur within these 531 decisions.[16]

Using these coding rules, each poll-matched Supreme Court decision is classified as either "consistent" or "inconsistent" with nationwide public opinion, or as "unclear." The appendix lists all the poll-to-decision matches.

- In a "consistent" poll match, the decision agrees, in substance, with a majority (or occasionally, a plurality) in the poll question.[17] *Obergefell v. Hodges* (2015) and *U.S. v. Windsor* (2013), discussed in chapter 1, are both consistent decisions.
- In an "inconsistent" match, the decision disagrees, in substance, with a majority or plurality in the poll question.
- For a few instances of conflicting or evenly divided (within the .05 margin of error) poll results, the poll match is classified as "unclear."

Many matching poll questions clearly refer to a specific Supreme Court case. In *Ricci v. De Stefano* (2009) a 5-to-4 majority of justices overturned federal court decisions upholding a New Haven, Connecticut, decision to void civil service exam results for firefighters' promotions on racial grounds. A few days before the decision was announced, a CNN survey asked a nationwide adult sample a question clearly written to tap the issue:

> In a case currently before the Supreme Court, a city decided to use a test to determine which firefighters should receive promotions. No black firefighters scored high enough on the test to earn a promotion, so the city decided not to offer promotions to the white firefighters who got the highest scores on the test. Which of the following statements comes closest to your view? Those white firefighters were victims of discrimination and should get the promotions based on the test results. Because no black firefighters got high scores, the city should use a new test to make sure that blacks were not victims of discrimination.

A 65-to-31% poll majority supported the Court's soon-to-come decision upholding the white firefighters' claims. The 5-to-4 decision is accordingly "consistent" with nationwide public opinion. The five justices (Roberts, Scalia, Kennedy, Thomas, and Alito) in the majority agreed with nationwide public opinion. The four dissenting justices (Souter, Stevens, Ginsburg, and Breyer) disagreed with the polls.

Not all poll matches are worded as specifically as is the CNN poll question on *Ricci v. De Stefano*. A poll-to-decision match may be counted if the poll question asks about an issue and the legal dispute is a specific instance of that issue. In *Center for Biological Diversity v. Wolf* (2020), the Court denied an appeal of a lower court decision on the waiver of multiple federal statutes in building the so-called border wall along the U.S.-Mexican border. The matching Gallup poll question was, "Do you favor or oppose, or neither favor or oppose, building a wall along the U.S.–Mexican border?" These general-to-specific poll matches are very common. As another example, the *Bourgeois v. Barr* (2020) decision allowed federal death penalty executions to resume for the first time since 2003. Gallup's matching poll question was: "Are you in favor of the death penalty for a person convicted of murder?"[18]

Some Supreme Court decisions clearly disagree with nationwide public opinion. A well-known inconsistent decision is the so-called individual mandate provision of *NFIB v. Sebelius* (2012). A large (74-to-23%) majority in a Princeton Survey Research Associates survey opposed the individual mandate provision that required most individuals to have a health care policy or else pay a tax penalty. Accordingly, the 5-to-4 decision upholding that part of the Affordable Care Act is "inconsistent" with public opinion. Among the best-known inconsistent rulings are *U.S. Term Limits v. Thornton* (1995), on term limits for Congress; *Clinton v. City of New York* (1998), on the line-item veto; *Texas v. Johnson* (1989), on flag burning; *Citizens United v. Federal Election Commission* (2010), on corporate and union campaign funds; or *Brown v. Entertainment Merchants Association* (2011), on selling violent video games to minors.

About 1 in 20 poll-to-decision matches is classified as "unclear" either because of closely divided poll results (within the .05 margin of error) or because different timely polls reporting conflicting results. Examples include *Cooper v. Aaron* (1958), a school desegregation decision, and *Arizona v. U.S.* (2012), in part, on a state law criminalizing illegal immigrants seeking work, both due to closely divided polls. *Masterpiece Cakeshop v. Colorado Civil Rights Commission* (2018) and *Bush v. Gore* (2000) are instances of closely divided or inconsistent poll results.

Reweighting Procedures

Although pollsters have asked questions tapping attitudes on Supreme Court decisions since the 1930s, fewer poll matches, per term, exist for the Hughes, Stone, Vinson, and Warren Courts than for the Burger, Rehnquist, and Roberts Courts. Nor are all issues equally often polled. Disputes of widespread public interest are most frequently polled, for example, civil liberties and civil rights, crime and the death penalty, national security, and abortion. Pollsters seldom ask questions about trademarks and patents, the tax code, arbitration, price fixing, rivers and harbors, bankruptcy, monopolies, restraint of trade, sovereign immunity, court jurisdiction and procedures, federalism, administrative procedure, or intergovernmental relations. These seldom-polled topics, while important, elicit little interest from pollsters, the public, or the media. Pollsters ask more questions on non-unanimous than unanimous decisions. As a result, these 531 poll-to-decision matches are a diverse but nonrandom sample of Supreme Court decisions since the mid-1930s.

Nonrandom sampling presents a challenge in interpreting poll results. Pollsters deal with nonrandom sampling in several ways, some of which remedies are feasible here, others not. Pollsters may deliberately oversample difficult-to-contact respondents. Pollsters repeatedly attempt to contact potential respondents over several days or weeks to improve the randomness of a sample. Occasionally, pollsters use "snowball sampling" to identify difficult-to-identify respondents by asking ineligible respondents to name an appropriate person. Sometimes pollsters contact respondents in different ways, such as by both telephone and web-based panels. The Census Bureau imputes (i.e., estimates) information on missing households based on nearby households with known demographic or household information.

None of these otherwise useful methods is helpful for secondary survey research. Nor is it possible to reconstruct public opinion for long-ago Supreme Court decisions. This leaves the option of reweighting these 531 decisions back to the correct proportion of Supreme Court decisions. Reweighting nonrandom samples is a long-standing, widely accepted practice in survey research. Reweighting involves two steps: first, determining (or at least estimating) the "true" (correct) population numbers; and second, readjusting the sample proportions to the correct population figures based on theoretically important variables. Sometimes reweighting significantly changes the unweighted sample results, sometimes not. Chapter 3 compares unweighted and reweighted results for full, written decisions across Courts.[19] To preview the results: the unweighted and the reweighted results are very similar.

The resulting sample of 531 decisions yield similar estimates to many other accounts.[20] For example, the justices' career liberal-versus-conservative voting records in table 4.3 closely resemble other estimates (Martin and Quinn 2002; Bailey 2013; Bonica et al. 2017; Bonica and Sen 2021). As a caveat, those measures are differently constructed with different decisions and years. The Warren and late Hughes Courts appear as the least conservative Courts, while the Vinson and Rehnquist Courts are the most conservative. As in other accounts, the justices show behavioral drift over time. Current and recent justices' partisan ties and voting patterns are more closely linked than are those of earlier justices.

CONCLUSION AND DISCUSSION

This chapter outlined six different approaches to compare Supreme Court decisions with public opinion. Each method has its own strengths. The poll-matching method pairs a wide variety of specific decisions each with timely poll questions on the issue in dispute. Poll matching has three main strengths. First, poll matching provides specificity about public opinion by matching decisions with poll questions on that topic. Second, public opinion is clearly defined by using timely random samples of nationwide adults. Third, poll matching captures American attitudes across a wide range of Supreme Court decisions. These 531 poll-to-decision matches form a database offering a wide-ranging view on the modern Court's behavior as a representative institution. Through poll matching, one can study the Court as a whole, the justices individually, variations across time or issue, or even entirely hypothetical situations.

Using the poll-matching method helps to answer the question posed in chapter 1. If many, perhaps most, Americans now view the Court as a representative institution, does the modern Court so behave? Chapter 3 turns to the modern Court's record of representing American attitudes. Chapters 4 and 5 turn to the justices. Chapter 6 evaluates the Court's record and its future as a representative policymaker.

NOTES

1. Many authors employed the historical method to describe American attitudes absent any polling, among them Alexis de Tocqueville in *Democracy in America* (1848, 1966), James Bryce in *The American Commonwealth* (1900), and Walter Lippmann in *Public Opinion* (1922) and *The Phantom Public* (1925).

2. *The Will of the People* continues its analysis through the confirmations of Chief Justice Roberts and Justice Alito, reporting polling evidence for specific decisions and for the Court's approval ratings. See also Ansolabehere and White (2020).

3. Case studies are neither new nor limited to the American setting. Sheldon (1967) considers public opinion toward Communists in the United States, West Germany, Canada, and Australia.

4. Pildes (2011a) discusses the problems in assessing majority preferences.

5. The justices' votes to hear cases partly depends on whether they are likely to agree with public opinion on the outcome (Bryan 2020). Bryan and Owens (2017) point to the importance of certiorari in supervising states that are ideologically distant from the justices.

6. A poll match is classified as "unclear" if poll questions taken within a few weeks of the closest-in-time question conflict one with another.

7. By scattered evidence, some justices paid attention to polls in specific cases (e.g., Greenhouse 2012: 76).

8. For the former, see Marshall (1989: 31–36; 2008: 6–8). For a recent instance of reading public opinion by noting widespread consumer complaints, see Justice Kavanaugh's opinion in *Barr v. American Association of Political Consultants* (2020): "Americans passionately disagree about many things. But they are largely united in their disdain for robocalls. The Federal Government receives a staggering number of complaints about robocalls—3.7 million complaints in 2019 alone. The States likewise field a constant barrage of complaints." Justice Kavanaugh called public reaction "a torrent of vociferous consumer complaints." The justices also estimate public opinion through other indicators such as Congressional legislation (Clark 2011), presidential actions (Collins and Eshbaugh-Soha 2019), or even election returns (Harvey and Friedman 2006). See also Friedman (1993).

9. See also Gibson, Pereira, and Ziegler (2017); Jamieson and Hennessy (2007); and the periodic Annenberg Civics Knowledge surveys available at www.annenbe rgpublicpolicycenter.org.

10. A counterargument is a three-part sequence of poll questions. Respondents are initially asked their opinion on an issue; then asked one or more follow-up questions providing seemingly conflicting information to determine how many will change their mind; then asked their opinion on the issue again. Often a third to half of respondents change their initial answer. Pollsters occasionally ask counterarguments during polls on Supreme Court decisions. For example, a December 2019 Kaiser/Ipsos survey asked a counterargument question about *June Medical Services v. Russo* (2020), reporting that numerous respondents changed their answer on the follow-up question. While interesting, the final responses from counterarguments are never included in the poll matches used herein.

11. Kugler and Strahilevitz's study of public opinion on privacy issues (2015: 229–34; 2017) reviews several caveats.

12. Giving respondents an explicit option of "don't know" has long passed out of fashion in survey research. A few poll questions used here offer respondents a range of choices, typically with five answers ranging from strongly favor to strongly oppose and including a middle position. Such responses are recoded into just two categories, either favor or oppose; the middle position is treated as a response of don't know or no opinion.

13. For a recent discussion of this increasingly debated controversy, see McFadden and Kapoor (2021).

14. Because the coding scheme classifies poll-to-decision results as either consistent, unclear, or inconsistent, few minor sampling biases and variations in poll results would result in a different outcome.

15. A Supreme Court decision ordering a lower court to reconsider its own ruling is counted as a final decision only if the Supreme Court's ruling is sufficiently clear; a summary affirmation or a summary reversal can likewise be counted as a substantive decision. "Finality" is only for a particular dispute and is usually resolved within one or two years. The Supreme Court sometimes overturns one of its own precedents, often many years later. Chapter 3 returns to this issue.

16. A few Supreme Court rulings that delay a disputed law or policy or legal challenge past a critical deadline are counted as a substantive decision. Among these are *Department of Commerce v. New York* (2019) on adding the so-called citizenship question to the 2020 Census, and *Merrill v. People First of Alabama* (2020) and related cases on voting procedures. This counting rule assumes that no similar cases later arise through the end of the 2019–2020 term.

17. In very rare instances, dicta may be coded. If a Court opinion explicitly states a position on an issue raised in a matching poll question, although it does not apply that position to the instance at hand, the general principal is coded. *Louis K. Liggett Co. v. Lee* (1933) explicitly allowed additional taxes for chain stores while disallowing Florida's so-called county-counting rule. Accordingly, *Liggett v. Lee* is coded as "consistent" with a Gallup poll question showing a 56-to-32% majority in favor of "requiring chain stores . . . to pay special taxes." Dicta in a decision may be compared

with a poll question even if the poll question does not ask about the particulars in the case and if the dicta is elsewhere used. Based on the well-known language in footnote 4, rather than on the so-called filled milk issue, *U.S. v. Carolene Products Co.* (1938) is coded as consistent with a Gallup poll question: "Should the Supreme Court be more liberal in reviewing New Deal measures?" *Wickard v. Filburn* (1942) is also widely cited on this issue.

18. A Gallup survey of October 1–13, 2019, reported 56% in favor, 42% opposed, and 2% no opinion. Surveys by Abt for Pew and NORC from 2018 with slightly different wording show similar results.

19. For purposes of reweighting, the correct proportions of decisions are taken from the *Supreme Court Compendium* (2015).

20. Racek (2014), using slightly different coding rules, reports that poll-matched Roberts Court decisions from 2005 through 2011 were 63% consistent with nationwide public opinion, nearly identical to the 62% figure reported herein.

Chapter 3

The Norm of Representation

This chapter asks three questions about the modern Court's representative role by using the methods outlined in chapter 2. First, how often and when do Supreme Court decisions represent American public opinion? Second, does the Court represent Americans equally as well as do other policymakers? Third, do Supreme Court decisions themselves sway public opinion?

This chapter examines the Supreme Court as a collective policymaker. Chapters 4 and 5 turn to the individual justices. Opinions differ as to which is the better approach. The argument for focusing on the Court collectively is that, as a practical matter, decisions matter most. Dissents or concurrences may be a guidepost for future decisions but have little immediate importance as public policy. The Court's decisions win the most attention from the media, politicians, and the public. By contrast, the argument for focusing on the justices individually is that justices cast the actual votes. Decisions are simply byproducts of the individual justices' votes. Focusing on the individual justices highlights important patterns in representation as a judicial role. Since Court watchers use both approaches, so does this book.

PATTERNS IN REPRESENTATION

Most Supreme Court decisions agree with nationwide polls and thereby represent public opinion. Since the mid-1930s, three-fifths (61%) of poll-matched Supreme Court decisions were consistent with poll majorities (or occasionally pluralities). A sizeable minority (34%) of decisions were not. A few (6%) decisions are "unclear" due to closely divided or conflicting poll results. Excluding the few unclear decisions, nearly two-thirds (64%) of Supreme Court decisions agreed with public opinion, while the remaining

36% did not. Again, setting aside "unclear" matches, 64% of full, written decisions, per curiam decisions, and summary affirmations agree with the polls—a figure identical to the 64% figure for cert denials, denials of a stay or habeas corpus.

Reweighting by type of issue or by caseload does not greatly change these results. By Court, the results are very similar for both the weighted and the unweighted sample of all poll-matched decisions. Table 3.1 reports these estimates.[1] The unweighted and reweighted results, by Court, for full, written decisions, per curiam decisions, and summary affirmances (only) are nearly identical: 74% versus 70% consistent, respectively, for the Hughes Court; 50% and 50% (Stone Court); 55% and 60% (Vinson Court); 62% and 65% (Warren Court); 67% and 67% (Burger Court); 61% and 61% (Rehnquist Court); and 74% and 73% (Roberts Court).[2]

The percentage of consistent decisions can also be reexamined by reweighting caseload. Since the mid-1930s, the Supreme Court has decided about 11,000 full, written (merits) rulings, per curiam decisions, and summary affirmations. Over time, this output changed greatly, particularly so with fewer grants of certiorari during the Rehnquist and Roberts Courts.[3] As a result, the number of poll-to-decision matches, per term, increased over time, but the number of full, written decisions fell. This creates a possible bias. To correct for this, the (reweighted) figures in table 3.1, per Court, were applied to the actual number of full, written decisions, per Court. This adjustment makes little difference. The (reweighted) estimate for the percentage of consistent decisions since the 1935 term is 63%, a figure nearly identical to the 64% unweighted estimate.

In short, by various estimates, three-fifths to two-thirds of modern Court decisions represent public opinion. This estimate is relatively stable over time, slightly rising since the 1960s. Opinions may vary as to whether this

Table 3.1 Percentage of Supreme Court Decisions Consistent with Public Opinion, by Court

	Consistent, Unweighted Results (%)	Consistent, Reweighted Results (%)	Number of Cases
By Court:			
Hughes	71	65	28
Stone	52	54	23
Vinson	65	57	26
Warren	61	61	59
Burger	65	65	125
Rehnquist	63	64	161
Roberts	69	68	80

Note: Data excludes instances of conflicting and evenly divided polls. The percentage of inconsistent decisions equals 100% minus the percentage of consistent decisions.
Source: Data collected and analyzed by the author and listed in the appendix.

estimate falls below, meets, or exceeds expectations. The modern Court's record of representing public opinion is well above a hypothetical 50:50 standard. Even so, some accounts treat this figure as unimpressive and suggest that public opinion seldom directly influences the Court (Devins and Baum 2019: 32–33). This chapter compares the modern Court's record to that of other policymakers, concluding that the modern Court matches the record of other federal policymakers. The modern Court also brings lower court decisions, state and local policies, and the Court's own precedents back into line with contemporary opinion. Chapters 4 and 5 turn to the individual justices.

Significant variations in representation occur across Courts, across issues, by public interest, and by the circumstances surrounding a decision. Table 3.1 reports the percentage of decisions that agree with public opinion, by Court era, offering both unweighted and reweighted estimates. By either estimate, all seven modern Courts mostly agreed with the polls. The Burger, Rehnquist, and Roberts Courts did so nearly two-thirds of the time.[4]

Table 3.2 reports on issues involved. Most modern Court decisions agree with public opinion across nearly all issues. Even so, wide variations exist.

Table 3.2 Percentage of Supreme Court Decisions Consistent with Public Opinion, by Issue

	Consistent (%)	Number of Cases
Overall Results:	64	
By type of issue:		
Labor, unions, strikes	57	63
Crime, courts, police	69	86
Education, schools	72	50
National security, war, foreign policy, communism, terrorism, immigration	47	59
Abortion, morality, privacy, sex	69	54
Race, integration	72	54
Business regulation, taxes, lawsuits	78	82
Elections, voting, campaign finance	66	35
Federalism, intergovernmental relations, disputes between branches	49	41
Free speech, dissent, obscenity, media	54	52
Social welfare, poverty	70	10
Transportation, commerce	92	13
Religion	58	31
Health care, hospitals, health insurance	61	28
Families, children, family law	83	18
Women's rights claims	64	14
LGBTQ rights claims	73	15

Note: Data excludes "unclear" poll matches. Summing the number of cases across types of issues in this table exceeds 502 since some decisions involve multiple issues.
Source: Data collected and analyzed by the author and listed in the appendix.

Decisions on transportation, commerce, family law, and business cases most often agree with the polls. Decisions on national security, federalism, intergovernmental relations, and first amendment claims least often do. These large variations help to explain why case studies report widely different findings and merit further attention.

The State of Public Opinion

Supreme Court decisions especially often agree with public opinion when the dispute ranks among Americans' "most important problem" on Gallup's often-asked question. On a top-ranking concern, 72% of decisions agree with the polls. When the issue in dispute is at least among the public's top-five concerns, 62% of decisions agree with the polls. When the issue is of less widespread concern, 64% of decisions agree with the polls.

The modern Court is less sensitive to one-sided polls. For about half of the poll matches, public opinion was very one-sided. For example, on *Ricci v. De Stefano* (2009), previously described in chapter 2, Americans favored the Court's decision by a 65-to-31% margin—a "poll margin" of 34% (or 65% minus 31% equals 34%). Poll margins that equal or exceed 30% are considered as "landslide" margins. As a hypothesis, possibly the justices might best be able to discern (and follow) public opinion when the polls are one-sided. Often the polls divided more closely. For example, by a 46-to-40% plurality, the polls disagreed with the *Thornhill v. Alabama* (1940) decision permitting labor union picketing—thus, a much smaller poll margin of only 6%. When the polls are very one-sided (a "landslide" poll margin) the decision agreed with public opinion 66% of the time. By comparison, the Court agreed with public opinion 63% of the time when the polls divided more closely. Although consistent with expectations, the difference is small. Public interest better predicts consistent decisions than do one-sided poll margins.

Representation in part depends on the public's liberal-versus-conservative leanings. When public opinion is conservative on a dispute, the Court's decisions agree with the polls 59% of the time. When public opinion is liberal, that figure is 70%. For the few (only 14) decisions on which there was no obvious ideological dimension, that figure is 79%.

Described otherwise, and again setting aside decisions with no clear ideological content, public opinion was ideologically conservative 55% of the time and liberal 45% of the time. The Court's decisions leaned in a more liberal direction; its decisions were conservative only 46% of the time but liberal 54% of the time. In short, the modern Court somewhat better represented liberal views than conservative views. Chapter 4 returns to ideology from the perspective of the justices.

Another way to view how often Supreme Court decisions and public opinion align is to look only at the Court's most important decisions. So-called super precedents (or sometimes: "super-duper precedents") have the greatest lasting impact and capture the most attention from the media, legal scholars, politicians, and public opinion (Landes and Posner 1976, Gerhardt 2006). Super precedents have broad and lasting importance and often signal a new course for the Court and the lower federal and state courts. Accounts vary as to how many decisions fall into this category. Questions asked at Senate confirmation hearings may feature a few decisions such as *Brown v. Board of Education* (1954), *Roe v. Wade* (1973), or *Planned Parenthood of Southeastern Pennsylvania v. Casey* (1992). Some lists include many more such decisions (Gerhardt 2006, Barrett 2013), including decisions as long ago as *Marbury v. Madison* (1803).

Do super precedents agree with contemporary public opinion? Many but not all do. One recent list (Pasley 2019) includes 21 such decisions since the early 1930s that can be poll-matched, ranging in time from *Near v. Minnesota* (1931) to *Obergefell v. Hodges* (2015). Slightly over half (55%) of these super precedents agreed with public opinion; a third (32%) disagreed with the polls; on a few (14%) decisions, the polls were closely divided or inconsistent.

Unanimity and Close Votes

Do unanimous or very one-sided votes signal a decision consistent with public opinion, while closely divided votes signal an inconsistent decision?[5] No such pattern appears. Sixty-four percent of unanimous decisions agreed with the polls, compared to 56% of decisions with near-unanimous votes (typically 8-to-1 or 7-to-2). Decisions with more closely divided votes (e.g., 6-3 or 5-4) agreed with the polls 65% of the time. In short, no clear relationship exists between a decision's vote split and representation.

Time and Representation

The modern Court now spans over nine decades. Are there significant variations over time in how well the Court represents public opinion? Figure 3.1 depicts the percentage of consistent decisions by five-year moving averages from 1937 through 2020.[6] Except for brief periods, half or more of decisions always agreed with public opinion since the 1930s. A notable exception is for several Warren Court years during the early 1960s.

The early 1960s were clearly an anomaly. Today, only a dwindling number of older Americans can remember the Warren Court. Most Americans today have a lifelong experience with a Court most of whose decisions represent

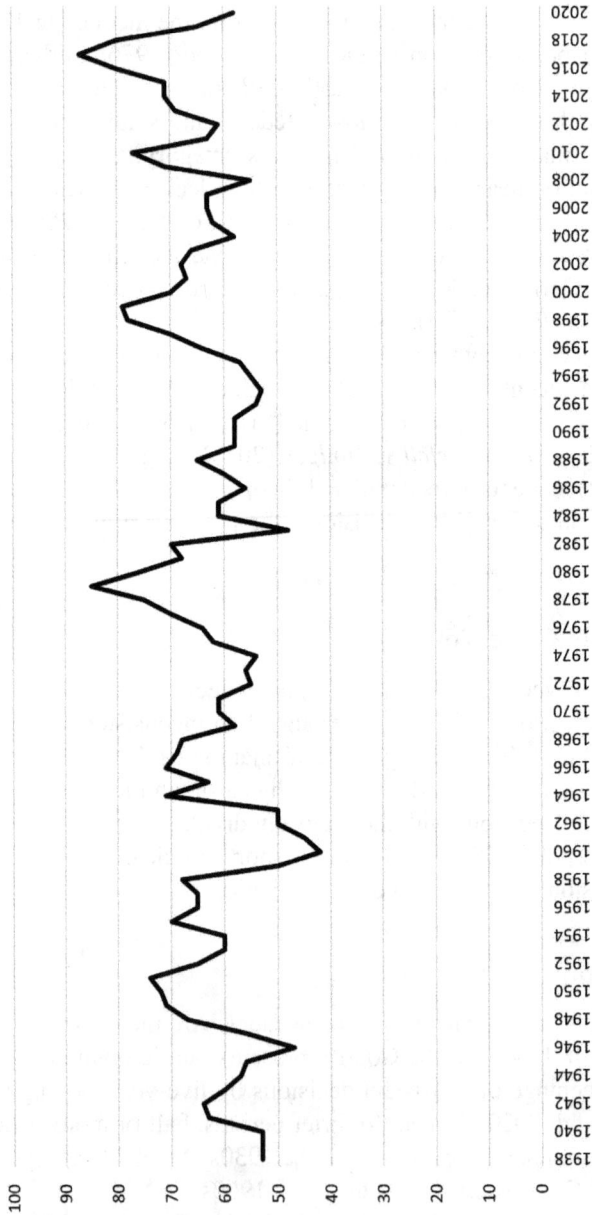

Figure 3.1 Percentage of Supreme Court Decisions Consistent with Public Opinion, Five-Year Moving Averages, 1938–2020. *Source:* Data collected and analyzed by the author and listed in appendix.

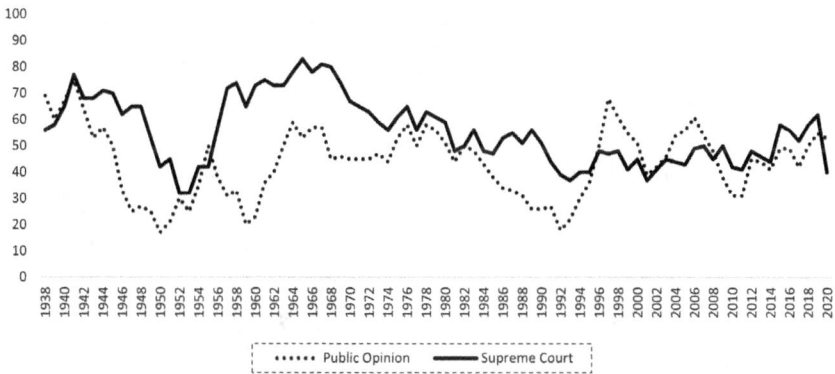

Figure 3.2 Percentage Liberal for Public Opinion and Supreme Court Decisions, Five-Year Moving Averages, 1938–2020. *Source:* Data collected and analyzed by the author and listed in appendix.

public opinion. Nor in the memory of most Americans today has the Court produced a steady stream of high-profile, unpopular decisions. This experience may have produced a settled expectation among Court watchers that most Supreme Court decisions will represent public opinion. Not surprisingly, when the Court announces a high-profile, unpopular decision, the Court's popularity ratings may drop dramatically in the short term. The widely unpopular flag-burning decisions offer an example. From just before until just after the *Texas v. Johnson* decision in 1989, those expressing "a great deal of confidence" in the people running the Supreme Court dropped from 34% to 17% three weeks later. By NORC's figures, a year thereafter, that number was back to 35%. Chapter 6 returns to this issue.

Figure 3.2 offers another look by comparing the percentage of liberal Supreme Court decisions versus the percentage of times public opinion was liberal on poll-matched decisions, again for five-year moving averages. The public opinion measure in figure 3.2 is analogous to the well-known public mood measure except that it is based on poll-matching, reported in percentages rather than indexed, and depicted for running five-year time periods. The Court was sometimes out of sync with American public opinion, mostly by handing down decisions that were more liberal than was public opinion, particularly so during the Stone and Warren Courts. Only occasionally was the Court more conservative than was public opinion. Roberts Court decisions closely matched public opinion.

Coincidental Representation

Table 3.3 presents the results in another way. If public opinion and the justices were in line ideologically, high levels of representation could occur

Table 3.3   Percentage of Conservative Decisions, by Ideology of Public Opinion

Public Opinion Is Conservative (%)	Public Opinion Is Liberal (%)	Court	Conservative Decisions If Public Opinion Is Conservative (%)	Conservative Decisions If Public Opinion Is Liberal (%)	Difference (Responsiveness) (%)
31	69	Hughes	50	22	28
65	35	Stone	40	25	15
77	23	Vinson	70	50	20
53	47	Warren	39	15	24
54	46	Burger	56	23	33
58	42	Rehnquist	66	41	25
50	50	Roberts	71	37	34
59	41	Overall	59	30	29

Note: Data excludes "unclear" poll matches.
Source: Data collected and analyzed by the author and listed in appendix.

by happenstance. For example, if public opinion had always been liberal during the generally liberal Warren Court, that would produce a high level of representation but only coincidentally so. As the first two columns in table 3.3 report, different Courts face very different public opinion environments—sometimes more conservative, sometimes more liberal. Table 3.3 reports for each modern Court the percentage of times public opinion was ideologically conservative or liberal. Table 3.3 then reports the percentage of conservative decisions by whether the polls were conservative or liberal. The last column in table 3.3 reports a summary measure of responsiveness—that is, how often decisions change ideologically depending on the polls' ideology.

As the final column in table 3.3 shows, all seven modern Courts were somewhat responsive to public opinion. That is, all seven Courts more often produced conservative decisions when the polls were conservative than when the polls were liberal. That said, not all Courts had the same ideological leanings. The Roberts and Vinson Courts best represented conservative poll majorities; the Warren and Stone Courts least well did so. The Warren Court best represented liberal poll majorities; the Vinson Court least well did so. Compared to earlier Courts, the Roberts, Rehnquist, and Burger Courts rank as quite responsive to public opinion. When the polls were conservative, the Vinson, Roberts, and Rehnquist Courts produced conservative decisions about two-thirds of the time. Given liberal public opinion, the latter two Courts produced liberal decisions about three-fifths of the time; the Vinson Court did so only half the time. Chapter 4 applies this schema to the individual justices in naming the "great" and "near-great" justices on representative role.

Artifacts and Representation

Does survey timing or question wording affect the level of representation?[7] As a possibility, Supreme Court decisions might better represent public opinion if the poll question occurs post-decision, if the poll question mentions the Supreme Court as authoring a decision, or if both occur. If so, representation might merely be a byproduct of survey timing and question wording. In survey research, such concerns are termed artifacts and merit careful attention.

Testing for artifacts involves running two tests. First, when did the pollster ask the poll question: before versus after the decision was announced? Second, if the poll question followed the decision's announcement, did the question explicitly mention the Supreme Court as authoring the decision?

Survey timing or question wording does not affect representation. The level of representation is identical (64% of decisions are consistent, either way) whether the poll question came before, versus after the decision was announced. Further, if a post-decision poll question explicitly mentioned how the Court ruled in a decision, 59% of decisions agreed with the polls—versus 66% consistent for post-decision poll matches that did not explain how the Court ruled.

Both results suggest that the Court cannot favorably influence public opinion through an "endorsement effect." Case studies and experiments offer mixed results on the Court's persuasive abilities. By these real-world, real-time results, most Supreme Court decisions agree with the polls, but the Court cannot favorably sway public opinion by announcing a decision.[8]

If these two tests seem too indirect, there is still another test. Sometimes identically worded poll questions are available both shortly before and shortly after the Court announces its decision.[9] When identically worded poll questions are available both soon before and after a decision, poll shifts only reflect reactions to the decision and ensuing commentary, since long-term events and demographic changes cannot affect the poll shifts. As an example, six weeks before the *Obergefell v. Hodges* (2015) decision was announced, a poll question reported 56% favored and 39% opposed "allowing gays and lesbians to marry legally?"[10] Three weeks after the decision, those figures were 54% and 38%, respectively. The poll change was small (only 2%) but moving opposite to the decision.

Past studies show a variety of short-term poll shifts, mostly small, with only modest net shifts. From the Hughes Court through the Burger Court, the average poll shift was virtually zero with slightly more negative than positive shifts. Only for liberal (or activist) decisions did modestly positive poll shifts occur, averaging about 5% *toward* the Court's position after two years (Marshall 1989: 145–56). For the Rehnquist Court, short-term shifts averaged 3% but *away from* the Court's decisions, again with more negative than positive shifts, and under no conditions with poll shifts toward the Court's decision (Marshall 2008: 131–37). Long-term post-decision poll shifts, those that occur over at least a decade, show mostly small positive poll gains for the Court's decisions.

Much like its predecessors, the Roberts Court failed to win short-term support for its decisions. Identically worded poll questions are available both before and after 16 Roberts Court decisions. The average poll shift favoring the Court's decision is very small: only four-tenths of 1%. For liberal decisions, average poll support dropped by a third of 1%; for conservative decisions, average poll support rose by nine-tenths of a percent. For full, written decisions, average poll support rose by two-tenths of a percent; for all other decisions, average poll support rose by seven-tenths of a percent. The important point is that all these average poll shifts are essentially zero.[11] As for earlier Courts, the Roberts Court could not move the poll numbers in its favor.[12] Simply put, the modern Court cannot win public approval for its decisions.[13]

To summarize these findings: most Supreme Court decisions agree with public opinion, but this finding cannot be "explained away" as polling artifacts or as an endorsement effect. Supreme Court decisions do not greatly influence American attitudes on specific issues. The modern Court is representative but unpersuasive.

Explaining these largely null results is somewhat speculative but lies partly in Americans' limited attention to the Court and partly in the Court and the justices' limited popular appeal. True, in recent years, the Court has been more popular than Congress or the executive branch. Yet the Court's approval ratings are still apparently insufficient to sway public opinion. Further, the justices themselves are neither highly visible nor highly popular. In a March 6–9, 2021, *Economist*/YouGov nationwide survey, for example, between a third and a half of Americans had no opinion of each justice. Americans expressed about as many unfavorable as favorable opinions of the justices. The most popular justice, Sonia Sotomayor, had recently administered the oath of office to Vice President Kamala Harris. Justice Sotomayor was favorably viewed by 38% of Americans and unfavorably by 26% of Americans—a net +12% approval rating. The other justices had very small positive or negative net approval ratings: +7% for Thomas, +5% for Gorsuch and Kagan, +4% for Alito and Breyer, −1% for Roberts, −2% for Barrett, and −4% for Kavanaugh. Respondents' opinions mostly divided along partisan lines.[14] Chapter 6 returns to this issue.

POLL CORRECTION AND POLL UPDATING

The Supreme Court uses two important ways to bring judicial decision-making into closer alignment with current public opinion. Through "poll correction," the

Court selectively overturns lower court rulings that are inconsistent with public opinion. The Court also poll corrects state and local laws and policies, although not federal laws and policies, as described later in this chapter. Through "poll updating," the Court selectively overturns its own now-unpopular precedents. The poll-matching method makes it possible to evaluate both practices.

Poll Correction and the Lower Courts

Almost inevitably, if the Supreme Court grants certiorari and hears arguments on an appeal, a state court, a federal district court, a federal appeals court, an agency court, or some combinations thereof have already ruled on the dispute. Indeed, the Court often refuses to grant certiorari until lower courts have fully considered an issue and not until federal appeals courts disagree. As a result, one can compare nearly all Supreme Court decisions to a lower court decision. The question is: Does the Supreme Court better represent nationwide public opinion than do the lower courts?

As an example, the Roberts Court's decisions in *Chiafalo v. Washington* (2020) and *Colorado Department of State v Baca* (2020) agreed with the polls and upheld a state's right to require that presidential electors vote for the candidate who won that state's popular vote. The unanimous *Chiafalo* decision upheld a decision by the Washington state Supreme Court. Both the Roberts Court and the Washington state Supreme Court's rulings agreed with nationwide public opinion.[15] The Supreme Court's per curiam decision in *Baca* overturned a federal appeals court decision in favor of a "faithless elector." Thus, the Supreme Court's per curiam decision in *Baca* "poll corrected" the Tenth Circuit Court of Appeals decision.

On all its decisions (setting aside the few instances of original jurisdiction and excluding "unclear" poll matches), the Supreme Court agreed with nationwide public opinion 64% of the time and disagreed with the polls 36% of the time.[16] By comparison, the last lower court decision agreed with nationwide polls only 51% of the time and disagreed with nationwide polls 49% of the time. Overall, then, since the mid-1930s, the Court's net poll correction rate is 13% (or 64% minus 51% equals 13%). Supreme Court decisions bring lower court decisions more closely into alignment with nationwide public opinion.

Poll correction against the lower courts is a regular feature of Supreme Court decision-making. Poll correction exists across time, across issues, and across different lower courts. Over time, poll correction rates against the lower courts have risen. For the Warren, Burger, Rehnquist, and Roberts Courts, net poll correction rates range from a high of +27% for the Roberts Court to a low of +4% for the Warren Court. Across the earlier, more lightly polled Hughes, Stone, and Vinson Courts, the combined net poll correction rate is +3%.

The Supreme Court widely practices poll correction by major issue and by the dispute's level of visibility. For economic cases (those involving business and labor regulation, taxation, significant federal spending, or such issues), the poll correction rate is +15% (63% consistent for the Supreme Court versus 48% consistent for the last lower court). For fundamental freedom cases, the poll correction rate is also +15% (63% consistent for the Supreme Court versus 48% consistent for the last lower court). For decisions on crime and courts, the poll correction rate is +21% (69% consistent for the Supreme Court versus 48% for the last lower court). For First Amendment cases, the poll correction rate is a smaller, albeit still positive, +4% (54% consistent for the Supreme Court versus 50% consistent for the last lower court).

The modern Court poll corrects both high- and low-visibility disputes. For decisions involving Gallup's top-ranked "most important problem," the poll correction rate is +15% (73% consistent for the Supreme Court versus 58% consistent for the last lower court). For all issues that ranked among Americans' top-five concerns, the poll correction rate is also +15% (64% consistent for the Supreme Court versus 49% consistent for the last lower court). For decisions that do not involve a top-five public concern, the poll correction rate is also +15% (64% consistent for the Supreme Court versus 49% consistent for the last lower court).

The Supreme Court is equally or more often consistent with American public opinion than any type of lower court. The Court's poll correction rate is +16% against the federal appeals courts (67% consistent for the Supreme Court versus 51% consistent for federal appeals courts). The Court's poll correction rate is +19% against the federal district and specialized courts (66% consistent for the Supreme Court versus 47% consistent for federal district and specialized courts). Only against state courts (usually state supreme courts) is there no apparent difference: 55% consistent with the polls both for the Supreme Court and for state courts.[17]

Another way to look at poll correction is to compare certiorari grants versus denials of certiorari or of habeas corpus or a stay. Since the mid-1930s, two-thirds (67%) of lower court decisions on which the Supreme Court declined to grant certiorari (or to grant a stay or habeas corpus)—thereby leaving the lower court decision in effect—agreed with nationwide polls, versus 33% that did not. Now compare these figures to lower court decisions for which the Supreme Court did grant certiorari. When the Supreme Court granted certiorari, only 49% of lower court decisions agreed with nationwide polls versus 51% that did not. The difference of 18% suggests that the Court much more often grants certiorari on unpopular than on popular lower court rulings.

As this suggests, poll correction proceeds in two ways. First, the Supreme Court disproportionately denies certiorari on lower court decisions that agree with nationwide polls, but more often grants certiorari on unpopular lower court decisions. Second, if granting certiorari, the Court disproportionately overturns unpopular lower court decisions. These results address a common pattern whereby the Supreme Court grants certiorari in order to reverse a lower court decision. The net effect of the Court's review-to-reverse norm is that poll correction leads to better representation. Studies relying on the public mood measure report similar results (Calvin, Collins, and Eshbaugh-Soha 2011; Hall, Kirkland, and Windett 2015).

Poll correction against lower courts is a regular feature of Supreme Court behavior. Why exactly poll correction exists against the lower courts merits attention. Possibly, the justices better understand and more highly value nationwide public opinion than do lower court judges. Lower court decisions may better reflect regional, state, or local opinion than nationwide opinion (Owens and Wohlfarth 2017, 2019). Compared to the Supreme Court, lower courts are less free to abandon now-unpopular legal precedents. Federal district and appeals court judges are less closely scrutinized during their Senate confirmations than are the justices. Whatever the causality, poll correction brings lower court decisions closer to contemporary American attitudes.

At first impression, poll correction might seem of only modest importance. The Supreme Court now grants certiorari, holds hearings, and then issues an opinion on only 1% or 2% of all appeals each term. That figure, taken alone, underestimates the importance of poll correction. As lower courts apply poll-corrected decisions to future disputes, many lower court decisions will come into line with nationwide public opinion; other policymakers, both public and private, may change their decisions; and interest groups may bring lawsuits accordingly (Ballingrud 2021; Barak-Coren 2021; Driver 2021; Fix and Kassow 2020; Fix, Kingsland, and Montgomery 2017; Parmet 2021; Rice 2014).

Stare Decisis, Precedents, and Poll Updating

Another norm involves the Supreme Court's overturning of its own earlier rulings. *Stare decisis*—the idea that courts should follow earlier decisions—is undoubtedly an important but flexible norm (Brenner and Spaeth 1995; Segal and Spaeth 1996; Schauer 2019). On average, the Supreme Court overturns its own earlier decisions once or twice a term, occasionally more often. Sometimes a Supreme Court decision openly states that it is overturning a precedent, typically describing the earlier decision as wrongly decided or as no longer workable. Occasionally, dissenting justices accuse the majority of overruling a precedent by degree or even *sub silentio*, that is, without expressly so saying.[18]

Does overturning precedent bring judicial policy-making more closely into alignment with current public opinion? Usually, it does. In 42 poll-matched decisions, the Supreme Court overturned one of its own earlier decisions.[19] When this happens, the new decision more often agrees with contemporary public opinion than did the precedent overturned. Of these 42 decisions that overturned a precedent, the new decision agreed with timely polls 71% of the time, disagreed with the polls just 19% of the time, and was unclear (because of conflicting or closely divided polls) 10% of the time. Setting aside the few unclear cases, decisions overturning a precedent agreed with the polls 79% of the time and disagreed with the polls 21% of the time. This pattern is termed "poll updating," a practice roughly analogous to poll correcting lower court decisions. The poll updating rate is +58% (i.e., 79% consistent for the new decision minus 21% consistent for the precedent equals 58%). In short, overturning precedent usually brings past Supreme Court decisions into agreement with current American attitudes.

Poll updating exists across time, across issues, and across the age of the overturned precedent. For the more lightly polled Hughes, Stone, and Vinson Courts, 71% of the new (overturning) decisions agreed with contemporary polls while 29% did not. For the Warren Court, the figures are 78% and 22%, respectively; for the Burger Court, 80% and 20%; for the Rehnquist Court, 89% and 11%; for the Roberts Court (through the 2019/20 term), 75% and 25%. By these consistent results across Courts, poll updating is a longstanding norm at least dating back to the 1930s.

Poll updating exists across issues. On economic cases, 91% of the new (overturning) rulings were consistent with contemporary polls, versus 9% not. On crime-related decisions, 84% of the new decisions were consistent, versus 16% not. On race-related decisions, 71% of the new decisions were consistent with the polls, versus 29% not. For the remaining decisions, mostly on civil liberties, 73% of the new decisions were consistent with the polls, versus 27% not. These results suggest that poll updating is not limited to a narrow part of the Supreme Court's docket.

Poll updating occurs about equally often regardless of the age of the precedent overturned. If the overturned precedent was relatively recent (i.e., no more than 15 years old) the new (and overturning) decision agreed with the polls 80% of the time, versus 20% not. If the precedent was older than 16 years, as is often the case, the new ruling was consistent with the polls 78% of the time, versus 22% not.

Both poll correction and poll updating are important, although heretofore little studied. Both practices bring judicial policy-making more closely into alignment with modern public opinion.[20] Both practices merit more scholarly attention. One should not underestimate the importance of poll correction and poll updating by looking only at the exact number of lower court decisions or precedents overturned. By poll correcting an unpopular lower court decision or by poll updating an unpopular precedent, the Court signals that lower state and federal courts and other policymakers should so revise their own decisions and the Court encourages (or discourages) future litigation (Ballingrud 2021; Barak-Coren 2021; Driver 2021; Fix and Kassow 2020; Parmet 2021; Rice 2014).

POLL CORRECTION AND FEDERAL, STATE, AND LOCAL POLICYMAKERS

Does the Supreme Court poll correct federal, state, and local laws and policies? Among these 531 poll-matched Supreme Court decisions are 230 legal challenges to a federal law or policy. One should not assume that all federal laws and policies agree with the polls. In fact, poll support for disputed federal laws and policies varies widely. Two well-known *popular* federal laws and policies are the employer mandate in the Affordable Care Act and the Trump Administration's decision to resume death penalty executions. Two *unpopular* federal laws and policies are the Affordable Care Act's individual mandate provision and the Trump Administration's decision to divert military funding to build a wall along the U.S. Mexican border. Many other decisions occur on either side of the counter-majoritarian divide.

Overall, about two-thirds (63%) of federal laws and policies agreed with public opinion when the Court considered the lawsuit. A third (32%) of disputed federal laws and policies disagreed with the polls. On a few disputes (6%), the polls were evenly divided or inconsistent. Once again setting aside instances of unclear poll matches, two-thirds (66%) of disputed federal laws and policies agreed with the polls but a third (34%) did not. Although methodologies and time periods vary, these estimates and those for the states and localities, reported next in the chapter, resemble estimates elsewhere (Monroe 1979, 1998; Page and Shapiro 1983; Sutton 1973; Erikson 1976).

Does the modern Court poll correct against federal laws and policies? The short answer is no. Two-thirds of challenged federal laws and policies agreed with the polls. When the Court has done its work, two-thirds (66%) of its decisions agree with public opinion and a third (34%) do not. The result is a zero net poll correction rate.

Even so, whether the disputed federal law or policy agrees with public opinion still matters. If a challenged federal law or policy agrees with the polls, the odds that the Court will uphold it are three-to-one. That is, the Court upheld 75% of popular federal laws and policies and overturned the remaining 25%. If a federal law or policy *disagrees* with the polls, there are only even odds that the Court will uphold it as overturn it (i.e., 53% of unpopular federal laws and policies were upheld, 47% were overturned).

The Roberts Court's record resembles that for earlier Courts. The Roberts Court upheld 67% and overturned 33% of popular federal laws and policies. For unpopular federal laws and policies, the Roberts Court upheld about half (48%) while overturning about half (52%). Summarizing these results: the Court treats popular federal laws and policies much more favorably than unpopular ones.

The picture for disputes over state and local laws and policies is different. Within this sample of poll-matched Supreme Court decisions are 308 challenges to state or local laws and policies. Compared to federal laws and policies, state and local laws and policies that reach the Supreme Court less often agree with public opinion. Only 57% of challenged state and local policies agreed with the polls, versus 43% that did not, again setting aside instances of closely divided or inconsistent polls. Further, the Supreme Court more often poll corrects state and local policies than it does federal laws and policies. By comparison, two-thirds (65%) of Supreme Court decisions on disputed state and local laws agreed with the polls, versus 35% that did not. This is a poll correction rate of +8% (65% minus 57% equals 8%).

The modern Court is less deferential to state and local than to federal laws and policies. If a state or local policy agreed with timely polls, the Court upheld it 61% of the time (versus a 75% figure for federal laws and policies). If the state and local policy was unpopular, the Court upheld it only 25% of the time (versus a 53% figure for federal laws and policies). As a result, the Court's decisions on disputed state and local policies agree with the polls two-thirds of the time but through a more aggressive pattern of poll correction.

Taken together, the evidence is clear. Most Supreme Court decisions represent current American attitudes. The modern Court poll corrects against the lower courts and against state and local governments, but not against federal laws and policies. When the Court overturns its own precedents, the new decisions better reflect contemporary public opinion than did the old. The impact of poll correction and of poll updating should not be underestimated. Both practices often affect many existing laws, policies, privately made decisions, and lower court decisions beyond the one immediately in question (Ballingrud 2021; Barak-Coren 2021; Driver 2021; Fix and Kassow 2020; Fix, Kingsland, and Montgomery 2017; Lindquist and Corley 2013; Hoekstra 2005; Parmet 2021). Poll correction and poll updating discourage disfavored laws and policies from being enacted in the future; encourage interest groups and litigants to sponsor future litigation (Rice 2014); and pressure lower courts, legislatures, and agencies to shape their decisions accordingly.[21]

Does all this make the Supreme Court a voice of the people? Opinions will differ as to what standards should apply. True, not every Supreme Court decision agrees with public opinion. The perfection standard, however, is very exacting and one that no other public policymaker would meet. Supreme

Court decisions *as often* reflect American attitudes as do federal laws and policies under review; *more often* do so than lower federal court decisions that reach the Court upon appeal; *more often* do so than state and local laws and policies under review; and *more often* do so than precedents overturned. Whatever the causality, representing public opinion is a consistent modern norm across time, Courts, and issues.

CONCLUSION AND DISCUSSION

Most Supreme Court decisions represent American public opinion. This pattern holds up across all seven modern Courts, across most if not quite all issues, and across both grants and denials of certiorari. The modern Court is a representative institution notwithstanding its tenuous formal ties to mass public opinion. Judging from these poll-matched decisions, Supreme Court decisions more often agree with nationwide public opinion than do disputed state or local policies and about equally as often as do disputed federal laws and policies. The modern Court often poll corrects lower court decisions and poll updates its own precedents. Thus far, the Roberts Court has equally well or even slightly better represented American attitudes than did earlier Courts.

Is representing public opinion an unstated norm? A norm is a colloquial term that denotes the Court's typical or customary behavior nowhere required by the Constitution or public law.[22] Over the years, norms come and go. During the Court's earliest years, the justices announced their opinions seriatim, that is, one by one. That practice ended after John Marshall became Chief Justice in 1801. Until the early 1940s, dissents were rare. During the Stone Court, dissents and concurrences became a norm. Unanimity in the face of expected strong public criticism remained for a time an occasional practice but eventually fell out of favor (Zilis 2017). Unlike earlier Courts, the Roberts Court seldom, if ever affirms a lower court ruling that upheld a statute (Johnson and Whittington 2018).

Norms not only disappear but sometimes emerge (Howard 2015). The Court now routinely issues fewer than a hundred full, written decisions per term, far fewer than during the 1980s and before (Owens and Simon 2012; Heise, Wells, and Chutkow 2020). The Court now mostly grants certiorari to overturn a lower court ruling. Each justice now authors about an equal number of majority opinions, per term. The Court is generous in allowing the filing of amicus curiae briefs and in granting the Solicitor General's requests to appear. A justice who earlier voted one way usually, albeit not inevitably votes the same way in similar later disputes. The Court often reserves its "blockbuster" decisions for the last few days of each term. Justices increasingly speak and travel widely. Some justices sign lucrative book deals.

Justices often try to time their retirements to ensure a like-minded replacement. These modern norms are so well established that the occasional exception can spark widespread commentary.

A fair standard for judging whether representation is a norm is to compare it to other well-recognized modern norms. Were universal practice, with no exceptions at all, the proper standard to apply in judging whether a norm exists, one could not acknowledge most modern norms. As this chapter describes, between three-fifths and two-thirds of Supreme Court decisions agree with the polls, a figure that has been relatively consistent for many decades. By that standard, representing public opinion is as commonly practiced as are several other norms and should rank an unstated norm even if the justices' rhetoric does not wholly embrace that norm.

The representation norm operates in a largely predictable fashion. The Supreme Court best represents public opinion when the issue is among the public's most important problems. The representation norm is stronger if there is little chance of an adverse reaction. The Court more aggressively poll corrects state and local governments than federal policymakers. Poll updating brings the Court's precedents back into line with current public opinion.

That most Supreme Court decisions represent public opinion is of some consequence. Americans who pay at least passing attention to the Court and who fashion their expectations from experience may well expect that most Supreme Court decisions will agree with American attitudes. Over the decades, representation becomes a settled expectation. Such experiences and expectations buttress judicial symbols as a source of public support for the Court. Chapter 6 returns to this question.

Chapter 4 turns to nationwide public opinion and the individual justices. Chapter 5 then asks how well the modern Supreme Court and the justices represent specific groups. To preview the next two chapters, some justices far better represent public opinion than do others. Those justices who outpace the other justices comprise the representative "greats" or "near-greats." Some justices are representative laggards. The individual justices' behavior greatly affects whether the Court's decisions agree with American attitudes. Only one or two votes often make the difference in whether a decision agrees with public opinion. Further, some justices represent specific groups far better (or alternatively, far worse) than do others, and not always so in the expected fashion.

NOTES

1. Although the number of poll-matched decisions herein is nearly double that identified in earlier accounts, the percentages of consistent versus inconsistent

decisions remain nearly unchanged since earlier accounts through the Rehnquist Court (Marshall 1989: 78–79; 2008: 35).

2. Reweighting for the more lightly polled Hughes, Stone, and Vinson Courts is dichotomous: whether the case involved economic issues or not. Reweighting for the Warren, Burger, Rehnquist, and Roberts Courts is trichotomous: whether the case involves economic, crime, or other issues. Estimates for the "true" caseload use figures in the *Supreme Court Compendium* with estimates before 1946 and after 2013. Since it was not possible to identify the issues raised in denials of certiorari, there are no reweighted estimates for those decisions.

3. According to the *Supreme Court Compendium*, the number of signed and per curiam (after oral argument) opinions averaged about 110–120 during the Vinson and Warren Courts, about 150 during the Burger Court, about 90 for the Rehnquist Court, and only 73 for the Roberts Court through the 2013–14 term. The number of poll matches, per term, averages 3.5 during the Hughes, Stone, and Vinson Courts, and then increases to 4 for the Warren Court, to 7.9 (Burger Court), 8.9 (Rehnquist Court), and 5.4 (Roberts Court) through the 2019–20 term.

4. If the poll matches that were identified after this book's data analysis was completed, as reported in section 4 of the appendix, are also included, the Roberts Court results would be 67% rather than 69% consistent, excluding "unclear" matches.

5. During the time covered by this book, on average, about half of Court decisions were unanimous, according to the annual count in the *Harvard Law Review*; see also Sunstein (2015).

6. Beginning in 1937 there are always ten or more poll-to-decision matches, per year, for the five-year rolling averages reported in figure 3.1.

7. Since the late 1930s, survey research has identified many artifacts (commonly called "effects") including question wording, question order, question choice, seasonal, house, interviewer, mode, and setting effects.

8. Over longer periods of time, poll support sometimes moves slowly in favor of Supreme Court decisions (Ura 2014; Marshall 1989: 154–55; 2008: 134–36).

9. Some post-decision poll questions mention that the Supreme Court recently ruled on this issue and how so. The analysis just below evaluates the effect of this wording change.

10. Princeton Survey Research Associates, 5/12-18/2015 and 7/14-20/2015, conducted these surveys for Pew Research Center.

11. Six decisions had a negative pre-to-post poll shift; eight decisions had a positive shift; two decisions had no shift. The two largest poll shifts include one negative and one positive five-point shift in *Windsor v. U.S.* (2013) and *Center for Biological Diversity v. Wolf* (2019), respectively, with margins of error of 3%.

12. Fontana and Krewson (2020) offer similar evidence on Chief Justice Roberts's response to President Trump's criticism of "Obama judges."

13. Nor do presidential comments on high-profile Supreme Court decisions typically lead to significantly favorable poll shifts toward the president's position (Collins and Eshbaugh-Soha 2019).

14. Zilis and Borne (2021) point to post-decision media framing as a reason that the Court may not win popular approval for its decisions.

15. The poll match is: "In the U.S., the President is chosen by the Electoral College, comprised of 'electors' from all 50 states and the District of Columbia. Some people think that states should be able to require Electoral College electors to vote for the person who won the majority of votes in the state and not some other person. However, some people think that electors should be able to vote for whomever they want. What do you think? States SHOULD be able to require their 'electors' to vote for the candidate who won their state? States SHOULD NOT be able to require their 'electors' to vote for the candidate who won their state?" Source: SCOTUS Poll by YouGov, 4/29-5/12/2020. Of approximately 2,000 respondents, 61% said should be required, while 39% said should not.

16. Three-quarters (75%) of the few rulings on original jurisdiction agreed with public opinion and the remaining 25% disagreed.

17. The unexpected finding for state courts as the last prior court results from a slightly negative net poll correction rate against state courts for the Hughes, Stone, Vinson, and Warren Courts (a –12% combined rate) and thereafter a +8% poll correction rate for the Burger, Rehnquist, and Roberts Courts.

18. The Supreme Court sometimes decides a new case differently than a lower court decision on a point on which the Court had previously denied certiorari. An example is the landmark decision, *Loving v. Virginia* (1967), striking down state laws banning racial intermarriage. Eleven years earlier, the Court denied certiorari in *Naim v. Naim* (1956), thereby allowing states to bar interracial marriages. Since a cert denial is not, per se, a precedent, this analysis only includes overturned precedents that were full, written decisions.

19. Decisions that overturn precedent are taken from the Library of Congress' frequently updated list.

20. Decisions that are unpopular, when announced, are also overturned more quickly than are popular-at-the-time decisions (Marshall 2008: 139–52).

21. For recent reviews of the extensive literature on compliance with Supreme Court decisions, see Fix and Kassow (2020); Hoekstra (2009); Kastellec (2018); Graber (2017); Fix and Fairbanks (2020); Fix, Kingsland, and Montgomery (2017); Masood, Kassow, and Songer (2019); and Bosworth (2017).

22. The term "norm" typically describes behavior rather than substantive doctrine. Under one current norm on nominations, presidents typically nominate relatively young federal appeals court judges from their own party. Under another norm, the justices seldom grant certiorari until a conflict appears between lower federal courts. Under a recent retirement norm, justices try to time their retirement to ensure an ideologically like-minded replacement (Zigerell 2013; Chabot 2019; Benjamin and Vanberg 2016; Strayhorn 2020).

Chapter 4

The Justices' Representative Role

Judicial role is a long-studied, widely familiar concept. A role describes activities that some justices regularly perform but other justices do not. The constitution and public law define a few roles, but most roles are informal. Some roles are defined by Court custom. A justice' ability, talent, or inclination define other roles. The media, political elites, or the public define still other roles. A few roles are defined by other justices' behavior. Some roles come and go over the years. Judicial scholars seldom study representative role, that is, how well a justice reflects public opinion in his or her votes. Representative role differs from other now-familiar roles. This chapter first outlines several well-known judicial roles and then evaluates representative role.

The constitution defines the chief justice's role, the best-known role, but in little detail. A chief justice is nominated by a president and confirmed by the U.S. Senate just as are the other justices. By Court practice, the chief justice has several leadership responsibilities and unique responsibilities outside the Court, described further in the chapter. On rare occasion, the chief justice presides over a presidential impeachment trial in the U.S. Senate. Scholarly practice often describes Supreme Court eras by the presiding chief justice, just as journalists often report and comment on the chief justice. The chief justice earns a slightly higher salary than an associate justice. Another role defined by Court tradition is that the senior associate justice who votes differently than the chief justice will designate who authors the majority opinion when the chief justice is not in the majority.

Many roles are defined neither by the constitution, nor by law, nor by Court practice, but rather by a justice's efforts and abilities. These include being an intellectual leader (e.g., as Justices Powell, Rehnquist, and Scalia), a task leader (e.g., Justices Brennan, Powell, and Rehnquist), or an argument leader at hearings (e.g., Justices Scalia, Ginsburg, or Sotomayor). The social leader role has largely disappeared into history (Black, Owens, and Wedeking 2016; Danelski 2016). Some justices frequently speak in public, represent the Court at Congressional hearings, or attend numerous national or international conferences.

Not all judicial roles win plaudits. In recent years, a few justices have become minor celebrities through their personal histories; recent confirmations; book tours; appearances at political meetings, media interviews, television or film biographies; or appearances at mock trials, sports, or musical events. As of the Court's 2019–2020 term, Justices Ruth Bader Ginsburg and Brett Kavanaugh ranked highest on the FameFlux ranking of celebrities at number 306 and 637, respectively. Most justices barely register even as minor celebrities.[1] Celebrity justices are an emerging judicial role although many legal scholars take a dim view (Hasen 2016; Lerner and Lund 2010; Sherry 2020). Historically, a few justices played the role of Court curmudgeon; Justice McReynolds is universally so described (Abraham 2008: 138–41). Several justices take on no identifiable roles, leading scholars to rank most of them as below average or even as a failure. Few justices take on more than one or two informal roles at a time.

The justices' voting patterns define another role. Often, although not always, the justice least closely aligned with either the Court's current liberal or conservative voting bloc is the tiebreaker in five-to-four votes (Enns and Wohlfarth 2013; Lauderdale and Clark 2012). Court watchers sometimes describe the tiebreaker role as the median justice or as the "most dangerous" justice. The tiebreaker role is entirely unofficial and different justices can fill this role depending on how other justices split their votes.

Sometimes a role involves a justice's personal background. Symbolic representation occurs when a justice has the same background as a politically important but underrepresented or never-before-represented group. Often a president and the media stress the importance of symbolic appointments, at least the first time for such a nomination. In 1967, Thurgood Marshall became the first Black justice. In 1981, Sandra Day O'Connor became the first woman justice. Both justices' symbolic status won heavy media attention beginning with their nominations and continuing throughout their Court tenure. Typically, a symbolic role is reserved for the first such appointee; later justices who fit into the same category are less often so described until the novelty value fades away (Escobar-Lemmon et al. 2016). Symbolic roles involve no official duties since politics, the public, media attention, and Court history entirely define this role. Sometimes a symbolic role translates into policy representation for the group so represented, sometimes not (Marshall 2008: 107–21).[2] Chapter 5 returns to this question, reporting only mixed evidence that symbolic representation leads to policy representation.

Court watchers have carefully described all these judicial roles. By comparison, representative role has won little attention. Representative role is different from the roles just described. It is neither a constitutional, nor a legal, nor a formal role. Nor does representative role necessarily require special effort or ability. Nor does it depend on other justices' voting patterns. Nor does it require the justice to be a tiebreaker. Nor does it necessarily involve a justice's gender, religion, region, or race. Representative role may not be a highly valued role that the justices seek out. Indeed, several high-ranking justices on representative role have made ambivalent or negative comments on the importance of representing public opinion (e.g., Rehnquist 1987: 236). By the evidence presented next, representative role is little correlated with most other roles.

Representative role is empirically defined solely by how often a justice's votes agree with public opinion or some part thereof. Aside from their votes, the justices' hidden motives (Posner 2008) do not play into how representative role is measured. The justices have several reasons to be concerned about public opinion, including succeeding with the Court's legislation wish list (Ura and Wohlfarth 2010); avoiding Congressional Court-curbing (Clark 2011; Nelson and Uribe-McGuire 2017); preserving the Court's approval ratings and sense of legitimacy; winning greater compliance in lower courts, state legislatures, and agencies; avoiding criticism; and perhaps for a few justices preserving their celebrity status. Some justices may simply prefer to stay within the outer bounds of public opinion (Primus 2010). Not every justice's voting patterns strongly reflect public opinion. Focusing on representative role directs our attention outside rather than inside the Court. Chapter 3 focused on how often, when, and why Supreme Court decisions represent public opinion. This chapter turns to the individual justices. Chapter 5 then evaluates how well the Court and the justices represent specific groups in American society.

MEASURING REPRESENTATIVE ROLE

Measuring an individual justice's representative role is straightforward and mostly follows the procedures described in chapter 2. A justice's votes are poll matched to public opinion on issues in Supreme Court decisions and each justice's votes are classified as consistent, inconsistent, or unclear. The same procedure is used to compare a justice's votes to the views of specific groups of Americans by race, gender, education, or partisanship. Chapter 1 provided examples by comparing Americans' attitudes on marriage equality with the justices' votes in *U.S. v. Windsor* (2013) and *Obergefell v. Hodges* (2015). When coding the individual justices, mostly only votes on full, written decisions are counted since denials of certiorari, denials of habeas corpus, or denials of a stay seldom describe how the justices voted.[3] As elsewhere, chapters 4 and 5 include the justices' poll-matched votes from the mid-1930s through the 2019–2020 term.[4]

COMPARING THE JUSTICES ON REPRESENTATIVE ROLE

The 48 justices who served on the modern Court differ considerably on representative role. Table 4.1 ranks 43 justices for whom at least a dozen votes can be poll matched. At the top of the list, over 70% of Chief Justice Hughes and Justices Brandeis, Minton, Owen Roberts, and Whites' votes agreed with nationwide public opinion. Ranking just behind, at over 60%, are Justices Powell, and Clark, and Chief Justices Stone, Vinson, Rehnquist, and John Roberts. These 11 justices' votes most often agreed with public opinion. They are obviously a varied lot. Five served as chief justice. Several won plaudits for their Court tenure, others not so. These 11 justices include both Republicans and Democrats, and both liberals and conservatives. Their service spans the entire modern Court.

At the other extreme are 11 justices whose votes agreed with the polls less than half of the time, including Justices McReynolds, Butler, Sutherland, Black, Murphy, Rutledge, Marshall, Kavanaugh, Souter, Stevens, and Brennan. These justices are also a varied lot as to when and how long they served on the Court, their partisan affiliation, and their judicial philosophies. In between the top and the bottom groups fall the remaining justices who cast at least a dozen poll-matched votes.

As table 4.1 indicates, the justices differ in how often their votes agree with public opinion. Why so? To begin: Does representative role vary by the appointing president, by the appointing president's political party, or by the appointing president's reputation? Table 4.2 combines the justices' votes, by appointing president, and reports the percentage of the justices' votes that agree with the polls, by appointing president.

Representative role varies by appointing president but is not linked to an appointing president's partisanship. Republican presidents' appointees voted consistently with the polls 57% of the time. For appointees of Democratic presidents, the figure was 56% consistent.

"Great" presidents do not necessarily appoint great justices on representative role. Many rankings of presidential greatness exist, most of them compiled by polling historians, legal scholars, journalists, or political scientists.[5] Among the presidents who appointed justices to the modern Court, Presidents Franklin Roosevelt, Woodrow Wilson, and Harry Truman usually rank as

Table 4.1   Justices Ranked by Agreement with Public Opinion

Rank	Justice	Justices' Votes That Agree with the Polls (%)	Number of Votes
1	Hughes* (Chief Justice), 1930–1941	78	23
2	Brandeis*, 1916–1939	73	15
3 (tie)	White, 1962–1993	70	184
	Owen Roberts*, 1930–1945	70	40
	Minton, 1949–1956	70	20
6	Powell, 1972–1987	69	102
7	Stone* (Chief Justice), 1925–1946	67	42
8	Clark, 1949–1967	64	53
9 (tie)	Rehnquist (Chief Justice), 1972–2005	63	218
	John Roberts* (Chief Justice), 2005–	63	68
11	Vinson (Chief Justice), 1946–1953	62	21
12 (tie)	Kennedy, 1988–2018	60	164
	O'Connor, 1981–2006	60	153
	Stewart, 1958–1981	60	114
	Burger (Chief Justice), 1969–86	60	102
16 (tie)	Scalia, 1986–2016	59	168
	Reed, 1938–1957	59	63
18 (tie)	Breyer*, 1994–	58	137
	Kagan*, 2010–	58	50
	Jackson, 1941–1954	58	36
21(tie)	Frankfurter, 1939–1962	56	71
	Harlan, 1955–1971	56	61
	Warren (Chief Justice), 1953–1969	56	55
	Fortas, 1965–1969	56	16
25 (tie)	Alito*, 2006–	55	66
	Burton, 1945–1958	55	38
	Gorsuch*, 2017–	55	22
28	Douglas, 1939–1975	54	136
29	Blackmun, 1970–1994	53	153
30 (tie)	Thomas*, 1991–	52	157
	Ginsburg, 1993–2020	52	142
32	Sotomayor*, 2009–	51	57
33 (tie)	Brennan, 1956–1990	49	175
	Souter, 1990–2009	49	103
35	Black, 1937–1971	48	123
36	Stevens, 1975–2010	47	206
37 (tie)	Murphy, 1940–1949	46	33
	Rutledge, 1943–1949	46	22
39	Kavanaugh*, 2018–	44	18
40	Marshall, 1967–1991	43	148
41	Sutherland*, 1922–1938	42	12
42	Butler*, 1923–1939	38	16
43	McReynolds*, 1914–1941	32	19

* A justice whose tenure partly predates the modern Court or who remains on the Court after the 2019–2020 term.

Notes: Data excludes "unclear" votes (those with conflicting or closely divided poll results within the .05 margin of error). Two justices (Stone and Rehnquist) served as an associate justice before becoming Chief Justice. Chief Justice Hughes served as an associate justice between 1910 and 1916. The remaining five justices cast fewer than a dozen poll-matched votes, including Justices Byrnes, 1941–1942 (75%, 4 votes); Goldberg, 1962–1965 (70%, 10 votes); Cardozo, 1932–1938 (64%, 11 votes); Van Devanter, 1911–1937 (46%, 11 votes); and Whittaker, 1957–1962 (33%, 9 votes).

Source: Data collected and analyzed by the author and listed in appendix.

Table 4.2   Presidential Appointees' Agreement with Public Opinion

Appointing President	Number of Justices Appointed Herein	Justices' Votes That Are Consistent (%)	Total Number of Votes
Taft* (R)	1	45	11
Wilson* (D)	2	50	34
Harding* (R)	2	38	29
Coolidge* (R)	1	67	42
Hoover* (R)	3	72	74
Roosevelt (D)	8	53	496
Truman (D)	4	68	136
Eisenhower (R)	5	54	416
Kennedy (D)	2	69	193
Johnson (D)	2	45	164
Nixon (R)	4	61	577
Ford (R)	1	46	205
Reagan (R)	3	60	485
G.H.W. Bush* (R)	2	52	260
Clinton* (D)	2	55	279
G.W. Bush* (R)	2	59	134
Obama* (D)	2	54	107
Trump* (R)	2	50	40

* A president whose justices partly predate the modern Court or whose justices remain on the Court after the 2019/20 term; (R), a Republican Party president; (D), a Democratic Party president.
Notes: Chief Justices Stone and Rehnquist are counted under the president who originally appointed them (Coolidge and Nixon, respectively). President Trump's third appointee, Justice Barrett, joined the Court after the 2019–20 term and is not included here.
Source: Data collected and analyzed by the author and listed in the appendix.

great or near-great presidents. Some recent lists include Presidents Lyndon Johnson, Dwight Eisenhower, John Kennedy, and Ronald Reagan. Near the bottom of recent lists are Presidents Coolidge, Nixon, Ford, Harding, Hoover, and George W. Bush.

There is no obvious relationship between presidential greatness and justices' rankings on representative role. The appointees of Presidents Hoover, Kennedy, Truman, and Coolidge average highest on representative role. At the bottom are the appointees of Presidents Wilson, Ford, Johnson, Taft, and Harding. For the eight presidents whose appointees both began and ended their service during the modern Court (to date), the appointees of Presidents Kennedy, Truman, Nixon, and Reagan rank more highly. Those of Presidents Eisenhower, Roosevelt, Ford, Johnson, and Trump trail behind. For each of the last five presidents' appointees (each president with two justices apiece through the 2019–2020 term), the justices' average is only middling.

As an obvious follow-up question: Do otherwise highly regarded justices rank highly on representative role? Just as with ranking presidents, ranking the justices may seem subjective but several lists are available, compiled mostly by surveying judicial scholars. As do American presidents, the justices vary greatly in their rankings. Some justices consistently rank near the top; others rank near the bottom. Comiskey (2004: 87–93, 2006) reports ratings for justices appointed during the 1900s (through Ginsburg and Breyer).[6] Breaking the modern Court's justices into three groups, the 10 top-ranked justices cast votes 59% of which agreed with the polls. For the 21 middle-ranked justices, the figure was 57%, a figure identical to that for the bottom-ranked 11 justices. In short, measures of judicial greatness are unrelated to representative role. Stated differently, legal scholars and political scientists who rate the justices apparently do not much value representative role.

Few of the justices' background experiences, roles, orientations, or personal traits are strongly tied to representative role. Gender is not. Fifty-six percent of votes cast by the four women justices agree with the polls, nearly identical to the 57% figure for male justices. Family background as a proxy for social class is uncorrelated with representative role. Ethnicity and race somewhat matter. Only 48% of the (combined) votes of the Court's three racial minorities—Justices Marshall, Thomas, and Sotomayor—agreed with the polls. For the remaining justices, the average is 58% consistent. Chapter 5 returns to representation by gender, race, education, and partisanship.

Perhaps surprisingly, confirmation votes are not strongly linked to representative role. Justices confirmed unanimously or nearly so (with fewer than 10 dissenting votes) do not much differ from justices confirmed with 10–25 dissenting votes. Excepting Justice Rehnquist, the six justices confirmed but with more than 25 dissenting votes averaged only slightly below average on representative role.[7]

Nor is past campaign experience linked to stronger representative role. Several justices ran for elective office before coming to the Court, including local, statewide, Congressional, and presidential bids. Until the 1960s, prior campaign and elective experience was common among the justices, although not since then. Fifty-six percent of votes cast by justices with past campaign experience agreed with the polls—versus a near-identical 57% figure for the remaining justices. As a cohort, only President Truman's appointees with U.S. Senate experience rank highly in representative role.[8]

Very few prior career experiences correlate strongly with representative role. For example, a few justices had prior experience as an advocate for a social group or movement—most notably, Justices Brandeis, Marshall, and Ginsburg. Justice Brandeis is a highly consistent justice, but Justices Ginsburg and Marshall rank only middling or lower. Twenty-four justices—most notably including Justices Frankfurter, Ginsburg, Kagan, and Scalia, and Chief Justice Stone—had sustained prior experience as law school professors. Several other justices' such experience was only intermittent and early in a justice's career. Having an academic career, however, is uncorrelated with representative role.

At one time, many justices had prior military experience, although that is no longer true. Fifteen of these justices had prior military experience. Overall, there is little relationship between military experience and representative role—but with one exception. All five justices (Rehnquist, Kennedy, Clark, Vinson, and Breyer) who served in the military but who were not officers scored as above average on representative role. Officers at all levels (by rank, from lieutenant to colonel) compiled only a mixed record.

At one time some justices pursued significant off-the-Court roles. As notable examples, Justice Jackson served as chief prosecutor at the Nuremberg war crime trials and Chief Justice Warren chaired the commission that investigated President John Kennedy's assassination. A few justices were presidential confidants, perhaps most notably, Justice Fortas. Of justices who served in significant off-the-Court activities, Justices Brandeis, Burger, Hughes, Jackson, Reed, Owen Roberts, Stone, and Vinson all scored as above average on representative role.[9] The remaining such justices (Douglas, Fortas, Frankfurter, Murphy, and Warren) mostly rank as about average.[10] Justices who are active in off-the-Court roles rank as above average in representative role, although the causality is difficult to discern.

Matthew Hall's book, *What Justices Want* (2018), evaluates 34 recent justices on the "Big Five" personality traits: extraversion, conscientiousness, agreeableness, neuroticism, and openness. For example, on extraversion, Justices Kagan, Sotomayor, and Ginsburg rank at the top, while Justices Burton, Rutledge, and Murphy rank at the bottom. By this account, none of these "big five" personality traits correlate strongly with representative role. As elsewhere, representative role appears to be largely a stand-alone trait unrelated to past experiences, personality traits, or other judicial roles except chief justice status. By another account (Black, Owens, Wedeking, and Wohlfarth 2020: 34–42, 270–85; 2021) using different measures of conscientiousness, however, highly conscientious justices behave very different from their less conscientious brethren. Highly conscientious justices more closely follow public opinion as measured by the public mood, perhaps because conscientious justices seek broader information. Results described later in this chapter show that "great" and "near-great" representative justices mostly rank as above average (and often as far above average) on conscientiousness (Black, Owens, Wedeking, and Wohlfarth 2020: 42). Only a few exceptions appear; Chief Justice Warren and Justice Marshall rank as highly conscientious but rank only as middling or lower on representative role; Chief Justice Stone ranks low on conscientiousness but high on representative role.

Now, consider ideology. As table 4.3 indicates, some justices nearly always vote in a liberal direction, while others nearly as often vote conservative. A liberal's hypothetical "dream Court" would comprise the nine most liberal justices: Murphy, Douglas, Ginsburg, Kagan, Warren, Fortas, Brennan,

Table 4.3 Representation and the Justices' Ideological Behavior

Justice	Consistent (%)	Conservative Votes Overall (%)	Conservative When Public Opinion Is Conservative (%)	Conservative When Public Opinion Is Liberal (%)	Difference ("Swing") (%)
Hughes*	78	26	50	13	37
Brandeis*	73	19	33	10	23
Minton	71	50	58	14	44
White	70	50	68	28	40
Owen Roberts*	70	33	52	21	31
Powell	68	48	63	24	39
Stone*	67	28	44	17	27
Clark	65	41	55	20	35
Rehnquist	63	77	83	61	22
John Roberts*	63	66	81	55	26
Vinson	62	65	71	60	11
Kennedy	60	63	70	53	17
O'Connor	60	63	69	53	16
Stewart	60	35	51	26	25
Burger	60	65	74	53	21
Scalia	59	79	82	71	11
Reed	59	33	45	20	25
Breyer*	58	26	42	16	26
Kagan*	58	13	24	4	20
Jackson	58	49	58	38	20
Frankfurter	57	39	50	27	23
Harlan	56	42	55	38	17
Warren	56	12	22	4	18
Fortas	56	11	13	0	13
Burton	56	59	63	50	13
Alito*	55	91	94	90	4
Gorsuch*	55	82	100	67	33
Douglas	54	16	23	8	15
Blackmun	53	31	36	25	11
Thomas*	52	83	85	81	4
Ginsburg	52	16	19	13	6
Sotomayor*	51	8	12	4	8
Brennan	49	11	15	7	8
Souter	49	29	36	21	15
Black	48	23	22	24	2*
Stevens	46	22	25	18	7
Murphy	46	17	14	21	7*
Rutledge	44	22	29	16	13
Kavanaugh*	44	94	100	90	10
Marshall	43	7	7	2	5
Sutherland*	42	75	75	75	0
Butler*	38	89	71	92	21*
McReynolds*	32	86	88	85	3

*(first column), a justice whose service began prior to the poll-matching era or who continued to serve on the Court after the 2019/20 term; *(final column), a swing score that is not in the expected direction.

Note: Percentages in the third, fourth, fifth, and final columns exclude the few votes without a clear ideological content. To compute a justice's percentage of liberal votes, subtract the figure in column three from 100. Chief Justice status and dates of service appear in table 4.1.

Source: Data collected and analyzed by the author and listed in the appendix.

Sotomayor, and Marshall. These nine justices' votes average 52% consistent. At the other extreme, a hypothetical "dream Court" for conservatives would comprise the nine most conservative justices: Sutherland, Rehnquist, Scalia, Gorsuch, Thomas, McReynolds, Butler, Alito, and Kavanaugh. These nine justices' votes average 49% consistent. Both imaginary Courts fall well below the representative role average of 60% for the remaining justices. Ideological rigor, whether liberal or conservative, results in low rates of representing public opinion. The discussion at table 4.3 returns to this issue.

An intriguing question is whether and how a justice's preferred approach to judicial interpretation ties into representative role. As an example, two of Justice Anthony Kennedy's preferred approaches were an expansive notion of individual liberty and a strongly held view of the states' importance in federalism disputes.[11] In his "liberty" votes on gay rights, religious freedom and expression, free speech, and race, 60% of Justice Kennedy's votes agreed with public opinion. On federalism votes, only 46% of his votes agreed with public opinion. In short, Justice Kennedy's preferred approaches made no net difference in representative role for his "liberty" votes and led to a below-average level of representation on federalism disputes.

Many other justices have preferred approaches to deciding cases. Justices Scalia, Thomas, and Gorsuch advocate originalism or textualism. By these standards, the text or historical meaning of the constitution and constitutional amendments should dictate modern-day rulings. In the abstract, it is not clear whether a devotion to originalism and textualism would lead a justice to agree with modern-day public opinion. In any case, these three justices rank as about average on representative role (at 59%, 52%, and 55%, respectively).[12]

The "living constitution" is another interpretative method, albeit one that is difficult to define with great precision. One advocate explains the idea as a common law constitution that is strongly influenced by evolving precedent, major statutes, and modern popular concepts of rights, and "one that can protect fundamental precedents against transient public opinion" (Strauss 2010: 3; see Friedman and Smith 1998; Eskridge and Ferejohn 2001). In another account: "living constitutionalism . . . is the practice of interpreting the Constitution, usually in a nonhistorical way, to meet the needs of the present" (Friedman and Smith 1998: 10). Most "living Constitution" decisions are liberal by conventional meaning. Most (86%) major such decisions as described in Ackerman (2007), Balkin (2009), and Strauss (2010) agree with public opinion; 11% disagree; the remaining 13% are "unclear." Other lists may produce different results.

Cass Sunstein (1999, 2005, 2006) describes minimalism as another approach. Under minimalism, a justice prefers narrowly written decisions that focus on the specific facts in a case. As a result, Supreme Court decisions develop incrementally in cautious small steps rather than in abrupt and sweeping shifts. Sometimes this is described as making decisions that are "narrow and shallow" rather than "bright lines" (Sunstein 1999), or, more colloquially, "O'Connorism" (Maveety 2008). Although judicial minimalism describes rulings rather than justices,[13] terms, or entire Courts by chief justice,[14] a few justices comprise the modern Court's better-known minimalists, particularly Justices Sandra Day O'Connor, Felix Frankfurter, and Chief Justice John Roberts (Sunstein 2006, 1999; Shapiro 2016).[15] All three justices score at or above average on representative role. That the leading modern-day advocates or landmark decisions for originalism, textualism, the "living Constitution," and minimalism alike all score at or above average on representative role suggest that devotion to a particular judicial philosophy is neither a certain link nor a bar to representative role.

Along with ideological moderation, serving as chief justice is closely linked to a stronger representative role. Combined, 63% of the seven Chief Justices' votes (including Justices Stone and Rehnquist's votes only when they served as chief justice) agreed with the polls, versus a 56% figure for the associate justices. Six of the modern Court's seven chief justices (all except Warren) rank as above average on representative role. Arguably, serving as chief justice sensitizes a justice to public opinion (Biskupic 2019: 8–10, cf. 299–301; Christenson and Glick 2015b: 406; Fettig and Benesh 2016).[16] Badas (2021) draws similar conclusions using the public mood measure. The chief justice serves in many roles that the other justices do not. This list of duties is extensive and steadily grows. A chief justice circulates a discuss list, leads the discussions on granting certiorari and on deciding cases, and presides over oral arguments (Bartels and Wininger 2016; Cameron and Clark 2016; Vining and Wilhelm 2016). A chief justice has unique duties outside the Court including leading the Judicial Conference of the United States, selecting members of the Foreign Intelligence Surveillance Court, selecting a director for the Administrative Office of U.S. Courts, chairing the Federal Judicial Center's board, and appointing judges to the Judicial Panel on Multidistrict Litigation. A chief justice serves as the Smithsonian Institution's chancellor, administers the oath of office to new presidents, and upon rare occasion presides during a presidential impeachment trial at the U.S. Senate. The chief justice's name is also widely used as a shorthand for an era—most recently, the Roberts Court.

TENURE, REPLACEMENTS, AND REPRESENTATIVE ROLE

Over recent decades, the justices changed in several important ways. Nominees are now typically younger, without experience in elective office, and nearly all career federal judges who graduated from prestigious law schools. Newly appointed justices typically go on to spend two decades or longer on the Court, leaving only upon death or retiring at old age. As the justices grow steadily older and remain on the Court, they usually become the last of their cohort still in public office.

Time and tenure affect representation in two ways. First, as the justices' tenure lengthens, their votes steadily less well represent American attitudes. Second, when new justices join the Court, they better represent American attitudes than did the former justices whom they replaced. Studying the impact of tenure and replacements requires looking at representation across time for those justices who joined the Court since the mid-1930s. Beginning with President Franklin Roosevelt's first appointee, Justice Hugo Black, one can track the justices' poll-matched votes over time. As justices leave the Court, one can also compare how often the retiring and newly confirmed justice's votes agree with public opinion.

A first question, then, is whether a justice's votes less well represent public opinion as a justice serves longer? The answer is mostly yes. Consider those justices who served into a second decade. During these justices' first decade on the Court, 61% of their (combined) votes agreed with public opinion (see also Sharma and Glennon 2013). During the justices' second decade, that figure fell to 54%. Some justices served into a third decade or occasionally into a fourth decade; these justices' (combined) votes agreed with the polls only 50% of the time during their third decade or thereafter.[17]

Declining representative role over a justice's tenure is not surprising. Many justices "drift" ideologically over time, mostly becoming more liberal rather than more conservative in their voting patterns (Epstein and Segal 2005: 136–37; Epstein et al. 2007; Martin and Quinn 2007; Owens and Wedeking 2012; Sharma and Glennon 2013; Gooch 2015). So, too, do most justices drift in their representative role over time and usually away from, not toward public opinion. Two-thirds of the modern Court's justices better represented public opinion during their first decade, compared to their second decade or beyond. The exceptions are rare, and the pattern is increasingly strong over time. Before President Lyndon Johnson appointed Justice Thurgood Marshall to the Court, only about half the justices showed a decline between their first and second decade. Thereafter, over two-thirds of the justices did.

The decline in representative role continues into the justices' third decade. Only three justices (most dramatically, Justice Breyer) significantly better represented public opinion during their third decade than during their first decade.[18] Most justices drift further and further away from public opinion. For a few justices, the decline is particularly striking. During his first decade on the Court, 63% of Justice Blackmun's votes agreed with the polls; that figure fell to 52% during his second decade, then to 33% thereafter. For Justice

Brennan, the figures across decades are 70%, 56%, and 35%, respectively. For Justice Marshall, the figures are 54%, 43%, and 24%. These extreme over time declines merit further scholarly attention.

Advocates of judicial term limits seldom point to declining representative role, at least not directly so. Instead, scholars point to the declining physical health or mental acuity of elderly justices or to a president's inability to appoint new justices. Several advocates of term limits recommend a fixed tenure of 18 years, thereby ensuring presidents an appointment to the Court every two years. The poll-matching evidence, described earlier, raises the question: Is there a tipping point after which representative role declines? Breaking down poll-matched votes by shorter five-year periods, representative role does not vary across the first two half-decades of tenure, but falls across the next two half-decades, until reaching only a random level of agreement with the polls thereafter.[19] From the perspective of maximizing representative role, a fixed term of 9 years would be better than 18 years (see also Badas 2019b). Still, the often mentioned 18-year term would stem the drop-off in representational role that ordinarily occurs during a justice's third decade on the Court. Chapter 6 discusses term limits at greater length.

A second question asks whether newly appointed justices better represent public opinion than did their predecessor? Again, the answer is mostly yes. Answering this question requires comparing a new justices' representative role score for his or her *first* five years to that of the recently retired or deceased justice who previously held the seat for that former justice's *last* five years. The earliest replacement since poll matching became possible was in 1937 when Justice Hugo Black replaced Justice Willis Van Devanter. During his first five years, 79% of Justice Black's votes agreed with public opinion, but during his last five years on the Court, only 50% of Justice Van Devanter's votes agreed with public opinion. The difference (an increase of 29%) represents the common pattern. About three-fifths of judicial replacements led to an increase in representative role. Across all replacements since the mid-1930s, the prior justices' votes agreed with the polls 53% of the time during their last five years—versus a 59% figure for newly appointed justices during their first five years.[20] Overall, the average net replacement effect is a 6% increase in representative role. The replacement effect is slightly larger (+10%) for justices appointed after President Lyndon Johnson left the White House.

Many replacements lead to only a small net change in representative role, but some replacements have large consequences. Borrowing from a sports analogy, the seven "best trades" for increasing representative role were Justice Clark replacing Justice Murphy (a 40% increase), White for Whittaker (+37%), Breyer for Blackmun (+32%), Thomas for Marshall (+29%), Black for Van Devanter (+29%), Powell for Black (+27%), and Goldberg for

Frankfurter (+27%). The seven "worst trades" for representative role were Justice Marshall replacing Justice Clark (a 41% decrease), Harlan for Jackson (−31%), Whittaker for Reed (−26%), Ginsburg for White (−26%), Jackson for Stone (−17%), Fortas for Goldberg (−14%), and Frankfurter for Cardozo (−8%).

IDEOLOGY, THE ATTITUDINAL MODEL, AND REPRESENTATIVE ROLE

Among the most compelling explanations of judicial behavior is that the justices often vote their liberal-versus-conservative preferences.[21] Academics and journalists alike mostly view the justices' ideological leanings as a broad and sweeping concept that applies across a wide variety of disputes. Among political scientists, the attitudinal model is a widely accepted explanation for the justices' voting behavior at least on high-profile, nonunanimous decisions.

Conceded, none of the justices vote perfectly along a single liberal-conservative ideological dimension (Fischman 2019; Lauderdale and Cark 2012; Unah and Hancock 2006). Even Justice Alito, a very conservative justice, sometimes casts a "liberal" vote. Even Justice Sotomayor, a very liberal justice, occasionally casts a "conservative" vote. Justices may vote against their usual ideological preferences to respect a recent or important precedent. For example, Chief Justice Roberts's tie-breaking concurrence in *June Medical Services v. Russo* (2020), striking down Louisiana's so-called admitting privileges provision, cited the similarity between the Louisiana law and a Texas provision recently struck down in *Whole Woman's Health v. Hellerstedt* (2016).

Some justices carve out a specific legal area on which their votes deviate from their usual voting patterns. Justice Gorsuch casts "liberal" votes on Indian treaty rights claims.[22] Justice Thomas sometimes casts "liberal" votes on economic cases.[23] Justice Kennedy's "liberal" votes on gay rights claims are well known. These exceptions may significantly impact case outcomes. Justice Kennedy's theory of liberty, for instance, led to five-member liberal decisions on several poll-matched gay rights claims, including *Lawrence v. Texas* (2003), *U.S. v. Windsor* (2013), and *Obergefell v. Hodges* (2015), causing each decision to agree with the polls.[24]

The attitudinal model is so important that representative role should be so reexamined. That is, some justices might rank highly on representative role, but only because public opinion aligns with their usual judicial ideology. Consider Justice Thurgood Marshall, one of the modern Court's most liberal justices. When poll majorities were ideologically liberal, Justice Thurgood Marshall almost always (98% of the time) agreed with the polls, but the correlation is arguably spurious. Justice Marshall also nearly always voted liberal when poll majorities were conservative (doing so 93% of the time). Thus, when the polls were liberal, Justice Marshall nearly always represented public opinion, but when the polls were conservative, he rarely did. Justice Marshall's representative role score is well explained simply by how often the polls are liberal.

Not all justices are like Justice Marshall. Some justices usually vote conservative when the polls are conservative but vote liberal when the polls are liberal. The justices vary considerably on this pattern (herein termed a "swing"). Almost all justices show at least a small swing; a few justices show an unusually large ideological swing. Table 4.3 reports how often each justice voted consistently with the polls; how often each justice voted in a conservative direction; then how often each justice voted conservatively depending on whether public opinion itself was liberal or conservative. The last column of table 4.3 reports a swing score, indicating how responsive each justices' votes were to ideological shifts in public opinion. Table 4.3 includes justices with at least a dozen poll-matched votes.

Almost all the justices show at least a small swing in the predicted direction. That is, nearly all justices more often vote conservative when the polls are conservative than when the polls are liberal. Only for the extremely liberal or conservative justices (or those with very few poll-matched votes) is the swing near zero or in the unexpected direction. For a few justices, the swing is very large—indicating a great deal of ideological flexibility. For the 16 justices included both in Bailey and Maltzman (2008: 379) and table 4.3, the average effect size for public opinion is about half that for precedent, deference to Congress, or protection of speech.[25]

As table 4.3 indicates, some justices score highly on representative role, but mostly because public opinion during their tenure happened to align with the justice's own ideology. Historically, American public opinion was unusually liberal on decisions during the late Hughes Court, while public opinion was unusually conservative on decisions during the Stone and Vinson Courts.[26] This pattern did not persist. Since the 1950s, the polls have been about equally often liberal as conservative on poll-matched cases. When this occurs, about half of a highly ideological justice's votes will agree with public opinion, but about half will not. Ideologically, flexible justices will agree with the polls at a much higher rate.

If public opinion on cases that reach the Supreme Court is about equally often conservative as liberal—as it has been since the mid-1950s—increasing the Court's rate of agreement with public opinion heavily depends on whether the Court has at least one ideologically flexible justice whose votes shift with public opinion. Sometimes there are two such justices but rarely more. Such justices are unusually flexible, mostly voting conservative when poll majorities are conservative, but voting liberal when poll majorities are liberal. Highly flexible justices, although never especially numerous, have an outsized effect on decisional representation. When the Court is closely balanced between conservative and liberal justices, one or two justices with high swing scores can increase the Court's rate of agreement with public opinion from about 55% to 60% or higher. This chapter shortly returns to representation at the decisional level.

WHO ARE THE GREAT AND NEAR-GREAT REPRESENTATIVE JUSTICES?

Which justices then best represent public opinion? As table 4.3 indicates, most justices have only middling to low representative role scores and low swing scores. Such justices typically vote their ideological leanings and only slightly respond to public opinion. Mostly these justices' votes agree with public opinion roughly half the time. Their votes hover just above or below the half-way mark on representative role if public opinion on disputes that reach the Court is about equally often conservative as liberal.

Some justices better represent American attitudes. At the top, five justices stand out as having *both* very high representative role scores and unusually large swing scores that exceed 30%. These justices' votes mostly agree with the polls whether the polls are conservative or liberal. Justices Tom Clark, Sherman Minton, Lewis Powell, Owen Roberts, and Byron White comprise the modern Court's "great" representative justices. As this chapter earlier noted, representative greatness is essentially uncorrelated with other rankings of judicial greatness. Four of these five justices usually rank as average on lists of judicial greatness; Justice Minton usually ranks near the bottom. Notably, all five justices are from long past Courts. As Devins and Baum (2019), among others, argue, presidents now choose more ideologically predictable nominees.

Ten justices fall into the next group of "near-great" justices. These 10 justices score above average on representative roles and have above average swing scores. However, their votes better represent only conservative or, alternatively, liberal public opinion, but not both. They include five chief justices: Charles Evans Hughes, Harlan Stone, Warren Burger, William Rehnquist, and John Roberts. Justices Louis Brandeis, Stanley Reed, Felix Frankfurter, Robert Jackson, and Potter Stewart also rank as near-greats.

Exactly why do these 15 justices so well represent public opinion? Notably, several are chief justices. As the "first among equals," the chief justice may be reluctant to allow decisions to drift too far away from American attitudes (Fettig and Benesh 2016). Five of the modern Court's seven chief justices rank as among the great or near-great justices. Chief Justice Vinson also well represented public opinion.

For some of these 15 justices, evidence suggests an interest in public opinion. Chief Justice Rehnquist (1986) authored a thoughtful law journal article on the importance of public opinion in judicial decision-making. Justice Owen Roberts and Chief Justice Hughes are famous for their critical votes supporting New Deal legislation during the late 1930s (Devins 1996: 253–54; Leuchtenburg 2005: 1198; Knowles 2021). Several of these 15 justices engaged in public advocacy, campaigned for elective office for themselves or a candidate, served in elective office, or held a top appointive post before joining the Court. Admittedly, others did not, and several justices with such experiences do not rank among the great or near-great justices.

The 15 great and near-great justices mostly played a centrist and sometimes even an inconsistent line. Henry Abraham's classic study (2008: 159) describes Owen Roberts as a justice who "would lastingly please neither political wing," who "established a (voting) record of inconsistency probably difficult to equal," and who "tended to vacillate jurisprudentially." Another author wrote that "no one could say with confidence where (Owen Roberts) would wind up" (Leuchtenburg 2005; see also Knowles 2021: 149–54).[27] Justice Clark had "a cautious, innovative, independent streak" (Abraham 2008: 193). Justice White had an "independent and . . . utterly nondoctrinaire career . . . that defies categorization other than . . . it was considerably more conservative in some realms . . . than might have been anticipated" and pursued a "not easily predictable, cautious, often irritating centrist course" (Abraham 2008: 219–20). Justice Powell was "committed to a case-by-case approach" and was "cautious and conservative, yet moderate and nondoctrinaire by inclination and commitment, (and) comfortable in the Court's center" (Abraham 2008: 247–48). Justice Minton was "universally and justly regarded as a failure" but took a sometimes liberal, sometimes conservative stance depending on the issues involved in a case (Abraham 2008: 195–96).

THE IMPACT OF HIGHLY REPRESENTATIVE JUSTICES

What impact do great and near-great representative justices have on the Court's collective decision-making? To preview this section, some great or near-great justices have an oversized impact on how well Supreme Court decisions represent public opinion. This concept is termed "decisional impact."

Moving from the individual justice level to the collective decision-making level requires some parsing of votes. This proceeds as follows. First, to affect a decision's outcome, a justice must cast a tie-breaking vote, either singly or in combination with another justice.[28] Adding an extra vote to a

five, six, seven, or eight-member majority does not affect the resulting decision. Second, a justice's tie-breaking vote counts as having decisional impact
whether or not that vote departs from the justice's normal ideological voting
pattern. Third, as a practical necessity, the estimates offered just below only
include decisions with recorded votes. Decisions without recorded votes
(including nearly all denials of certiorari, denials of a stay or of habeas corpus, as well as most per curiam decisions) do not figure into the estimates
below which report the "net" effect on decisional representation.[29] That is, a
swing justice may sometimes provide a tie-breaking vote but one that results
in a decision that *disagrees* with poll majorities; these votes are subtracted
from the tie-breaking votes that result in decisions that *agree* with the polls.
Finally, the estimates below may report a justice's decisional impact singly
or in combination with another swing justice who served at the same time.

Consider the Roberts Court. Through its 2019–2020 term, only Chief
Justice John Roberts ranks as great or near-great on representative role. The
remaining justices who served (or continue to serve) on the Roberts Court
mostly posted middling or low representative role scores and low, often very
low swing scores. Taken alone, Chief Justice Roberts's votes raised the percentage of decisions that agreed with public opinion from 51% (what would
have occurred if he had always voted the other way) to 62%. The difference
of 11% significantly raised the Roberts Court's decisional representation
above the random-behavior level to nearly what it was (69% consistent).
Justice Kennedy had the second greatest impact. None of the remaining
Roberts Court justices had any significant decisional impact.

Now consider Justice Owen Roberts, a much earlier justice from the
late Hughes Court and the Stone Court, and one of five "great" justices on
representative role. Justice Owen Roberts's tie-breaking votes, taken alone,
raised the percentage of Supreme Court decisions that agreed with the polls
from 56% to 63%. All of Justice Roberts's decisional impact occurred during
the Hughes Court. Justice Roberts's tie-breaking votes include several critical votes favoring New Deal legislation during the late 1930s. By the early
1940s, a liberal majority comprised President Franklin Roosevelt's appointees reduced Justice Roberts's net decisional impact to zero. A swing justice's
decisional impact, taken singly, may be a net positive for representation, but
in magnitude may vary depending on how the other justices vote.

If two "great" or "near-great" representative justices sit on the Court at the
same time, their impact on decision-making may be joint rather than singu-
lar. For several terms, Justices Minton and Clark—both "great" justices on
representative role—sat together on the Court. Taken both singly and jointly,
their votes raised the percentage of consistent decisions from 54% to 71%
for those terms. Most of that positive net impact on representation occurred
when Minton and Clark voted the same way. The decisional impact of two

justices was only slightly less for the decade between 1962 and 1971 when both Justices White and Stewart sat on the Court. Taken both singly and jointly, Justices White and Stewart's votes raised the percentage of consistent decisions from 53% to 62% for those terms.

Another way to look at the impact of the justices' votes is to compare how often Supreme Court decisions would represent public opinion if the highest versus the lowest scoring justices sat on the Court. A purely hypothetical Court comprised the nine justices whose votes *most often* agreed with public opinion includes Justices Brandeis, Minton, White, Owen Roberts, Powell, and Clark; Chief Justices Hughes and Stone; and either Chief Justice Rehnquist or John Roberts. This Court's decisions would agree with public opinion 89% of the time. By contrast, another hypothetical Court comprised the nine justices who *least often* agree with public opinion includes Justices Black, Stevens, Murphy, Rutledge, Kavanaugh, Marshall, Sutherland, Butler, and McReynolds. That hypothetical Court's decisions would represent public opinion only 33% of the time. None of the seven modern Courts, by Chief Justice, and no natural court reached these extremes. Again hypothetically, if nine justices sat on the Court and each justices' votes agreed with public opinion exactly half of the time, then the Court's decisions would agree with public opinion half the time and disagree half the time.[30]

An interesting question is how politicians or ordinary Americans might react to such extremes—particularly so to very low rates of representation. Occasionally, a high-profile decision leads to sharply divided partisan approval ratings toward the Court. After the *Bush v. Gore* (2000) decision, grassroots Democrats' approval ratings of the Court sharply dropped, but grassroots Republicans' approval ratings rose. A similar reaction followed the 2010 decision upholding most of the Affordable Care Act, then with dropping approval ratings by Republicans and rising approval ratings by Democrats. After a year or two, these short-term poll shifts typically fade. What is entirely unclear is the likely impact on the Court's approval or legitimacy ratings if only a third of its decisions agreed with public opinion for a prolonged time. With several low-scoring justices on representative role, coupled with an absence of any "great" or "near-great" justices on representative role, this is a possibility, albeit one that has not yet happened. Chapter 6 returns to this issue.

IDEOLOGICAL BALANCE AND REPRESENTATION

Ideologically flexible justices have an oversized positive impact on decisional representation that ideologically consistent justices, whether liberal or conservative, do not. Even with just one or two ideologically flexible justices,

Supreme Court decisions will likely represent public opinion over 60% of the time despite most justices not being ideologically flexible at all. This assumes that there are about as many liberal justices as conservative justices. The Roberts Court's high rate of agreement with public opinion is a recent example.

Many questions arise: for example, what would happen to the rate of decisional representation if the Court grew ideologically unbalanced?[31] What if there were one more conservative (or alternatively, liberal) vote than there is? What if there were two additional conservative (or alternatively, liberal) votes than there are? What if there were three additional conservative (or alternatively, liberal) votes than there are? These scenarios are hypothetical, but new appointments sometimes upset the ideological balance on the Court and yield this result. Recent examples include replacing the very conservative Antonin Scalia with the (presumably) much more liberal Merrick Garland (who was not confirmed) or replacing the very liberal Ruth Bader Ginsburg with the (presumably) much more conservative Amy Coney Barrett.[32] Chapter 6 returns to the question of Court packing, which might add as many as four new justices.

Consider the Roberts Court's first 15 terms. Figure 4.1 shows how many decisions would have agreed with public opinion if there had been one, two, or three additional conservative (or alternatively, liberal) votes than there were. Figure 4.1 again sets aside instances of evenly divided or conflicting poll results and denials of certiorari for which there are no recorded votes. The results are striking. Were there one more conservative vote, per decision, than there was, the percentage of Roberts Courts decisions consistent with public opinion would have dropped from 68% to 62%. For each additional conservative vote, the percentage of consistent decisions would have dropped further—to 59% with two additional conservative votes, then to 57% with three additional conservative votes.

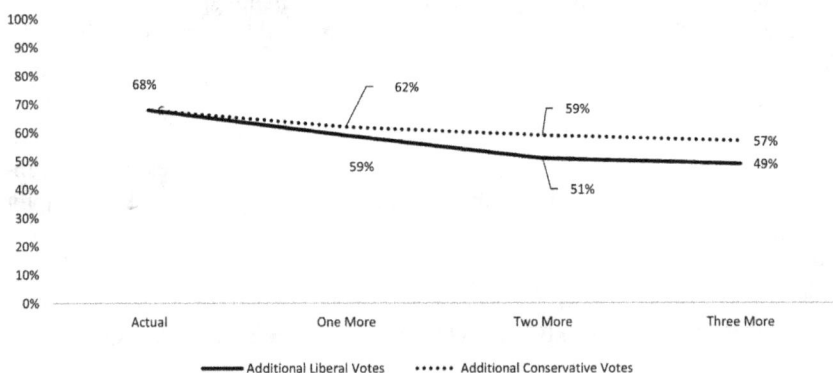

Figure 4.1   **Percentage of Roberts Court Decisions Consistent with Public Opinion, by Different Ideological Vote Changes.** *Source:* Data collected and analyzed by the author and listed in the appendix.

A similar pattern appears with additional liberal votes. The percentage of consistent decisions would have dropped from 68% to 59% with one additional liberal vote, then to 51% with two additional liberal votes, and then to 49% with three additional liberal votes. These results resemble hypothetical changes for the Rehnquist Court or earlier Courts (Marshall 2008: 52–56). In short, ideologically unbalanced Courts usually mean low levels of representation.

In recent decades, three realities have encouraged an ideologically closely balanced Court. First, recent presidents have carefully screened their nominees. Republican presidents only picked conservative justices and Democratic presidents only picked liberal justices (Dorf 2007; Devins and Baum 2019; Hitt 2013; Cameron, Kastellec, and Mattioli 2019). Since the 1990s, presidents, particularly so Republican presidents, avoided the "mistakes" of earlier presidents (Epstein and Segal 2005: 62–65, 130–32; Cottrell, Shipan, and Anderson 2019).[33] Second, each recent president appointed about the same number of justices—two apiece for Presidents George H. W. Bush, Clinton, George W. Bush, and Obama, and three for President Trump. Third, most justices now try to time their retirements to ensure that an ideologically like-minded justice will replace them (Epstein and Segal 2005: 38–40; Zigerell 2013). Sometimes they succeed, sometimes not, depending upon a justice's health and ideological stance and confirmation uncertainties (Ward 2003; Chabot 2019). An unexpected death sometimes upsets this pattern, as witness in 2020 the liberal-to-conservative switch from Justice Ginsburg to Justice Barrett. Even with an unexpected death, opposition political party control of the Senate can sometimes forestall an ideological rebalancing on the Court, as witness the death of Justice Scalia, the Republican-majority Senate's refusal to vote on Merrick Garland's nomination, and then Justice Gorsuch's confirmation after President Trump's election.

Three changes might unsettle a closely balanced Supreme Court. Expanding the number of justices—commonly called court packing—would likely upset the pattern of a closely balanced Court by allowing a president to add several very conservative (or alternatively, very liberal) justices. So might a sudden string of deaths or retirements—depending on exactly which justices died or retired and which party controls the White House and the Senate. So would a lengthy stretch of one-party control in national politics. None of these circumstances would likely bode well for decisional representation. Time will tell whether these changes transpire.

CONCLUSION AND DISCUSSION

Focusing on the justices and their voting patterns best explains why and when Supreme Court decisions represent public opinion. Taken individually, the justices vary greatly in how often they agree with American attitudes. Some justices agree with the polls over two-thirds of the time; others do so less than half the time. Many justices are not especially responsive to public opinion and vote in nearly the same ideological fashion whether the polls are conservative or liberal. As a result, how well their votes represent public opinion depends on how often the polls lean liberal or conservative. In recent decades, the polls were conservative nearly as often as liberal on issues reaching the Supreme Court.

Some justices rise to a higher level. The "great" and "near-great" justices best represent public opinion. The five representative "great" justices—Owen Roberts, Tom Clark, Sherman Minton, Byron White, and Lewis Powell— flexibly agreed with both conservative and liberal poll majorities. Ten justices rank nearly as highly and comprise the representative "near-great" justices. These 15 justices have an outsized impact on whether the Court's decisions represent public opinion.[34]

Representative role is uncorrelated with other rankings of judicial greatness. Several greats and near-greats served as chief justice. Some had prior experience in public relations, election campaigns, elective office, or top appointive office. All these experiences may sensitize a justice to public opinion. Admittedly, explaining representative role is imprecise. Other justices with the same traits rank only as middling or low on representative role. Tenure is also important. Most justices best represent public opinion during their first decade on the Court.

By strong circumstantial evidence, nearly a third of the modern Court's justices favorably considered public opinion when voting. The evidence lies in the justices' voting patterns, particularly their rates of agreeing with public opinion and their swing scores. Historical and biographical accounts such as Abraham (2008) or Biskupic (2019: 9–10, 298–99, 326) offer supporting evidence. Depending on the Court's current ideological balance, the representative great and near-great justices' votes bring the Court's decisions more closely into line with American attitudes. Other justices show little evidence that they greatly value public opinion. Conceded, the great and near-great justices seldom explicitly justify their votes as representing American attitudes. Nor is it clear exactly how the great and near-great justices assess public opinion. Recent appointments mean that the number of great and near-great justices has dwindled over time.

This evidence adds to several accounts of judicial behavior. Epstein, Landes, and Posner (2013a) evaluate the justices' personal goals, which, by this account, for some but not all justices apparently include representing public opinion. Hall (2018) considers the justices' personality traits that appear independent of representing public opinion. By contrast, Black,

Owens, Wedeking, and Wahlforth (2020) argue that highly conscientious justices are the most likely to follow public mood trends. Devins and Baum (2019) argue that public opinion less influences the justices' votes than do the justices' network of elite friends and political allies. The evidence here supports their claim for many but not all justices. Epstein and Martin (2010) question how public opinion is linked to Supreme Court decision-making. By the evidence herein, the link is through the voting patterns of specific justices. Numerous accounts describe or advocate a particular interpretative method, such as minimalism, textualism, attention to precedent, judicial restraint, originalism, or the living Constitution. Other accounts focus on law clerks (Bonica et al. 2019); birth order (McGuire 2015); media coverage (Clark, Lax, and Rice 2015; Collins and Cooper 2012; Sill, Metzgar, and Rouse 2013); state success (Canelo 2020); presidential pressure (Collins and Eshbaugh-Soha 2019; Rogol, Montgomery, and Kingsland 2018); or amicus briefs and the solicitor general (Spriggs and Wahlbeck 1997; Collins 2008; Bailey, Kamoie and Maltzman 2005; Vladeck 2019). This chapter's evidence and an analysis of the poll matches listed in the appendix may clarify these theories' ties to representation.

In the attitudinal model (Segal and Spaeth 1993, 2002; Segal, Spaeth, and Benesh 2005), the justices usually vote their own liberal-versus-conservative leanings whenever a dispute has ideological undertones. The attitudinal model works well for most justices and increasingly so for recently confirmed justices. Conceded, some justices "drift" ideologically over time, hold judicial views that temper their ideological leanings, or make an occasional strategic move. When this happens, a justice's liberal-conservative leanings cannot explain his or her votes. Following public opinion is another anomaly. Several justices are less predictable ideologically, and when their votes shift, these shifts sometimes better represent public opinion. Such flexibility keeps the Court in line with public opinion. Most highly flexible justices served on past, sometimes long past Courts. As of this writing, Chief Justice Roberts is the sole surviving "great" or "near-great" representative justice. If presidents continue to pick justices with strong enough ideological leanings as to lead the justice to ignore public opinion, the balance will further shift back to the attitudinal model.

Chapter 5 takes a deeper dive by looking at representation by gender, race, education, and partisanship. How well the Court and its justices represent different groups of Americans varies a great deal. Some justices well (or, alternatively, poorly) represent nationwide public opinion, but not always so specific groups. Chapter 5 then examines symbolic representation. For example, do Black or women justices better represent Black Americans or American women than do white or men justices? Chapter 6 then evaluates the Court's likely future as a representative institution.

NOTES

1. Listed in descending order, the remaining justices and their FameFlux ranking are Clarence Thomas (1,137), Neil Gorsuch (1,240), Sonia Sotomayor (2,401), John Roberts (2,792), Elena Kagan (3,465), Stephen Breyer (5,282), and Samuel Alito (5,507).

2. Symbolic representation may provide recognition as well as policy results (Dovi and Luna 2020).

3. Occasionally, a justice writes a dissent from a cert denial in sufficiently clear terms to describe his or her position; if so, that is coded as a vote.

4. As a caveat, justices who served prior to the 1930s are included only for the final part of their tenure. Similarly, justices still serving as of the 2019–2020 term are included only for the earlier part of their tenure.

5. For a compilation of such lists, see Abraham (2008: 378–81). For CNN surveys of historians in 2000, 2009, and 2017, see "Presidential Historians Survey" for various years. Older rankings do not include recent presidents. See also Lindgren and Calabresi (2001).

6. Top-rated justices scored 3 or above; middle-rated justices scored between 2 and 3; low-rated justices scored below 2 (Comiskey 2004: 91, 2006). Other lists of top-ranked justices also show no clear patterns on representative role (Schwartz 2000).

7. Closely divided Senate confirmation votes are mostly a recent phenomenon. Except for confirmation votes on Justice, and then Chief Justice Rehnquist (68-to-26 and 65-to-33, respectively), the six narrowly confirmed justices are all more recent: Justices Thomas (confirmed 52-to-48), Alito (58-to-42), Sotomayor (68-to-31), Kagan (63-to-37), Gorsuch (54-to-45), and Kavanaugh (50-to-48). Combined, these six justices' votes were 54% consistent, 46% not. In October 2020, Justice Barrett was confirmed 52-to-48.

8. Justices Minton, Byrnes, and Burton's votes, combined, agreed with public opinion 72% of the time, a record akin to Chief Justice Hughes's votes (78% consistent).

9. Chief Justices Rehnquist and Roberts both presided over an impeachment trial (Presidents Clinton and Trump, respectively). Both Rehnquist and Roberts rank above average in representative role.

10. Justices Byrnes and Van Devanter had too few votes to classify accurately. Listings for military service and off-the-Court roles are taken from the *Supreme Court Compendium*.

11. For descriptions of Justice Kennedy's notion of liberty, see Barnett (2003); Bhagwat and Struhar (2012); Biskupic (2019: 298–99); Colucci (2009); Knowles (2008, 2009); Shapiro (2010); and Shapiro (2016). Justice Kennedy sometimes included references to international law and policy in his opinions; Justice Breyer (2015) recently justified considering foreign law.

12. Fallon (2018: 132–48) reviews several other judicial theories such as non-originalist (or "living Constitution") tests, various balancing tests, judicial restraint, natural law, or Reflective Equilibrium Theory; see also Breyer (2005, 2011).

13. Sunstein's lists of well-known minimalist decisions (1999, 2006) yield very mixed results on representation. Nearly half of the so-described minimalist decisions disagree with public opinion.

14. As Posner and Sunstein (2016) note, the justices can be very flexible about their preferred methods of judicial interpretation.

15. Some accounts so describe Justices Jackson, Stevens, Kennedy, Souter, Breyer, and Ginsburg (Sunstein 1999: 9; 2005: 29, 107, 181–82). These justices' records of representing nationwide public opinion vary widely. For another description of minimalism, see Bickel (1962). For a review and criticism of minimalism, see Devins (1999) and Siegel (2005). Sunstein (1999: 6–8) describes originalism, majority rule, independent interpretative judgments, and democracy-reinforcement as competing judicial theories.

16. Danelski and Ward (2016); Mark and Zilis (2018); and Vining and Wilhelm (2012) describe aspects of the chief justice's role.

17. For those justices who served into a third decade or longer, their votes agreed with public opinion 60% of the time during their first decade, 53% of the time during their second decade, and only 50% of the time during the third decade or thereafter.

18. The other two were Justice Ginsburg and Chief Justice Rehnquist.

19. Representative role figures average 59%, 60%, 55%, 54%, and 50%, respectively, for the first four half-decades and then thereafter. As a caveat, the number of justices still serving declines sharply after the fourth half-decade.

20. This figure includes two switches in which an associate justice was appointed as Chief Justice (Stone and Rehnquist), but exclude the two switches involving Justice Byrnes, who resigned from the Court prior to serving five years. This section does not count switches involving Justices Gorsuch and Kavanaugh since neither justice has yet served five years on the Court.

21. This book adopts conventional meanings for the terms liberal and conservative. This book uses the term "liberal" since it is more widely used than "progressive." A liberal position includes support for claims by a labor union versus a corporation; for campaign finance restrictions; for higher taxes or greater government regulations; for low-income, free speech, liberal, controversial, or unpopular groups; or for those accused or convicted of crimes. A conservative vote is the opposite. Over recent decades, conservative legal groups have often asserted legal claims and exceptions are coded, as appropriate (Metroka 2018). The attitudinal model did not as accurately describe the justices' behavior during the Court's early decades when the justices feared that the Court lacked legitimacy and thus followed a norm of consensus that obscured differences in the justices' preferences (Parker 2018).

22. See, for example, *Washington State Department of Licensing v. Cougar Den Inc.* (2019), *Herrera v. Wyoming* (2019), and *McGirt v. Oklahoma* (2020).

23. See, for example, *Wyeth v. Levine* (2009) and *Geier v. American Honda Motor Company* (2000).

24. Justice O'Connor's concurrence in *Lawrence v. Texas* (2003) created a 6-3 vote.

25. The comparison is inexact since Bailey and Maltzman (2008) report on different decisions and time periods.

26. The polls were conservative on only 31%, versus liberal on 69% of Hughes Court decisions, excluding the few decisions with no clear ideological content. For the Stone and Vinson Courts, the polls were conservative 65% and 77% of the time, respectively, versus liberal 35% and 23% of the time, respectively. For the Warren Court the figures are 53% conservative, 47% liberal; for the Burger Court, 54% conservative, 46% liberal; for the Rehnquist Court, 58% conservative, 42% liberal; and for the Roberts Court, to date, 50% conservative, 50% liberal.

27. To Leuchtenburg (2005), Chief Justice Hughes was not so much a consistent centrist as he was erratic in shifting from one side to the other.

28. This measure of impact does not account for a justice's impact during the certiorari or opinion-writing stages.

29. A justice's tie-making vote counts as letting the last lower court decision stand.

30. I appreciate John Connolly's assistance in computing these estimates.

31. The Appendix's last section presents evidence on an "unbalanced" (6-to-3) partisan and ideological Court following the 2019–2020 term. Excluding "unclear" poll matches, 63 percent of decisions agreed with public opinion and the remainder did not. These conclusions are limited due to the short time involved (through December 2021), the small number of poll matches, and mixed patterns of ideological voting. Given that no membership changes occur, more terms will yield clearer conclusions. For the prior closely balanced (2019–2020) term, the percentages were 69% consistent and 31% inconsistent, again excluding "unclear" poll matches.

32. As a caveat, the Senate never voted on Judge Garland's nomination and Justice Barrett cast no votes until after this book's data analysis.

33. Cameron, Kastellec, and Mattioli (2019) argue that many so-called mistakes should not be so characterized, since some earlier presidents did not highly value ideology in nominating justices, operated with different Senate confirmation norms, and had fewer attractive and ideologically consistent potential nominees.

34. Fallon (2018: 159–67) argues that more centrist justices would protect the Court's sociological and moral legitimacy, urging presidents to nominate and Senators to confirm more such justices.

Chapter 5

Representing Group Opinions

Chapter 3 asked how well Supreme Court decisions represent nationwide public opinion and chapter 4 examined the individual justices' records. Representation can also occur at a different level—that is, by groups. This chapter asks how well the Supreme Court or its justices represent several groups in American society—by gender, race, partisanship, and education.

Drilling down to the group level is both important and feasible. Most modern Court decisions represent majority public opinion, but this does not necessarily mean that a decision equally well represents all groups. As chapter 1 pointed out, *Obergefell v. Hodges* (2015) agreed with majorities of grassroots Democrats, independents, women, men, whites, and those with a high school or college education—but not with majorities of Republicans or Blacks. Group identities are important to many Americans, as witness large differences in voting behavior or attitudes on issues by gender, race, partisanship, or education. Further, group identities are very stable over time or even nearly immutable, readily visible, and socially meaningful.

One should not simply assume that policymakers equally well represent all groups. By one well-known account, public policy typically represents both nationwide majorities and most groups, but when groups differ in their attitudes, public policy best represents the affluent (Gilens 2005). As well, attitude differences between groups are sometimes very large. Many accounts describe variations in representation by race and ethnicity (e.g., Abrajano and Poole 2011), education and income (Bartels 2008; Ellis and Ura 2011; Jacobs and Skocpol 2005; Gilens 2005, 2011; Wlezien and Soroka 2011), gender (Lizotte 2020), or partisanship (Hopkins and Stoker 2011). When attitudes differ from one group to another, many Americans identify closely with their own group.[1]

Measuring how well Supreme Court decisions and individual justices' votes represent group opinion is also feasible. Pollsters routinely ask about respondents' demographics, if only properly to reweight the completed interviews. When interpreting poll results, pollsters routinely point out large differences (commonly called the "gaps") between groups. When archiving their data, pollsters often include these demographics. As a result, one can nearly always break down nationwide poll results on Supreme Court decisions by important social and demographic groups such as gender, race, partisanship, and education.

Whether the Court represents some groups better than others is an open question. Presidents sometimes nominate justices who will appeal to certain groups. In 1980, President Reagan, for example, promised to appoint the Court's first woman justice (and did). Thirty years later President Biden promised to appoint the first Black woman justice should an opening occur. All recent presidents nominated justices from their own political party. That a president would nominate a justice from the other political party is now almost unimaginable. Further, Senate confirmation votes are now almost straight-line party votes.

This chapter's approach to identifying winners and losers is similar to studying the success rates of businesses or labor unions; federal, state, or local government; or other organizations by measuring their win-loss rates on cases that the group initiated, sponsored, financed, or supported with an amicus brief. Here, the groups are not government, interest groups, or litigants, but rather large and important population groups each with tens of millions of identifiers. The bottom line, though, is the same: Which groups win or lose?

THE MODERN COURT AND GROUP OPINIONS

Has the modern Court equally well represented all groups or, alternatively, has the Court better represented some groups than others? Table 5.1 presents results since the mid-1930s and compares the Warren Court (a more liberal Court) with the Roberts Court (the current and a more conservative Court). The figures in each cell of table 5.1 report the percentage of decisions that agree with a majority (or occasionally a plurality) of each group's opinions. Table 5.1 includes full, written decisions, per curiam decisions, and denials of certiorari or of habeas corpus.

Since the mid-1930s, Supreme Court decisions about equally often represented all ten groups at rates between 61% and 66%, as reported in the first column of table 5.1. Two reasons help to explain this even-handed pattern of representation. First, majorities of ten groups often hold the same opinions. Poll majorities of men and women differ on only 9% of Supreme Court decisions. On 15% of these decisions, those with less than a high

Table 5.1   Percentage of Supreme Court Decisions That Represent Opinion, by Group

Group Considered	Entire Modern Court Period (%)	Warren Court Only (%)	Roberts Court Only (%)
By gender:			
Men	66	62	69
Women	64	62	68
By race:			
Whites	66	62	69
Blacks	64	69	56
By Partisanship:			
Republicans	61	62	65
Democrats	65	69	59
Independents	65	62	68
By education:			
Less than High School	63	60	63
High School	65	62	67
College Degree or More	66	64	71

Note: To determine the percentage of decisions that *disagree* with a group's views, subtract the percentage in each cell from 100. Data does not include instances of evenly divided group opinions (within the .05 margin of error) or of conflicting polls.
Source: Data collected and analyzed by the author and listed in appendix.

school education, differ from those with a college education or more. Blacks and whites differ more often—on 21% of these decisions. Republicans and Democrats differed the most often—on 27% of these decisions. Second, these groups are themselves broad and diverse, each numbering at least tens of millions of Americans. Possibly, Supreme Court decisions better (or worse) represent smaller, better-defined groups such as Northern college-educated white men or low-income Blacks. Unfortunately, very small groups' attitudes cannot be reliably measured from polls.[2]

Table 5.1 compares how well each group fared during the Warren Court, a liberal Court, versus the mixed-to-conservative Roberts Court. Men and women fare equally well during each Court although both groups fare better under the Roberts Court. Whites fared better during the Roberts Court than during the Warren Court. Blacks fared less well than whites during the Roberts Court. Blacks fared worse under the Roberts than under the Warren Court. Republicans fared a little better under the Roberts Court than under the Warren Court. Democrats fared less well than did Republicans during the Roberts Court. Democrats also fared less well during the Roberts Court than the Warren Court. Better educated Americans fared better than the less well-educated during both Courts and particularly so during the Roberts Court. These shifting win-loss records show how changing ideology and Court membership can advantage or disadvantage different groups.

Arguably, a narrower measure better measures whom the Court favors. That is, when groups differ in their views, who wins? Political scientists often ask this question, and by several accounts, policymakers often favor the better educated and more affluent (Gilens 2012; Marshall 2016: 115). Since the justices are affluent and well-educated compared to the average American, this possibility merits consideration. Comparisons can also be made by gender, partisanship, and race.

When groups disagree, does the Court favor some groups rather than others? For this subset of decisions, the modern Court appears as relatively even-handed. Since the mid-1930s, when men and women disagree in their preferences, Court decisions favor women 53% of the time and men 47% of the time. When Democrats and Republicans disagree, the Court favors Democrats 53% of the time and Republicans 47% of the time. When the better educated disagree with the least well educated, the Court agrees with better educated Americans 54% of the time and with the less educated 46% of the time. When whites and Blacks disagree, the Court agrees with whites 53% of the time and Blacks 47% of the time. As a caveat, this analysis draws only on those decisions when groups differ. Through the 2019–2020 term, the Roberts Court generally follows historic patterns with two exceptions. When groups disagree, Roberts Court decisions favor whites 65% of the time and Blacks only 35% of the time, while favoring the better educated 63% of the time and the less educated only 37% of the time.

JUSTICES, REPRESENTATION, AND GROUPS

Chapter 4 ranked how well the justices represented nationwide public opinion. This chapter asks which justices best (or worst) represent each of 10 groups' views. A justice can represent majority of American views but poorly represent some specific groups' views. So can the reverse occur. Comparing each justice's votes with a particular group's attitudes views representation from a group perspective. The following text describes each group's hypothetical "dream Court" and "nightmare Court" based on how well the justices represent group preferences.

This analysis follows several counting rules. Each justice's vote on each decision either agrees or disagrees with a group's views on a specific case. Per curiam decisions and most denials of certiorari or of habeas corpus that do not report the individual justices' votes are not included. Nor are justices scored who cast very few poll-matched votes. This excludes a few justices with short tenure (e.g., Justices Byrnes or Whittaker) or who only served briefly at the start or end of the modern Court (e.g., Justices Cardozo). As a caveat, some justices who sat on the Court before modern polling cast many earlier votes that cannot be poll matched; similarly, justices who remain beyond the 2019–2020 term may cast many future votes.

Representation by Race

Which justices best represented Black Americans? Across the modern Court, the justices who most often agreed with the views of Black Americans are Chief Justice Hughes (83% of his votes did); Justices Fortas and Owen Roberts (tied at 73%); Chief Justice Stone (at 71%); Chief Justice Warren and Justices Brandeis and Kagan (all tied at 67%); and Justice Jackson (at 66%). Rounding out Black Americans' hypothetical "dream Court" is a five-way tie between Justices Brennan, White, Sotomayor, Douglas, and Minton, each of whose votes agreed with Black Americans' views 65% of the time.[3] As this "dream Court" for Black Americans suggests, a justice who represents all Americans at only middling or low rates may much better represent a specific group.

By comparison, which justices least well represented Blacks' views? On Black American's nine-member purely hypothetical "nightmare Court" are Justice Burton (only 49% consistent); Justice Scalia and Chief Justice Burger (both at 47% consistent); Justices Gorsuch and Thomas (both at 42%); and Justices Alito (at 37%), Sutherland (at 33%), Kavanaugh (at 28%), and McReynolds (at 22%).

Now, compare the hypothetical dream Court for white Americans—Chief Justice Hughes (78% consistent); Justices Minton and Owen Roberts (both at 70%); Justices White and Reed (both at 69%); Chief Justice John Roberts and Justice Powell (both at 67%); and Chief Justices Stone (at 66%) and Rehnquist (at 64%).[4] By contrast, white American's nightmare Court would include Justices Sotomayor and Black (both at 48%); and Justices Stevens (at 47%), Marshall (at 46%), Murphy (at 45%), Rutledge (at 41%), Sutherland (at 33%), Butler (at 31%), and McReynolds (at 26%).

Representation by Political Party

Following these same procedures, a hypothetical dream Court for self-identified Republicans would include Justices Gorsuch (consistent at 86%), Kavanaugh (at 83%), Alito (at 73%), and Minton (at 70%); Chief Justices Roberts (at 69%) and Vinson (at 67%); and Justices White (at 66%); and Scalia, and Burton (both at 65%).[5] Republicans' hypothetical nightmare Court includes Justices Blackmun and Sutherland (both at only 44% consistent), Ginsburg (at 43%), Rutledge and Murphy (both at 41%), Butler (at 40%), Marshall (at 37%), Kagan (at 32%), and Sotomayor (at 29%).[6] As these rankings suggest, a copartisan president's appointments often provide better representation for that political party's supporters, but there are exceptions.

Predictably, for self-identified Democrats, the results are very different. Democrats' dream Court includes Chief Justices Stone (at 78%) and Hughes (at 77%); Justices Owen Roberts (at 72%), Brandeis (at 71%),

Minton (at 70%), Jackson (at 69%), Sotomayor and Kagan (both at 68%); and a tie between Justices Fortas and Reed (both at 67%).[7] Democrats' nightmare Court includes Justice Scalia (at only 50% consistent), Chief Justice John Roberts (at 49%), and Justices Thomas (at 44%), Gorsuch (at 41%), Sutherland (at 36%), Alito (at 35%), Butler (at 33%), Kavanaugh (at 28%), and McReynolds (at 22%).

Independents' dream Court includes Chief Justice Hughes (at 83% consistent); Justices Owen Roberts (at 73%), Brandeis (at 71%), Minton (at 70%), and White (at 69%); Chief Justices Stone (at 68%) and Vinson (at 67%); Justice Powell (at 66%); and Chief Justice Roberts (at 65%). Independents' nightmare Court includes Justices Fortas, Souter, Black, and Rutledge (all tied at 50%); Marshall (at 48%), Stevens and Murphy (both at 47%); Kavanaugh (at 44%), Sutherland (at 42%), Butler (at 38%), and McReynolds (at 26%).

Representation by Education

Americans vary greatly in their educational backgrounds, and education is a rough proxy for income and status. Those without a high school education are typically the least advantaged, least affluent, and least well-organized Americans. For the least well-educated Americans—that is, those without a high school education—a hypothetical nine-member dream Court includes Chief Justice Hughes (at 74% consistent); Justices Brandeis (at 71%), Gorsuch (at 70%), and White (at 69%); Chief Justice Stone and Justice Owen Roberts (both at 68%); Chief Justices Vinson and Rehnquist (both at 67%); and Chief Justice John Roberts and Justice O'Connor (both at 63%).[8] By comparison, the least well-educated Americans' nightmare Court includes Justices Black (at 47% consistent); Stevens, Sotomayor, and Marshall (all at 45%); Sutherland and Rutledge (both at 42%), Kavanaugh (at 36%), Butler (at 38%), and McReynolds (at 26%).[9] Once again, the best and worst lists include a mix of Republicans and Democrats and of conservative and liberal justices.

For those with a high school education, a dream Court includes Chief Justice Hughes (at 83% consistent); Justices Owen Roberts (at 73%), Minton and White (each at 70%); Chief Justice Stone and Justices Powell and Brandeis (all at 67%); and Chief Justices Rehnquist (at 64%) and Vinson (at 62%).[10] By comparison, a nightmare Court includes Justices Black and Blackmun (tied at 49% consistent); Justices Marshall, Stevens, and Murphy (each at 45%); and Justices Kavanaugh (at 44%), Rutledge (at 43%), Sutherland (at 42%), Butler (at 38%), and McReynolds (at 36%).[11]

Holding a college education (or more) was at one time a rarity, although about a third of adult Americans now do. College-educated Americans are the most affluent group of Americans by education and in that sense the most privileged. College-educated Americans' dream Court includes Chief Justice

Hughes and Justice White (both at 71% consistent); Justices Minton (at 68%), Powell and Jackson (at 67%), Owen Roberts (at 64%); Chief Justice Stone and Justice Clark (both at 63%); and Justice Frankfurter and Chief Justice John Roberts (tied at 62%).[12] College-educated Americans' nightmare Court includes Justices Brennan (at 51% consistent), Rutledge and Gorsuch (both at 50%), Stevens (at 48%), Marshall (at 45%), Sutherland (at 42%), Kavanaugh (at 39%), McReynolds (at 35%), and Butler (at 29%).

Representation by Gender

Men and women comprise especially large and diverse categories, each group now numbering over 150 million Americans. Men's hypothetical dream court includes Chief Justice Hughes (at 78% consistent); Justices Gorsuch (at 73%); White, Owen Roberts, and Powell (each at 70%); Chief Justice Roberts (at 69%); Justices Powell (at 68%) and Minton (at 67%); and Chief Justices Stone and Rehnquist and Justice Clark (each tied at 64%). Men's nightmare Court includes Justices Black (at 48% consistent), Stevens (at 47%), Murphy, Rutledge, and Marshall (each at 45%), Sotomayor (at 43%), Sutherland (at 42%), Butler (at 38%), and McReynolds (at 32%).

For women, a hypothetical dream Court includes some but not all the same names: Chief Justice Hughes (at 78% consistent); Justices Owen Roberts (at 70%), White (at 68%), Brandeis (at 67%), and Clark (at 65%); Justice Powell and Chief Justices Roberts and Stone (all at 64%); and Chief Justice Rehnquist (at 63%).[13] Women's nightmare Court includes Justices Gorsuch and Black (both tied at 48%), Stevens (at 47%), Marshall (at 46%), Murphy and Rutledge (both at 45%), Sutherland (at 42%), Kavanaugh (at 41%), Butler (at 38%), and McReynolds (at 31%).[14]

All this suggests that representation is a complex issue. Since the 1930s, the Court represented all ten groups examined here at roughly similar rates. For individual justices, this is not necessarily true. Some justices such as Chief Justice Hughes and Justice White represent nationwide public opinion at high rates and do so across all or nearly all groups. At the other extreme, a few justices poorly represent nationwide public opinion and equally poorly represent all or nearly all groups—at the extreme, Justice McReynolds. Many justices represent some groups better than others. Justices Scalia, Alito, Gorsuch, and Kavanaugh, and Chief Justice John Roberts, all hold spots on Republicans' dream Court, but all five hold spots on Democrats' nightmare Court. Justices Sotomayor, and Kagan rank on Democrats' dream Court but both justices rank on Republicans' nightmare Court.

Compared to earlier justices, the Court's current and recent justices mostly better represent their appointing president's copartisans, versus supporters of the other party. Figure 5.1 depicts the voting "partisanship spread"—that

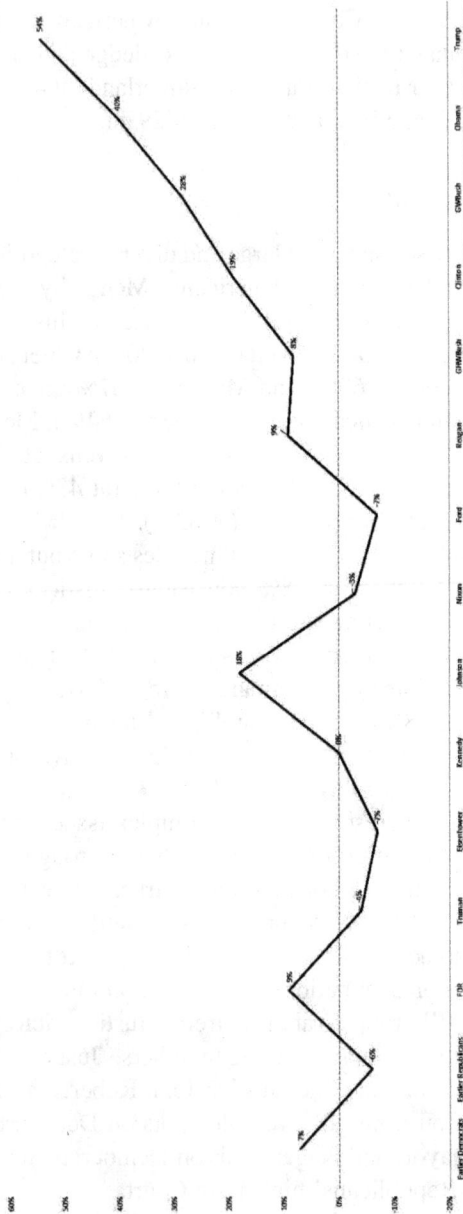

Figure 5.1 Justices' Average Voting Partisanship Voting Gaps, by Appointing President. *Source:* Data collected and analyzed by the author and listed in the appendix.

is, the difference between how well each president's appointees represented that president's copartisans and how well justices agree with supporters of the other political party. Figure 5.1 goes back to President Roosevelt's appointees.

The trend is striking. Until President Clinton's appointments, the partisanship spread was usually small and sometimes even negative.[15] Earlier presidents' appointees no better represented the presidents' copartisans than the supporters of the other political party. Beginning with President Clinton, each new set of justices acted in an increasingly partisan manner—that is, much better representing the president's copartisans than the other party's supporters.[16] With President Trump's first two appointees, Justices Gorsuch and Kavanaugh, the partisanship spread reached historic highs.[17] That many Americans noticed this pattern is not surprising. Chapter 6 returns to this issue.

SYMBOLIC REPRESENTATION AND THE MODERN COURT

For many years, all the justices were white men. Eventually that changed. Diversity on the Court first came through appointments by different geographic regions, followed by justices from both major political parties, then by Catholic and Jewish justices, and in time followed by Black, women, and Hispanic justices (Epstein and Segal 2005: 56–66). In part, these changes resulted from presidents' increased interest in diversity and in part from a growing number of plausible nominees mostly on the federal appeals courts (Cameron, Kastellec, and Mattioli 2019).

As the justices became in some ways more diverse, in other ways, they became less so. At one time, the justices came from a variety of academic and career backgrounds. Yet all current and recent justices graduated from elite law schools and made careers as high-ranking academics and government appointees and as federal appeals court judges. No longer do many justices have experience in the military,[18] in elective office, in business, or in law enforcement. Diversity on the Court remains in other ways limited. As of the 2020–2021 term no longer do any Protestants sit on the Court, nor are any justices of Indian or Mexican- or Cuban- or Asian-American heritage, disabled, openly gay or lesbian, or Islamic.[19]

This section asks whether symbolic nominees represent their group any better than do the other justices. It might seem logical that they would. Sometimes justices specifically cite the impact of a law or policy on their own symbolic group. Justice Sotomayor's dissent (with Justice Kagan) in *FDA v. American College of Obstetricians and Gynecologists* (2021) specifically cited the adverse effect of a policy requiring that women, particularly low-income women of color, pick up mifepristone in person during the coronavirus pandemic.[20] Few written opinions suggest symbolic representation so pointedly. Using poll matching, this section asks whether symbolic representation is commonplace.

The evidence on dream Courts or nightmare Courts does not suggest that symbolic nominees inevitably better represent their own groups than do the other justices. This section reexamines this question more narrowly. The test here compares a symbolic nominee's votes only to the votes of those justices who heard the same dispute. For example, Justice Thurgood Marshall's votes are compared only to the votes of white justices who sat with him on the Court and who voted on the same disputes. This approach thereby offers an apples-to-apples comparison.

Consider, then, Justice Thurgood Marshall. Sixty-two percent of Justice Marshall's votes agreed with the views of Black Americans. That figure compares to 57% of the votes cast by white justices who sat during Justice Marshall's tenure. Broken down by the justices' partisanship, during Justice Marshall's tenure the white justices who were Democrats agreed with Black Americans in 62% of their votes. White Republican justices agreed with Black Americans 53% of the time. Thus, Justice Marshall's votes represented Black Americans' views *exactly as often* as did the Court's white Democratic justices, but 9% *more often* than did white Republican justices. The difference over all other justices (of 5%) or, alternatively, over white Republican justices (of 9%) is termed the "bonus" for Black Americans. No such bonus exists comparing Justice Marshall solely to white Democratic justices.

The results are quite different for Justice Clarence Thomas, the Court's second and only other Black justice. Only 42% of Justice Thomas' votes agreed with the views of Black Americans. By comparison, 54% of all the other justices' votes who served during Justice Thomas' tenure agreed with Black Americans' views. Broken down by partisanship, that figure is 62% for Democratic justices and 50% for Republican justices. In short, Justice Thomas less often represented Black Americans' views than either the remaining Democratic or Republican justices. Black Americans received no bonus at all from Justice Thomas, quite the reverse.

Gender offers another comparison. Four women served on the Court through the 2019–2020 term. Table 5.2 reports how often each woman justice agreed with the views of American women, compared to the equivalent agreement rate for men justices who served during those times. Of the four women justices, only Justice O'Connor better represented women than did the men justices who sat at the same time—8% better. For women, this bonus is slightly larger than the bonus that Black Americans received from Justice

Table 5.2 Agreement Rates of the Four Women Justices Compared to Men Who Served during the Same Time Periods

Justice	How Often Did this Woman Justice Represent Women's Views? (%)	How Often Did All Men Justices Represent Women's Views? (%)	How Often Did Other Democratic Men Justices Represent Women's Views? (%)	How Often Did Other Republican Men Justices Represent Women's Views? (%)
O'Connor	61	53	52	54
Ginsburg	54	55	55	56
Sotomayor	53	57	58	57
Kagan	55	56	61	55

Source: Data collected and analyzed by the author and listed in the appendix.

Table 5.3 Agreement Rates of Black and Women Justices versus Other Justices, on Core Issues for Blacks and Women

Justice	How Often Did This Justice Agree with His or Her Own Group on Core Claims? (%)	How Often Did All Other Justices Who Served at the Same Time Agree with That Group on Core Claims? (%)	How Often Did Other Democratic Justices (Only) Who Served at the Same Time Agree with That Group on Core Claims? (%)	How Often Did Other Republican Justices (Only) Who Served at the Same Time Agree with That Group on Core Claims? (%)
Marshall	100 (Blacks)	65	82	52
Thomas	15 (Blacks)	51	89	33
O'Connor	83 (Women)	61	53	65
Ginsburg	70 (Women)	62	50	64
Sotomayor	75 (Women)	18	50	12
Kagan	50 (Women)	18	50	11

Source: Data collected and analyzed by the author and listed in the appendix.

Marshall. For Justices Ginsburg, Sotomayor, and Kagan, American women derived no bonus at all. As this suggests, symbolic representation can deliver a modest bonus for the group so represented, but not predictably so.

This section makes one final pass at finding evidence for symbolic representation. Table 5.3 includes only "core" cases—those presumably most closely related to the status of Blacks or women. This distinction is admittedly arbitrary since many other issues may be of equal or greater interest to Blacks, women, or partisan identifiers.[21] With that caveat, Black Americans' core issues include racial and civil rights disputes. Women's core issues include gender rights and reproductive rights claims. For Republicans and Democrats, core issues include disputes over elections and voting. As before, table 5.3 only compares justices who served during the same time.

The results in table 5.3 again provide mixed evidence for symbolic representation although with evidence that is narrower in scope. The number of justices is small; so are the number of core disputes and the number of other justices compared. Justices Marshall and O'Connor again stand out for symbolic representation. Both justices always or nearly always represented their own symbolic groups' views (Blacks and women, respectively) and both justices did so at much higher rates than do the remaining justices. Justice Ginsburg also produced a "bonus" for women in symbolic representation, albeit smaller in size. On core issues, both Justices Sotomayor and Kagan represent women's views much better than do all the men justices, mostly because current and recent Republican justices seldom support abortion rights or other gender rights claims. Justice Thomas seldom represented Blacks' views on racial claims, doing so less often than the remaining justices.

On partisan core claims over voting and elections, the evidence for symbolic representation is stronger but should be interpreted cautiously. At one time, the partisan divide was small on core partisan issues that reached the Court. Since the 1930s, Republican justices agreed with grassroots Republicans 56% of the time on election-related votes. Yet Democratic justices agreed with grassroots Republicans even more often—71% of the time. Not until the Clinton era appointees and thereafter did Republican justices better represent grassroots Republicans on partisan core claims than did Democratic justices (61% versus 40%, respectively). For grassroots Democrats, the pattern is quite different. Since the 1930s, Democratic justices always better represented grassroots Democrats on core partisan claims than did Republican justices (87% versus 45%, respectively), and this pattern did not much change over the decades. In short, partisanship led to symbolic representation only over the past three decades.

To summarize: symbolic representation may lead to policy representation but not necessarily so. Do symbolic nominations serve any other purpose? A symbolic nominee may more likely win Senate confirmation, as did Justice Clarence Thomas whose narrow Senate confirmation was likely aided by support from Black Americans (Overby et al. 1992; Badas and Stauffer 2018; Kaslovsky, Rogowski, and Stone 2021). A symbolic nominee may also increase support for the Court or its decisions both among those Americans so represented and perhaps even those who are not (Mansbridge 1999; Clayton, O'Brien, and Piscopo 2019). More evidence would be welcome.[22]

CONCLUSION AND DISCUSSION

Representing nationwide public opinion is not the end of the story. Some Courts and some justices represent specific groups better (or worse) than do others. In terms of representation, different groups often have very different "best" and "worst" lists of justices.

Many names that appear on different groups' best or worst lists offer little by way of surprise. Other names may be unexpected. For American women, all the justices on a hypothetical "dream Court" are men. The dream Court for Black Americans entirely comprises white justices, including a few long-ago Republicans. On Republicans' dream Court are three Democratic justices. On Democrats' dream Court are three Republicans. Two of nine names on Republicans' nightmare Court are Republicans. Two of nine names on Democrats' nightmare Court are Democrats.

Mixed evidence appears on whether symbolic representation leads to policy representation. Justice Thurgood Marshall does not rank on Black Americans' dream Court, while Justice Clarence Thomas ranks on Black Americans' nightmare Court. None of the four women justices (through the 2019–2020 term) rank on either women's dream Court or nightmare Court. Symbolic representation can lead to policy representation on a group's "core" issues but only sometimes so. Justices Thurgood Marshall and Sandra Day O'Connor are the standouts.

Why is symbolic representation so far from an all-encompassing explanation for representation? All 10 groups compared here are themselves large and diverse. Sometimes majorities of a group's identifiers do not support what appears to be a group-based claim. Nor do large and diverse groups take opposing views on most disputes that reach the Supreme Court. Further, some justices have few ties to and less clearly value their symbolic group compared to a justice's preferred modes of legal reasoning. Some presidents pick symbolic nominees who only marginally identify with the group that nominee supposedly represents or with interest groups that purport to represent a group.[23] Presidents have several reasons to pick a symbolic appointee other than representing that group.

Symbolic and policy representation may have been more strongly linked in years past, although the lack of survey data before the 1930s makes that impossible to prove (Perry 1989, 1991). As well, stronger evidence for symbolic representation may occur in future years for a disabled, evangelical, openly gay or lesbian, Islamic, Indian, or Mexican- or Cuban- or Asian-American justice. The evidence for symbolic representation is also limited by the available polling data. Justice Scalia won minor fame as the first Italian American Catholic justice, but polls do not produce reliable samples for small groups. As a caveat, the number of justices is itself small, and the evidence here may not readily transfer to state and lower federal courts.

Most accounts of symbolic representation consider race and gender. Yet partisanship is now an important form of symbolic representation. At one time, Republican and Democratic justices' votes did not closely represent their own copartisans at the grassroots. The change in partisan representation is recent. For example, Justice Sandra Day O'Connor, a Republican appointee of President Reagan, cast votes that agreed with grassroots Republicans 64% of the time and that agreed with grassroots Democrats 58% of the time—a small partisanship voting gap of only 6%. After Justice Clarence Thomas joined the Court, the partisanship gap steadily grew for each successive president. For example, Justice Sonia Sotomayor's votes agreed with Republicans only 26% of the time but agreed with Democrats 68% of the time—a partisanship voting gap of 42%. Figure 5.1 depicts that change. The partisanship gap is steadily growing and for President Trump's first two appointees reached historic highs. Whether the partisanship voting gap for Justice Barrett and for future justices will be large is unclear.

Not surprisingly, many Americans view the Court as a partisan and representative policymaker. The nomination and confirmation process has grown highly partisan and ideological. Once confirmed, the justices do, in fact, better represent their own copartisans than the other party's supporters. These realities are well established. Chapter 6 returns to the Court's likely future as a representative institution.

NOTES

1. McClain et al. (2009) and Lu and Jones (2019) review this extensive literature.

2. Pollsters define Hispanics or Latinos in several different ways and often did not do so until recent years. Some of the group preferences reported in table 5.1 are not available through online archives since the data files are not available but can be determined from print materials. Poll samples are very small and yield high margins of error for narrowly defined groups such as Black college-educated respondents. Education is easier to compare consistently across broad time periods than income. As a caveat, the percentage of American adults who fall into some categories varies over time. For example, the percentage of adults with a college degree or more has steadily risen since the mid-1930s, whereas the percentage of adults with less than a high school education has dropped.

3. Closely following are Justices Marshall, Ginsburg, and Vinson, all tied at 62%.

4. Closely following are Justices Stewart, O'Connor, and Kennedy, and Chief Justice Vinson (all at 62%), and Justice Scalia (at 60%).

5. Closely following are Justices Jackson and Thomas, and Chief Justice Rehnquist (all at 64%) and Justice Clark (at 63%).

6. Closely following are Justices Stevens (at 45%), Breyer (at 46%), Brennan and McReynolds (both at 47%), and Souter and Black (both at 48%).

7. Closely following are Chief Justice Warren and Justices White and Powell (all tied at 65%); and Justices Sotomayor (at 64%), Stewart (at 63%); Frankfurter, Clark, and Ginsburg (all tied at 62%); and Brennan (at 61%).

8. Closely following are Justice Scalia (at 62%); and Justices Stewart and Minton (both at 60%).

9. Closely following are Justices Blackmun (at 48%) and Ginsburg (at 50%).

10. Closely following are Chief Justice Roberts and Justice Scalia (each at 61%).

11. Closely following is Justice Fortas (at 50%).

12. Closely following are Justice Burton, Kennedy, and Chief Justice Rehnquist (all at 61%); and Justices Reed, Fortas, O'Connor, and Chief Justice Warren (all at 60%).

13. Closely following are Chief Justice Vinson (at 62% consistent); Justice O'Connor (at 61%); Justices Minton, Kennedy, and Scalia (all at 60%); Justice Reed (at 59%); and Chief Justice Warren (at 57%). Justices Kagan (at 55%), Ginsburg (at 54%), and Sotomayor (at 53%) follow.

14. Closely following are Justices Blackmun (at 49%), Fortas (at 50%), and Souter (at 51%).

15. Beginning with President Franklin Roosevelt, a Democrat, the individual justices' partisanship spreads are: Black (+8%), Reed (+11%), Frankfurter (+2%), Douglas (+6%), Murphy (+17%), Jackson (+5%), and Rutledge (+18%). For President Truman, a Democrat: Burton (−11%), Vinson (−10%), Clark (−1%), and Minton (0%). For President Eisenhower, a Republican: Warren (−7%), Harlan (−2%), Brennan (−15%), and Stewart (−6%). For President Kennedy, a Democrat: White (−1%). For President Johnson, a Democrat: Fortas (+17%) and Marshall (+19%). For President Nixon, a Republican: Burger (−2%), Blackmun (−11%), Powell (−4%), and Rehnquist (+6%). For President Ford, a Republican: Stevens (−6%). For President Reagan, a Republican: O'Connor (+6%), Scalia (+15%), and Kennedy (+5%). For President George H. W. Bush, a Republican: Souter (−5%) and Thomas (+21%). A positive sign indicates that the justices more often voted with their appointing president's copartisans; a negative sign indicates the opposite. Only justices with at least a dozen poll-matched votes are included here. Justices Burton, Brennan, and Powell were crossover appointees—that is, were not affiliated with the president's political party—and their partisanship spread averages −10%.

16. Beginning with President Clinton, a Democrat, the justices' partisanship spreads are Ginsburg (+19%) and Breyer (+18%). For President George W. Bush, a Republican: Roberts (+16%) and Alito (+38%). For President Obama, a Democrat: Sotomayor (+42%) and Kagan (+39%). For President Trump, a Republican: Gorsuch (+48%) and Kavanaugh (+56%). See also Segal and Spaeth (2002: 217–22).

17. Justice Amy Coney Barrett is not included in this analysis. Modern polling is not available before the 1930s. For earlier Republican presidents' appointees who had at least a dozen poll-matched votes, the partisanship spreads are: Hughes (−20%), Sutherland (+4%), Butler (+3%), Stone (−20%), and Owen Roberts (−13%). For appointees of prior Democratic presidents, the partisanship spreads are McReynolds (−19%) and Brandeis (+27%). Justice Butler was a crossover appointee.

18. Among recent or current justices, only Breyer, Kennedy, and Stevens had prior military service.

19. Some consider Justice Amy Coney Barrett, although Catholic, to be evangelical. Her confirmation followed the 2019–20 regular term, and none of her votes are poll matched for this book's analysis.

20. "Due to particularly severe health risks, vastly limited clinic options, and the 10-week window for obtaining a medication abortion, the FDA's requirement that women obtain mifepristone in person during the COVID–19 pandemic places an unnecessary and undue burden on their right to abortion. Pregnancy itself puts a woman at increased risk for severe consequences from COVID–19. In addition, more than half of women who have abortions are women of color, and COVID–19's mortality rate is three times higher for Black and Hispanic individuals than non-Hispanic White individuals. On top of that, three-quarters of abortion patients have low incomes, making them more likely to rely on public transportation to get to a clinic to pick up their medication. Such patients must bear further risk of exposure while they travel, sometimes for several hours each way, to clinics often located far from their homes."

21. For recent reviews of the now-extensive literature on whether judges who are racial minorities and women decide cases different from white and male judges, see Boyd (2016), Boyd and Nelson (2017), and Boyd and Rutkowski (2020). For a critique of the concepts raised here, see Kirkpatrick (2020).

22. Solberg and Diascro (2020) and Moyer et al. (2020) discuss symbolic representation in the lower federal courts.

23. As a well-known example, in 1941, President Franklin Roosevelt nominated Associate Justice Harlan Fiske Stone, a Republican, as chief justice (Abraham 2008: 182–83; Mason 1956: 563–68). For evidence on Justices Thomas, Ginsburg, and Breyer, see Perry and Abraham (1998).

Chapter 6

Representation, Public Opinion, and the Modern Court

The U.S. Supreme Court is indisputably a representative institution. The Court's decisions inevitably produce winners and losers. Historically, the Court always better represented some claimants' interests than others, even if the list of winners and losers changed over time. Through the early 1800s, the Court's decisions favored businesses and the national government rather than the states. Until the Civil War, the Court's decisions supported slaveholders' interests. After the Civil War, the Court usually favored businesses and Southern segregationists. During the late 1930s, the justices narrowly began to uphold a greater federal role in the economy; soon thereafter, retirements and new appointments led to a sharp reversal in the Court's earlier pro-business position. The Warren Court decisions more often favored civil rights, accused criminals, and religious and political dissenters. The Rehnquist and Roberts Courts were friendlier to businesses and state and local governments (Epstein, Landes, and Posner 2013a: 399–401, 2017).

Examining representation need not stop with a particular claimant. How well the Supreme Court represents Americans at the grassroots level is a different but no less an important question. Beginning in the 1930s, it became possible to answer this question more precisely. Pollsters often queried Americans on disputes that reached the Court. The justices better signaled their views through dissents and concurrences. Academics offered mounting evidence on how the Court and its justices decide cases. Many, perhaps most, Americans came to view the Court as a representative, not solely a legalistic, institution.

This book relies on poll questions that closely match issues raised in specific Supreme Court decisions to answer three questions. First, how well has the modern Court and its justices represented American public opinion and key groups' attitudes? Second, how do Americans perceive that the Court

makes decisions in this increasingly partisan era? This chapter concludes with
a third question: How would current reform proposals affect the Supreme
Court as a representative institution?

BEING A REPRESENTATIVE INSTITUTION

To answer the first of these three questions: three-fifths to two-thirds of
poll-matched Court decisions agree with Americans' views. This record is
relatively consistent over time. By Chief Justice, all seven modern Courts
mostly agreed with timely public opinion. Over the past half-century, there
is remarkably little variation in this pattern. The Court agreed with American
views from just below to just above two-thirds of poll-matched decisions.

With few exceptions, this pattern is broad and deep. Across nearly all
issues, most Supreme Court decisions agree with public opinion. Nearly half
of national security and foreign policy, federalism and intergovernmental
relations, and free speech decisions represent public opinion. Two-thirds or
more decisions do so on crime, education, abortion and morality, race, business and taxes, transportation and commerce, social welfare and poverty,
families, and LGBTQ claims. Over two-thirds of decisions on Americans'
"most important problem" agree with the polls. Taken across time and issues,
the modern Court is a majoritarian institution. Opinions may differ on what
cutoffs should be used before so describing the Court. True, the justices are
unelected, indirectly appointed, and with life terms, but in its behavior, the
modern Court is not counter-majoritarian.

This is not to say that the Court cannot produce some notably unpopular
decisions. As did earlier Courts, the Roberts Court sometimes makes unpopular decisions. *Trump v. Sierra Club* (2019) favored the so-called border wall.
NFIB v. Sebelius (2012), in part, upheld the Affordable Care Act's individual
mandate. *Citizens United v. FEC* (2010) liberalized rules on campaign spending. Although winning widespread and sustained criticism, unpopular decisions are not the norm. High-profile unpopular decisions are even less the
norm.[1]

This robust pattern of representation is not an artifact of the Court's persuasive ability. The modern Court never had much ability to persuade public
opinion, at least not so in the short term. By some polling experiments and
case studies, public opinion can follow Court decisions. Yet using real-world,
real-time polling evidence, the modern Court is representative, but remarkably unpersuasive.

Several practices help the Court to represent public opinion. Poll updating and poll correction are modern judicial norms. Through poll updating,
the Court overturns now-unpopular precedents and brings its own decisions

back into line with contemporary public opinion. Through poll correction, the Court selectively overturns lower court rulings that disagree with nationwide polls. By these two practices, the Court signals that lower federal and state courts should change their own future decisions better to reflect nationwide public opinion. Poll updating and poll correction discourage localities, state legislatures, governors, Congress, the White House, and state and federal agencies from enacting policies likely to be struck down. Exactly how widespread these preventative effects are is difficult to measure with any great precision and merits more attention. Unfortunately, absent modern polls it is impossible to estimate the extent of poll updating and poll correction before the 1930s.

In representing public opinion, the modern Court is clearly a co-equal branch. The Court's decisions as often represent public opinion as do challenged federal laws and policies. The Court's decisions more often agree with public opinion than do challenged state and local laws and policies. This has implications for arguments about judicial activism and restraint (Whittington 2014). Many critics urge the Court more often to practice judicial restraint. Doing so might lower the Court's profile and avoid public, presidential, or Congressional criticism (Fallon 2018: 162–67). Yet practicing judicial restraint would not, per se, better bring Supreme Court decisions into alignment with public opinion. Often it would have the opposite effect.

The modern Court's majoritarian record extends further. Since the 1930s, three-fifths to two-thirds of the Court's decisions represented the views of all 10 groups studied here. This pattern varies somewhat by Court. Grassroots Republicans fared better than did grassroots Democrats during the Roberts Court. The reverse was true under the Warren Court. Yet variations in groups' win-loss rates are surprisingly small. Even with a supposedly unfriendly Court, all 10 groups studied here still "win" more than half the time.

Most justices' votes agree with public opinion over half the time although there is great variation. At the top are a few justices whose votes represent public opinion about two-thirds of the time and whose voting patterns shift according to whether American attitudes on a dispute are liberal or conservative. Chapter 4 names five justices as the representative "greats"—Owen Roberts, Tom Clark, Sherman Minton, Byron White, and Lewis Powell. Ten "near-great" justices represent public opinion nearly as well. These 10 justices include Chief Justices Charles Evans Hughes, Harlan Stone, Warren Burger, William Rehnquist, and John Roberts, as well as Justices Louis Brandeis, Stanley Reed, Felix Frankfurter, Robert Jackson, and Potter Stewart. In representing Americans' views, the great and near-great justices do much of the heavy lifting.

The 15 great and near-great justices include several names not usually found on other lists of judicial greatness. Representative role is seldom recognized as a measure of judicial greatness, perhaps in part because representative role is difficult to measure. Before the 1930s, representative role was virtually impossible to estimate. Most judicial scholars apparently value leadership skills, bold strokes, and a preferred and consistent ideology as measures of judicial greatness, not representing public opinion.[2]

Other justices do not represent public opinion as well as do the great and near-great justices. At the other extreme are several justices whose votes agree with public opinion less than half of the time. The least representative justices are typically either extremely liberal or extremely conservative and their votes do not well represent public opinion. Falling in between are the remaining justices whose votes represent public opinion a little over half the time.

How often Supreme Court decisions represent American attitudes depends on which justices sit on the Court. Chapters 4 and 5 imagine purely hypothetical Courts whose justices best or worst represent Americans' views nationwide or the views of ten groups of Americans. At the extremes, a hypothetical "dream" Court would produce decisions nearly nine-tenths of which agree with American views, but a hypothetical "nightmare" Court would do so only a third of the time. Since the 1930s, no Court has produced decisions at either extreme. How Americans would react if only a third of Supreme Court decisions agreed with public opinion is an interesting but speculative question. Very possibly, criticism of the Court would reach unprecedented high levels.

Some plausible explanations for why some justices best (or worst) represent public opinion do not bear up. "Great" presidents do not necessarily appoint top-ranking justices on representative role. Nor does representative role closely correlate with other measures of judicial greatness. Nor are a justice's preferred decision-making rationale, gender, ethnicity, or partisanship closely related to representative role.

A justice's position on the Court and length of tenure are tied to representative role. Nearly all chief justices represent public opinion at above-average rates. Most justices best represent public opinion during their first decade on the Court and thereafter "drift away." During their early tenure, most of the recently appointed justices' votes better represent public opinion than did the outgoing justices' votes during recently past terms. Growing length of service thereafter takes its toll on representation. The decline often begins after a justice's first decade on the Court. Since most justices now serve for at least two or three decades, longevity takes a serious toll on representation. Term limits proposals do not always explicitly discuss representation, but longevity usually reduces representation.

Some justices represent different groups in an even-handed way. Others do not. Chapter 5 names the hypothetical "dream" and "nightmare" Courts for 10 key groups: men, women, Blacks, whites, Republicans, Independents,

Democrats, the college-educated, those with a high school degree, and the less well-educated. A few justices such as Chief Justice Hughes and Justice White appear on many groups' dream Court. Others such as Justice McReynolds appear on multiple nightmare Courts. Some justices' voting records are more group specific. These justices appear on one group's dream Court but on another group's nightmare Court. Current and recent justices often do so, reflecting the nation's political polarization.

The evidence for symbolic representation is mixed to negative. A symbolic nominee may serve a president's immediate political goals, fulfill a campaign promise, or win extra votes for a problematic Senate confirmation. Once confirmed, though, a symbolic justice may or may not represent his or her group better than do other justices. Symbolic representation often exists only on a narrow set of core issues for the group involved. Even then, the record is uneven. A few symbolic justices gave their group a "bonus"—particularly so, Thurgood Marshall (for Blacks) and Sandra Day O'Connor (for women).

Partisanship is an important recent trend in representation. The justices' votes increasingly better represent their own grassroots copartisans than the other political party's supporters. This pattern became apparent three decades ago. Many earlier justices no better represented their copartisans' views than those of the other political party's supporters. Some did worse so. Since the 1990s, presidents more carefully choose their nominees (Dorf 2007, Devins and Baum 2019). Partisanship and ideology increasingly dictate presidents' nominations, grassroots support for the nominees, and Senate confirmation votes. So, too, is partisan representation increasingly common on the Court. On poll-matched votes, each recent president's appointees steadily better represent their own copartisans than the opposition party's supporters. President Trump's first two appointees, Justices Gorsuch and Kavanaugh, reached new heights of partisan representation. Whether this trend will continue is unclear but seems likely. That many Americans may understand partisanship as the modern meaning of group representation on the Court is not surprising. Americans react to events slowly but in meaningful, stable, and sensible ways (Page and Shapiro, 1982, 1992).

Some of these conclusions may seem paradoxical. Justices now vote in an increasingly partisan manner. Yet, most Supreme Court decisions continue to represent majority public opinion and the views of major groups. This seeming contradiction is resolved in two ways. On many disputes that reach the Court, majorities of different demographic and partisan groups hold the same view. As well, the Court has often been closely divided between liberals and conservatives, Democrats and Republicans, and with one or two (although seldom more) justices whose votes flexibly track public opinion. The recurring cycles of American elections, shifting partisan control at the White House and Congress, new appointments, and the presence of one or two "great" or "near-great" representative justices contribute to an even-handed pattern of representation. Whether these conditions will continue is unclear.

HOW AMERICANS PERCEIVE THE COURT

To answer the second of this chapter's three questions, most Americans now view the Supreme Court as an institution whose decisions at least sometimes represent the justices' ideological, partisanship, ideology, or social backgrounds. By some poll questions, about half of Americans believe that the justices *should* consider public opinion when making decisions, although far fewer perceive that the justices *do*. Measuring how Americans view the Court is not simple. Pollsters must translate the concept of representation into useable poll questions that respondents can understand. Depending on the poll question, at least a third to a half of Americans now view the Court as some sort of a representative policymaker. By some poll questions, well over half of Americans do. Only a quarter or fewer Americans say that the Court and its justices solely decide cases on legal grounds. If a poll question offers more options, half to three-quarters of Americans say that non-legalistic grounds sometimes or mostly affect the Court's decisions.

Describing overtime change in these perceptions is more problematic. The wide variety of poll question wording makes it difficult to ascertain with any great precision whether Americans increasingly perceive the Court as a representative policymaker. Without doubt, academic views have long since moved away from the view that the justices make decisions solely on legalistic grounds. Increased partisanship during the confirmations process, the justices' frequent split votes along partisan lines, politicians' criticisms, the declining number of ideologically flexible justices, and media coverage make it likely that Americans will increasingly view the Court as a representative institution.

Shifting approval ratings strongly suggest growing public perceptions that the Court is a partisan and representative institution. Republicans and Democrats at the grass roots nearly always shift their views of the Court whenever the White House shifts from Republican to Democratic control or the reverse. When the Court announces a high-profile decision favoring one party over the other, grassroots partisan approval follows suit. To paraphrase Mr. Dooley, a legendary cartoon character, approval for the Court follows the election returns.[3] These views are not unrealistic. The Supreme Court has been evolving into a partisan and representative institution for many years. Just as there seems no likelihood that the justices' behavior will soon change course, neither seems there much likelihood that Americans will come to view the Court as primarily a legalistic institution. If anything, Americans underestimate how greatly the Court is now a representative institution.

REFORM PROPOSALS AND THE COURT AS A REPRESENTATIVE INSTITUTION

This book evaluates the Supreme Court as an institution whose decisions represent Americans' policy views. By the evidence, the modern Court fares well. Since the 1930s, most poll-matched Supreme Court decisions agreed with American attitudes. Over recent decades, nearly two-thirds of Court decisions do—a figure equal to or better than other policymakers whose decisions the Court reviews. Many, and by some poll questions most Americans view the Court as a representative policymaker. So do most academics, journalists, and attorneys. This chapter's third and final question asks: How current reform proposals might affect the Court's future as a representative institution?

The Supreme Court now faces a multitude of criticisms. Although some criticisms are long-standing, the Court's critics have grown increasingly vocal. Notably, in April 2021, President Biden, by executive order, appointed a prestigious 36-member commission to evaluate possible changes in the federal courts.[4] Many of the current criticisms address representation.[5] This final section asks how proposed reforms might affect the Court's future as a representative institution.

Many proposed reforms do not explicitly aim at representation and seem unlikely to change how often Supreme Court decisions agree with public opinion. Televising the justices' hearings is a popular reform but not one obviously related to representation. So are complaints about the Court's so-called shadow docket. Requiring that the justices record their votes on grants or denials of certiorari or of a stay or on per curiam rulings would improve transparency and the vote split would interest attorneys and scholars. Yet so requiring would not clearly affect representation. Greater clarity on standards for recusals due to perceived conflicts of interest or travel paid for by outside groups fall into the same category—unless such standards were used to block specific justices from hearing specific appeals.

As another example, complaints sometimes arise that the Court often announces its highest-profile decisions during each term's last day or two. Yet a decision's announcement date has no obvious relationship to representation. Some proposals would limit the justices' often lucrative book contracts or their appearances at certain legal forums such as the Federalist Society or the American Constitutional Society. Other complaints arise about the justices' verbose writing style or the frequency of concurrences. Some critics would require a public listing of donors who spend large amounts of money on advertising campaigns supporting or opposing a nomination to the Court. None of these changes would necessarily affect representation. Worth noting, the Court might strike down some such requirements, if ever enacted.

Still other proposed changes might affect representation, but the effect is unclear. Since the 1980s, the number of full, written decisions has dropped despite an increase in appeals. The Court averaged about 180 petitions granted review, per term, during the 1980s but less than half that number during the 2000s. Increasing the number of full, written decisions might address complaints that the Court hears too few cases, but the likely impact on representation is modest. If long-standing patterns of poll correction continue, the Court might bring several additional lower court decisions back into agreement with nationwide public opinion, per term. Again, following historic patterns, the gain would be greatest if the additional decisions were on state and local laws.

Whether other proposals might bring more decisions into line with public opinion is often unclear since no such proposals have gone into effect. Term limits advocates aim to appoint justices on a more regular and predictable basis and force justices off the bench after a fixed number of years. Life tenure for federal judges is a historical oddity imitated by only a single American state. Under the best-known proposals, a president could make a new appointment every 2 years with a justice's tenure limited to 18 years (Calabresi and Lindgren 2006; Cramton 2007; Cramton and Carrington 2006; Cramton and Lindgren 2006; Chemerinsky 2014; Costello 2020).[6] Term limits would be a major change. With 18-year terms, a two-term president, given an agreeable Senate, could appoint four of the nine justices—making a great impact on the Court, albeit with each justice serving a somewhat shorter number of years.

Assessing how term limits would impact representation requires some counterfactual analysis (Black and Bryan 2016; Hemel 2021). Term limits would eliminate the longest-serving justices who mostly drift away from public opinion over the years. Term limits would also largely eliminate the practice of carefully timed retirements. Recently appointed justices are usually more attuned to contemporary public opinion and to Congressional and presidential goals (Sherry 2016: 912). Yet if presidents of either political party continue to nominate ideologically extreme justices, as is now the norm, term limits would not produce "great" or "near-great" ideologically flexible justices who promote representation. Improving representation would occur only through a very uncertain route. If control at the White House regularly shifted between Republicans and Democrats and if the Senate confirmed a president's presumably highly ideological and partisan nominees, then neither Democrats nor Republicans would long hold a stable majority on the Court. Whether a close and shifting partisan balance would better represent

American attitudes is unclear. Term limits might only result in more decisions made along partisan and ideological lines and fewer decisions that agree with public opinion. If one political party controlled the White House for three or more terms and continued to win Senate approval for its (again presumably highly ideological) nominees, the Court's decisions would almost certainly less well represent public opinion.

Term limits are among the more popular of proposed reforms. As chapter 1 reported, about two-thirds of Americans favor term limits rather than lifetime appointments.[7] Only televised hearings are as popular. Adding additional justices, commonly called Court packing, discussed later in this chapter, is decidedly less popular. Poll numbers notwithstanding, overcoming long tradition and the Constitution's wording ("The judges, both of the supreme and inferior Courts, shall hold their Offices during good Behavior") makes it difficult to enact term limits without a near-impossible constitutional amendment.

Daniel Epps and Ganesh Sitaraman (2019) propose two reforms, either of which might affect how often the Court's decisions represent American attitudes. One proposal, termed the Supreme Court Lottery, would expand the Court from 9 members to roughly 180 members by appointing every federal court of appeals judge as an associate justice (see also McGinnis 1999; Sonnert 2020). Cases would then be heard by rotating panels of nine judges, each panel with no more than five justices from a single political party, and with a 6-to-3 majority required to rule as unconstitutional a federal statute (and possibly a state statute). Alternatively, under the Balanced Bench Plan, the Court would consist of five Democratic justices and five Republican justices, who would together (two years in advance and either unanimously or by supermajority) select five federal judges to serve one-year non-renewable terms. Neither proposal prevents a president from picking ideologically extreme federal judges. Instead, the Supreme Court Lottery requires a supermajority rule for overturning federal (and perhaps state) laws; the Balanced Bench Plan would add rotating groups of five presumably centrist federal judges to the Supreme Court.

How either plan would affect representation is uncertain. The Supreme Court Lottery would likely result in nine-member panels closely balanced between liberals and conservatives. Yet with supermajority voting rule many federal and state policies, some of them unpopular, would likely remain in effect. The Balanced Bench Plan's addition of five presumably centrist federal judges might increase how often the Court's decisions agree with nationwide polls. These estimates are speculative since neither proposal has so far gone into effect.

Another proposal would shrink the number of justices from nine to eight, require that there be four Republican and four Democratic justices, and mandate that decisions be made by at least a 5-to-3 vote (Segall 2018).[8] Such a

Court briefly existed following Justice Scalia's death in 2016 until Justice Gorsuch joined the Court in 2017. Under this proposal, no longer could the Court make decisions, 5-to-4, along partisan lines. Possibly, this proposal might lead the justices more often to compromise on decisions. This plan would possibly reduce complaints that votes fall along partisan lines although the effect on representation is again unclear. Any four justices (whether Republicans or Democrats) who are satisfied with a lower court ruling could vote to leave that lower court ruling in effect. It is unclear whether this would increase the percentage of decisions that agree with public opinion.[9] As chapter 3 described, perhaps surprisingly, narrowly decided Supreme Court decisions no less often represent public opinion than do more one-sided decisions. Further, lower federal court rulings reviewed by the Supreme Court less often represent nationwide public opinion than do Supreme Court decisions.

Some proposals would strip the Supreme Court of appellate jurisdiction over specific issues. Historically, the best-known instance of jurisdiction stripping was a short-lived Congressional ban on hearing habeas corpus cases just after the Civil War. Since then, many critics proposed issue-specific jurisdiction stripping. Yet historical experience, modern legal views, the likelihood of tit-for-tat rounds of Congressional retaliation, qualms about foreclosing the courts to important issues, and the practical difficulties of implementation, all weigh against jurisdiction stripping (Bradley and Siegel 2017; Grove 2018; Epps and Sitaraman 2019; Fallon 2010; Fitzpatrick 2012; Tushnet 1999).

Whether jurisdiction stripping would better represent public opinion is unclear. Congress and the White House might use jurisdiction stripping to preclude an expected unpopular Court ruling or to send the justices a general warning not to stray too far from public opinion. Alternatively, Congress and the White House, when under unified party control, might use jurisdiction stripping to forestall the Court from overturning a controversial law or policy that lacks popular support. As chapter 3 reported, federal laws and policies only about equally often reflect public opinion as do Supreme Court decisions.

Public opinion has been consistently negative toward jurisdiction stripping. In 1936, a Gallup question reported a 59-to-41% majority opposing "limiting the power of the Supreme Court to declare acts of Congress unconstitutional." In four surveys between 1987 and 2005, by an average of 53% to 31%, Americans opposed limiting "the right of the Supreme Court to decide certain types of controversial issues" (Gibson 2007). Surveys by Marquette Law School and NORC in 2019, 2020, and 2021 reported that 62-to-38%, 58-to-41% and 56-to-43% majorities, respectively, opposed a plan to "limit the ability of the Supreme Court to review and set aside acts of Congress as unconstitutional." In a 2021 Annenberg survey, a 61-to-38% majority opposed the proposal that "when Congress disagrees with the Supreme Court's decisions, Congress should pass legislation saying the Supreme Court can no longer rule on that issue or topic." Perhaps not surprisingly, the Court's critics now seldom focus on jurisdiction stripping.

Some critics propose a so-called Court-packing plan to add several justices to the Court. Historically, the number of justices varied between 6 and 10 before settling at 9 in 1869. Those early changes sometimes aimed to better supervise the expanding lower federal courts, or at other times, to increase (or thwart) presidential control over the Court. President Franklin Roosevelt's ill-fated Court packing plan sought to increase the number of justices from 9 to 15, thereby allowing the president to name up to 6 new justices and ensure a supportive Court majority for New Deal legislation. After that plan failed, the idea of adding new justices to the Court seemingly faded away (Baum 2019: 12; Friedman 2000; Grove 2018: 514–17).

Court-packing regained popularity, at least among liberal Democrats, after Justice Scalia's death in 2016 when Senate Republicans refused to hold hearings on President Obama's nominee, federal appeals judge (and in 2021, Attorney General) Merrick Garland. In November 2016, President Trump unexpectedly won the presidential election and during his four years in office appointed 226 federal judges, including three Supreme Court justices. Justices Gorsuch and Kavanaugh joined the Court, followed by Amy Coney Barrett who won Senate confirmation barely two weeks before President Trump lost reelection. By then, many liberal Democrats backed a Court-packing plan, at least contingent on Democratic nominee Joe Biden winning the presidential election (Feldman 2020). During spring 2021, one such Congressional proposal sought to add four new justices, presumably all Democrats. The plan met mixed reviews and no action ensued.

Public opinion has so far opposed Court packing, albeit not overwhelmingly so. A 54-to-32% majority in a 2020 Abt/ABC/*Washington Post* survey opposed "increasing the number of United States Supreme Court justices, which would give the winner of the presidential election more influence over the court's makeup." A 2021 Monmouth University survey reported a 58-to-36% majority against adding more justices to the current nine-member Court. Surveys by Marquette Law School and NORC in 2019, 2020, and 2021 reported that by margins of 57-to-43%, 53-to-46%, and 51-to-48%, respectively, majorities opposed a proposal to "increase the number of justices on the United States Supreme Court." These poll results should be interpreted cautiously since Court-packing advocates have not yet won White House support, passed such a plan in Congress, or launched an expensive publicity campaign to support the plan (Bartels and Johnston 2020: 72).

Whether the Supreme Court would strike down as unconstitutional a partisan Court-packing plan, if enacted, is unclear (Bradley and Siegel 2017; Amar

2012). More the question here is: How would a partisan Court-packing plan affect representation? Almost certainly, Court packing would not increase the number of "great" or "near-great" representative justices who play a critical role in producing decisions that represent public opinion. Instead, Court packing would likely further raise the partisan and ideological stakes, reinforce the pattern of only very liberal Democrats or very conservative Republican appointees, and lead to a steadily increasing number of justices (Chilton et al. 2021). As chapter 4 suggests, highly ideological justices are unresponsive to public opinion. Court packing seems more likely to change the mix of winners and losers than to increase representation. This conclusion is tentative since no such plan has yet been enacted. As with other proposals, "There is no way to know beforehand what the implications will be down the road."[10]

Some critics recommend a particular interpretive approach such as minimalism (Sunstein 1999, 2005), judicial deference to the elected branches (Fallon 2018), a stronger commitment to civil rights and liberties (Chemerinsky 2014), or originalism (Scalia 1989; Gorsuch 2019; Paulson 2016; Sachs 2015). As chapter 4 noted, some justices closely associated with these theories rank as above average on representative role, but most are not the top-ranking justices. Instead, the top-ranking justices are ideologically flexible.

Possibly the justices themselves might take still other steps better to represent American attitudes by granting certiorari to appeals when federal, state, or local governments, lower courts, or the Court's own past decisions seem out of step with public opinion. To some extent the Court already does exactly this through poll correction and poll updating. For this strategy to bring the Court closer to public opinion would require a two-stage strategy: first, that the justices correctly identify unpopular laws and policies, lower court rulings, and Supreme Court precedents; and second, then overturn these. Alternatively, the justices could uphold popular policies, lower court decisions, or precedents either by denying certiorari or upon appeal. This strategy assumes that the justices highly value representation compared to other priorities.

Some Court watchers urge presidents to nominate and Senators to confirm centrist justices whose votes best reflect public opinion (Fallon 2018: 162–67). This is a key issue since new confirmations, taken alone, do not guarantee that a justice's votes will agree with public opinion. Historically, there were more "good trades" than "bad trades" on representation, but striking exceptions occur. Given the highly partisan and polarized state of American politics, the number of great and near-great justices on representative role has steadily dwindled. No new justice since Chief Justice John Roberts in 2005 ranks as great or near-great on representative role. Restoring the Senate filibuster—thereby requiring 60 votes for confirming a justice—might pressure presidents to nominate ideologically moderate justices (Epps and Sitaraman

2019), but given the present polarization of Congressional politics, that is unclear. The opposition party (given 41 votes) might refuse to allow a vote. Chapters 4 and 5 offer evidence that centrist justices best represent nationwide public opinion, although not necessarily so all groups. Conceded, there seems no likelihood either that presidents will nominate ideologically flexible justices or that the Senate will reinstate the filibuster for Supreme Court nominees. Were presidents and Senators to do so, the Court's decisions might better represent American attitudes.

Notwithstanding its many critics, the Court enjoys many strengths, and it is uncertain that *any* of these proposed changes will soon happen. One of the Court's strengths lies in how Americans view the Court. Confidence and approval in the Court vary with recent events, changing perceptions of the federal government, and the Court's agreement with public opinion and the public mood (Haglin et al. 2020). Even so, the Court usually enjoys better ratings than do the president, the executive branch, Congress, or top Congressional leaders. Figure 6.1 reports recent approval ratings. The Supreme Court is not always Americans' favorite institution; recently, the military's confidence ratings were higher. Yet in popular regard, the Court usually ranks well above the branches from which any major changes would necessarily come. There is no apparent groundswell of grassroots dissatisfaction with the Court. Nor, as chapter 3 indicates, has the Court recently produced an unusually high percentage of highly visible, unpopular rulings.

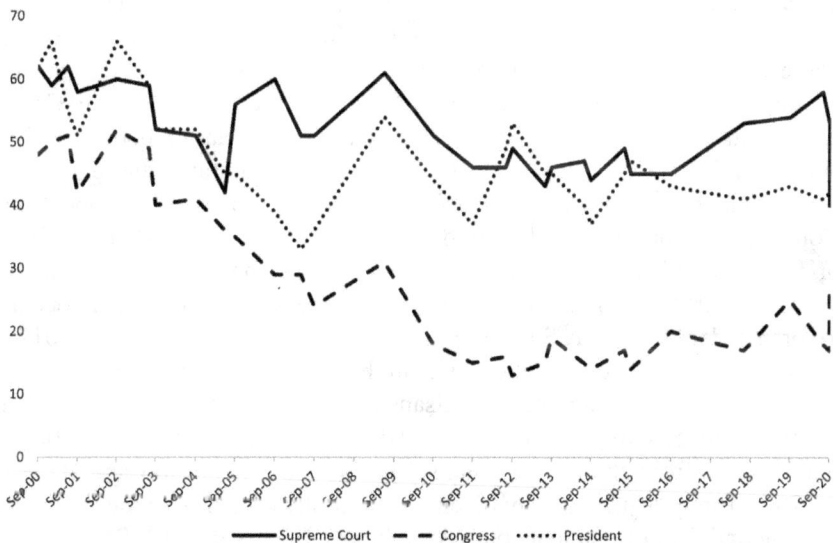

Figure 6.1 Approval Ratings for the Supreme Court, Congress, and the President.
Source: Data collected and analyzed by the author from Gallup polls, 2000 to 2020.

Americans' support for the Supreme Court goes beyond approval and confidence ratings. Diffuse support, or legitimacy,[11] indicates Americans' willingness ("a reservoir of good will") to protect the Court against institutional attacks. Surveys often use three to seven questions to measure diffuse support, including whether the Court can be trusted; attitudes toward jurisdiction stripping, other limits on the Court or even abolishing the Court; and perceptions that the Court is overly political. In the aggregate, the Court's diffuse support has remained relatively stable since the late 1980s, notwithstanding occasional offsetting partisan shifts in approval resulting from decisions such as *Bush v. Gore* (2000) or *NFIB v. Sebelius* (2010) (Nelson and Tucker 2021). In part, diffuse support depends on Americans being more influenced by decisions with which they agree than those with which they disagree, beliefs that the justices vote in a principled and sincere manner, early socialization and learning about the courts, and symbols of the judiciary such as courtrooms and robes (Gibson, Lodge, and Woodson 2014; Hansford and Coe 2019; Bonneau et al. 2017). Very likely, legitimacy depends on at least a mix of agreeable and disagreeable decisions (Gibson and Nelson 2014; Malhotra and Jessee 2014; Badas 2016; Bartels and Johnston 2020).[12] Compared to other nation's top courts, the U.S. Supreme Court is well regarded by the public (Gibson, Caldeira, and Baird 1998; Gibson and Caldeira 2011; Gibson and Nelson 2017; Sternberg, Brouard, and Honnige 2021).

Diffuse support is different from the Court's approval or confidence ratings (Gibson, Caldeira, and Spence 2003b; Gibson and Nelson 2016).[13] Through diffuse support, Americans may defend the Court's independence notwithstanding an unpopular decision or a highly politicized nominations battle (Armaly 2018a). Even so, diffuse support is not completely stable and may partly depend on whether Americans perceive that the Court reaches its decisions in a principled manner (Parker and Woodson 2020; Woodson 2018, 2019; Ramirez 2008). A string of unfavorable decisions can shrink the Court's reservoir of good feelings, as witness support for Court packing and Court curbing during the New Deal era (Badas 2019a) or Black Americans' declining support following the civil rights-friendly Warren Court (Gibson and Caldeira 1992). As well, the reverse may occur; favorable decisions may increase support (Armaly 2020a; Gibson 2017). Sustained attacks from well-known, highly partisan figures can depress support for the Court among copartisans (Armaly 2018b, 2020b; Clark and Kastellec 2015; Gibson and Nelson 2019; Rogowski and Stone 2019). So may attacks from the "sensationalist" news media (Johnston and Bartels 2010). So may a justice's involvement in controversial activities such as a presidential impeachment trial (Armaly and Enders 2021b). So may the growing emotional divide between partisans (Armaly and Enders 2021a).

So may a controversial nomination (Carrington and French 2021; cf. Krewson and Schroedel 2020). Even a single well-publicized, unpopular decision can temporarily depress diffuse support for the Court (Mondak and Smithey 1997; Durr 2000; Gibson, Caldeira, and Spence 2003a; Bartels and Johnston 2013; cf. Gibson and Nelson 2015; Nicholson and Hansford 2014; Christenson and Glick 2015b, 2019; Johnston, Hillygus, and Bartels 2014). The media's increased framing of Court decisions as strategic, not principled, may have the same effect on support for specific decisions (Hitt and Searles 2018).

The Supreme Court enjoys yet a final advantage: it is very difficult for its enemies to attack. Changes such as term limits would likely require a constitutional amendment. Jurisdiction stripping has uncertain effects and has long fallen out of favor. Enacting a constitutional amendment to overturn a particular decision seems a near-impossibility. Proposals to change the number of justices have not succeeded in a century and a half and fewer than half of Americans support such proposals. Political party control at the White House and Congress is often divided or with close partisan divisions in Congress. Under these circumstances, the most likely way to change the Court's decisions remains through new appointments, itself usually an infrequent event (Nemacheck 2021; see also Holden, Keane, and Lilly 2021).

To conclude, challenges to the Court—particularly Court packing—result more from the polarized partisanship of American politics than from a decline in how well the Court represents public opinion or from dropping public support for the Court. Since the mid-1930s, Supreme Court decisions have relatively well represented American attitudes. The Court's pattern of representation is mostly stable and even-handed. All 10 groups examined here "win" at the Supreme Court half to two-thirds of the time. The modern Court represents Americans' attitudes as well as do popularly elected officials. The Roberts Court has seen no decline in that record. True, the Court sometimes makes high-profile, unpopular decisions but that is not its typical behavior.

Will this pattern continue? The key links to representation are, first, a close ideological balance among the justices and, second, the presence of one or two ideologically flexible justices whose votes shift with public opinion. Until very recently, the Court remained closely balanced between liberal and conservative justices. The number of ideologically flexible justices dwindles as party sorting and polarization on and off the Court rise. Each recent president's appointees grow steadily more partisan in poll-matched decisions. To date, a closely balanced Court, coupled with one or two representative "great" or "near-great" representative justices, has kept the Court in line with American public opinion. Whether this balance will continue is a critical question, but the answer is now unclear.

NOTES

1. Pildes (2011a) offers four reasons why the Court sometimes makes high-profile, unpopular decisions. These include that the justices value but misunderstand majority public opinion; the justices favor judicial theories (e.g., originalism or a strong belief in minority rights) that disregard public opinion; the justices believe that their views will prevail, public opinion notwithstanding; and the justices vote their personal views without considering public opinion.

2. Pederson and Provizer (1993: 24–28) compile lists of "great" and "near-great" justices. The poll-matched justices therein have very mixed records on representative role.

3. The cartoon character, Martin J. Dooley, was a hypothetical Irish saloon keeper created by a Chicago-born journalist, Finley Peter Dunne. Mr. Dooley's many humorous pronouncements focused on the U.S. Supreme Court when he commented: "No matther whether th' constitution follows th' flag or not, th' Supreme Coort follows th' election returns" (Bander 1981).

4. In December 2021, the Commission produced its final report reviewing the pros and cons of various proposed reforms such as imposing term limits, adding additional justices, and limiting the Court's jurisdiction, but not taking positions on those issues. The report suggested a possible strengthening of the ethics code, clarifying the status of the emergency docket, and making audio recordings of hearings timelier available.

5. Other proposed reforms that primarily aim at different problems include increasing the number of justices and using panels to increase the number of appeals heard (George and Guthrie 2009) or fixing a retirement age to address frail health and mental decrepitude (Garrow 2000; Glock 2020).

6. Hemel (2021) proposes guaranteeing each president two appointments per term but without imposing term limits, thereby resulting in a flexible number of justices.

7. The sentiment is long-standing. A 1987 CBS/*New York Times* survey reported that only 16% of respondents said that the justices should serve for life, while 80% said that the justices should serve for a specific number of years. In a 1991 *Los Angeles Times* survey, only 21% of respondents favored life terms, while 51% favored terms of 10 or fewer years and 20% favored longer terms. In a 1938 Gallup survey, 70% of respondents said that "Supreme Court justices should be required to retire after reaching a certain age" with 70–75 as the average age given among those who favored an age limit.

8. For another argument criticizing simple majority rule on the Court, see Waldron (2014). Black and Bryan (2014a, 2014b) evaluate decision-making with eight justices, whether due to deaths, retirements, or recusals. Paulson (2016: 65–66) recommends an eight-member Court.

9. Segall offers a list (2018: 558–59) of important, narrowly decided (5-to-4) rulings made along liberal-conservative lines over the last quarter century. Excluding the "unclear" decision in *Bush v. Gore* (2000), three-quarters of these decisions agreed with public opinion and a quarter did not.

10. The quote is from an interview with Mark Tushnet in Illing (2020).

11. Fallon (2018) distinguishes between legal, moral, and sociological legitimacy. Diffuse support is a form of sociological legitimacy.

12. Upon occasion and perhaps for that reason, the Court announces a mix of ideological rulings together or just a few days apart (Hazelton 2021). In 2013, for instance, *Shelby County v. Holder*, a conservative decision, was followed the next day by *U.S. v. Windsor* and *Hollingsworth v. Perry*, both liberal decisions.

13. In part, diffuse support may be more stable, over time, because it is commonly measured by multiple questions, not by a single question as typically are approval or confidence. Badas (2019b) recommends using fewer (only three) but more specific questions to measure legitimacy.

Appendix
Poll-to-Ruling Matches and Issues

This appendix briefly describes each poll-matched issue and decision chronologically and is divided into four sections. In the first section are poll-matched Supreme Court decisions classified as consistent with public opinion. The second section lists decisions inconsistent with public opinion. The third section lists "unclear" decisions. The fourth section lists poll matches identified after the data analysis was completed, including decisions after the Court's 2020–2021 term. Chapter 2 describes the coding rules.

SECTION 1—SUPREME COURT DECISIONS CONSISTENT WITH PUBLIC OPINION

Press gag law—*Near v. Minnesota* (1931)
Chain store taxes—*Louis K. Liggett Co. v. Lee* (1933)
Milk prices—*Nebbia v. New York* (1934)
TVA—*Ashwander v. Tennessee Valley Authority* (1936)
Agricultural Adjustment Act of 1933—*U.S. v. Butler* (1936)
Foreign war debts—*Cummings v Deutsche Bank* (1937)
Social Security—*Helvering v Davis* (1937)
Wagner Act—*NLRB v. Jones & Laughlin Steel Corp.* (1937)
Minimum wage for women—*West Coast Hotel Co. v. Parrish* (1937)
Hugo Black to the Supreme Court—*Ex Parte Levitt* (1937)
Review of New Deal legislation—*U.S. v. Carolene Products Co.* (1938) and
    Wickard v. Filburn (1942)
Federal income taxes on salaries of state and local employees—*Helvering v.
    Gerhardt* (1938) and *Graves v. N.Y. ex rel. O'Keefe* (1939)
Sit-down strikes—*NLRB v. Fansteel Metallurgical Corp* (1939)

Protests—*Hague v. CIO* (1939)

Child labor constitutional amendment status—*Coleman v. Miller* (1939)

Undistributed profits tax—*Helvering v. Northwest Steel Rolling Mills* (1940)

Overtime pay—*U.S. v. Darby Lumber Co.* (1941)

Child labor prohibition—*U.S. v. Darby Lumber Co.* (1941)

Maximum hours legislation—*U.S. v. Darby Lumber Co.* (1941)

Minimum wages—*U.S. v. Darby Lumber Co.* (1941)

Regulating primary elections—*U.S. v. Classic* (1941)

Influencing votes of relief recipients—*U.S. v. Malphurs* (1942)

Fighting words—*Chaplinsky v. New Hampshire* (1942)

Death penalty for World War II spies—*Stephan v. U.S.* (1943), cert denied

World War II price controls—*Yakus v. U.S.; Bowles v. Willingham* (1944)

Draft registration by conscientious objectors—*Falbo v. U.S.* (1944)

Race in employment—*Tunstall v. Brotherhood of Locomotive Firemen and Enginemen* (1944)

Federal aid to rental housing—*City of Cleveland v. US.* (1945)

Nevada divorces—*Williams v. North Carolina* (1945)

Paying unemployment compensation—*Lawnix, International Shoe Co. v. Washington* (1945)

Japanese war criminals—*In re: Yamachita* (1946); *Homma v. Patterson* (1946)

Segregation within interstate commerce (buses)—*Morgan v. Virginia* (1946)

Punishment for German war criminals—*Milch v. U.S.* (1947) and companion cases

Coal mine strike—*U.S v. John L. Lewis and United Mine Workers of America* (1947)

Featherbedding—*U.S. v. Petrillo* (1947)

Portal-to-portal provisions for back pay—*Battaglia v. General Motors Corp.* (1948), cert denied and companion cases

Continuing rent controls—*Woods v. Miller* (1948)

Labor strike cooling-off period—*United Mine Workers v. U.S.* (1949), cert denied

State right-to-work ban on union or closed shops—*Lincoln Federal Labor Union v. Northwestern Iron & Metal Co.* (1949) and *A.F. of L. v. American Sash & Door Co.* (1949)

Controversial public speech—*Terminiello v. Chicago* (1949)

Contempt citations for the Hollywood Ten—*Trumbo v. U.S.* and *Lawson v. U.S.* (1950), cert denied

Anti-communist oath for labor officials to use NLRB—*American Communications Association, C.I.O., v. Douds* (1950)

Post Taft-Hartley Closed Shop—*National Maritime Union of America v. NLRB* (1950), cert denied

Communists in civil service jobs—*Garner v. Board of Public Works of Los Angeles* (1951)

Outlawing membership in the Communist Party—*Dennis v. US.* (1951)

Jurisdictional strikes—*International Longshoremen's and Warehousemen's Union v. Juneau Spruce Corp.* (1952)

Release time—*Zorach v. Clauson* (1952)

Rosenberg treason case—*Rosenberg v. U.S.* (1953) and prior rulings

School desegregation (first ruling)—*Brown v. Board of Education of Topeka, Kansas* (1954) and companion cases

Segregation in Washington DC schools—*Bolling v. Sharpe* (1954)

Radio lotteries—*FCC v. ABC* (1954)

School desegregation (second ruling, "all deliberate speed")—*Brown v. Board of Education of Topeka, Kansas* (1955) and companion cases

Minimum-set prices—*U.S. v. McKesson & Robbins, Inc.* (1955)

Foreign immunity—*National City Bank v. China* (1955)

Divorce residency requirements—*Granville-Smith v. Granville-Smith* (1955)

Testimony requirements for Congress—*Bart v. U.S.* (1955) and companion cases

Striking workers' vote—*Union Manufacturing Co. v. NLRB* (1955), cert denied

Miscegenation—*Naim v. Naim* (1956), vacated and remanded

Segregation on buses—*Gayle v. Browder* (1956)

Secondary boycotts—*Local v. NLRB* (1958)

Segregation in transportation facilities—*Boynton v. Virginia* (1960)

Racial voting in the South—*U.S. v. Raines* (1960)

Racial redistricting—*Gomillion v. Lightfoot* (1960)

Monopoly regulation—*U.S. v. DuPont* (1961)

Desegregation—*Peterson v. Greenville* (1963) and companion cases

Union dues for political purposes—*Brotherhood of Railway and Steamship Clerks v. Allen* (1963)

Desegregation of public parks—*Watson v. Memphis* (1963)

Reapportionment of state legislatures—*Reynolds v Sims* (1964)

Segregation within interstate commerce (motels and restaurants)—*Heart of Atlanta Motel v. U.S.* (1964) and *Katzenbach v. McClung* (1964)

Reapportionment of Congressional districts—*Wesberry v. Sanders* (1964)

News media coverage—*New York Times v. Sullivan* (1964)

School integration—*Griffin v. School Board of Prince Edward County* (1964)

Birth control—*Griswold v. Connecticut* (1965)

Required blood test for drunk drivers—*Schmerber v. California* (1966)

Federal voting registrars for the South—*South Carolina v. Katzenbach* (1966)

Preclearance provisions—*South Carolina v. Katzenbach* 1966)

Civil rights trial location—*City of Greenwood v. Peacock* (1966)

Private segregated parks—*Evans v. Newton* (1966)

Obscene materials punishable—*Mishkin v. New York* (1966)

Use (possession) of marijuana—*Glaser v. California* (1966), cert denied, and *Aguiar v. California* (1968), cert denied

Wiretapping—*Katz v. U.S.* (1967)

Schoolboy's haircuts—*Ferrell v. Dallas Independent School District* (1968), cert denied

Warrantless home searches in an emergency—*Chimel v. California* (1969)

Marijuana sale—*Oatis v. Nelson, Warden* (1969), cert denied

Immediate school desegregation—*Alexander v. Holmes County Board of Education* (1969)

Racial demonstrations and permits—*Shuttleworth v. Birmingham* (1969)

Federal voting rights for 18-to-20-year-olds—*Oregon v. Mitchell* (1970)

Residency requirements—*Oregon v. Mitchell* (1970)

Maximum family welfare grants—*Dandridge v. Williams* (1970)

Tax exemptions for churches—*Walz v. Tax Commissioner of New York* (1970)

Compulsory arbitration in a strike—*Boys Market, Inc. v. Retail Clerks Union* (1970)

Warrants and drug searches—*Vale v. Louisiana* (1970)

Right of government employees to join labor unions—*United Federation of Postal Workers v. Blount* (1971)

AFDC local cost-of-living adjustments—*Wyman v. Boddie* (1971)

Pentagon Papers case—*New York Times Co. v. U.S.* (1971) and *U.S. v. Washington Post Co.* (1971)

Criminal questioning—*Harris v. New York* (1971)

Gun registration—*U.S. v. Freed* (1971)

Warrantless electronic surveillance—*U.S. v. U.S. District Court* (1972)

Contraceptives to unmarried couples—*Eisenstadt, Sheriff v. Baird* (1972)

Ban on topless or bottomless bars—*LaRue v. California* (1972)

Work rules for welfare recipients—*New York State Department of Social Services v. Dublino* (1973)

Community standards test for obscenity—*Miller v. California* (1973)

Third trimester abortions—*Roe v. Wade* (1973)

Cross-district school busing—*Milliken v. Bradley* (1974)

Federal aid to parochial schools—*Wheeler v. Barrera* (1974)

Watergate tapes—*U.S. v. Nixon* (1974)

Pregnancy insurance coverage—*Geduldig v. Aiello* (1974)

Equal pay for women—*Corning Glass v. Brennan* (1974)

Student suspension hearings—*Goss v. Lopez* (1975)

Presidential impoundment—*Train v. City of New York* (1975)

Legal advertising standards—*Virginia State Board of Pharmacy v. Virginia Citizens Consumer Council* (1975)

Civil rights employment remedies—*Albemarle Paper Company v. Moody* (1975)

Offshore oil—*U.S. v. Maine* (1975)

Individual campaign contribution limit of $1,000—*Buckley v. Valeo* (1976)

PAC contribution limit of $5,000—*Buckley v. Valeo* (1976)

Public funding for presidential campaigns—*Buckley v. Valeo* (1976)

Limits on a candidate's personal spending—*Buckley v. Valeo* (1976)

Public disclosure of names of campaign donors of $100 or more—*Buckley v. Valeo* (1976)

Death penalty for first-degree murder—*Gregg v. Georgia, Profitt v. Florida,* and *Jurek v. Texas* (1976)

Karen Quinlan case—*Garger v. New Jersey* (1976), cert denied

Public housing—*Hills v. Gautreaux* (1976)

Limits on oil imports—*Federal Energy Administration v. Algonquin* (1976)

Pornography distribution to adults—*Smith v. U.S.* (1977)

Corporal punishment for students—*Ingraham v. Wright* (1977)

Medicaid funding for abortions—*Maher v. Roe* (1977)

Death penalty for rape—*Coker v. Georgia* (1977)

Contraceptives for teenagers—*Carey v. Population Services International* (1977)

Rights of homosexual schoolteachers—*Gaylord v. Tacoma School District, No. 10* (1977), cert denied

Women's pensions—*Los Angeles Dept. of Water and Power v. Manhart* (1978)

Adultery and fornication—*Hollenbaugh v. Carnegie Free Library* (1978), cert denied

Fixed racial quotas in educational admissions—*Regents of the University of California v. Bakke* (1978)

Affirmative action without quotas in educational admissions—*Regents of the University of California v. Bakke* (1978)

Warrants for newspaper searches—*Zurcher v. The Stanford Daily* (1978)

Teacher competency tests—*U.S. v. South Carolina* (1978) and *NEA v. South Carolina* (1978)

Snail darters—*TVA v. Hill* (1978)

Japanese tax policy—*Zenith Radio v. U.S.* (1978)

Random traffic checks by police—*Delaware v. Prouse* (1979)

Affirmative action programs in industry—*Steelworkers v. Weber* (1979) and *Fullilove v. Klutznick* (1980)

Veterans' job preferences—*Personnel Administrator of Massachusetts v. Feeney* (1979)

Libel suits—*Herbert v. Lando* (1979)

Criminal searches—*Payton v. New York* (1980)

PATCO strike—*Professional Air Traffic Controllers Organization v. U.S.* (1981), cert denied

Parental notification for teenage abortions—*H.L. v. Matheson* (1981)

Military registration for men—*Rostker v. Goldberg* (1981)

Warrantless searches—*Steagald v. U.S.* (1981)

Comparable worth pay—*County of Washington v. Gunther* (1981)

Safety regulations—*American Textile Manufacturers v. Donovan* (1981)

Prison overcrowding—*Rhodes v. Chapman* (1981)

Censorship of schoolbooks—*Board of Education, Island Trees Union Free School District, No. 26 v. Pico* (1982)

Tax Exemption for segregated schools—*Bob Jones University v. U.S.* (1983) and *Goldsboro Christian Schools, Inc. v U.S.* (1983)

Airbag requirement—*Motor Vehicle Manufacturing Assn. of the U.S. v. State Farm Mutual Automobile Co.* (1983)

Modifications in the exclusionary rule—*New York v. Quarles, Nix v. Williams,* and *U.S. v. Leon* (1984)

Holiday displays—*Lynch v. Donnelly* (1984)

Offshore oil—*Secretary of the Interior v. California* (1984)

Workplace surveys for illegal immigrants—*INS v. Delgado* (1984)

Lawsuits against the media—*Bose Corp. v. Consumer Union of U.S., Inc.* (1984)

Draft registration penalties—*Selective Service System v. Minnesota PIRG* (1984)

Preventative detention—*Schall v. Martin* (1984)

Clubs' right to discriminate among members by sex—*Roberts v. United States Jaycees* (1984) and *Board of Directors of Rotary International v. Rotary Club of Duarte* (1987)

Auto stops by police—*U.S. v. Hensley* (1985)

Parochial aid and teachers—*School District of the City of Grand Rapids v. Ball* (1985)

Student searches—*New Jersey v. T.L.O.* (1985)

No pass, no play rules—*Stamos v. Spring Branch Independent School District* (1986)

Lawsuits against the media—*Philadelphia Newspapers v. Hepps* (1986)

Teenager criminal punishment—*Tison v. Arizona* (1987)

Pregnancy leaves—*California Federal Savings & Loan Assn. v. Guerrera* (1987)

Plant closing tax—*Fort Halifax Packing Co. v. Coyne* (1987)

Federal funding cutoff for states with below-21 drinking age limits—*South Dakota v. Dole* (1987)

Bail availability—*U.S. v. Salerno* (1987)

Parental objections to school textbooks—*Mozert v. Hawkins Public Schools* (1987), cert denied

Principals' censoring high school newspapers—*Hazelwood School District v. Kuhlmeier* (1988)

Independent Counsel Act—*Morrison v. Olson* (1988)

Drug testing for safety employees—*Skinner v. Railway Labor Executives' Association* (1989)

Punitive damages—*Browning Ferris Industries of Vermont v. Kelco Disposal* (1989)

Public hospital restrictions on abortion—*Webster v. Reproductive Health Services* (1989)

Fetal viability tests—*Webster v. Reproductive Health Services* (1989)

Holiday displays—*Allegheny County v. Greater Pittsburgh ACLU* (1989)

Race in public contracts—*Richmond v. JA Croson Co.* (1989)

Race in hiring and promotions—*Martin v. Wilks* (1989)

Detentions after arrest—*Williams v. Ward* (1989), cert denied

AIDs testing of prison inmates—*Dunn v. White* (1990), cert denied

Student religious groups' use of school facilities—*Board of Education of Westside Community Schools v. Mergens* (1990)

Roadblocks for drunk drivers—*Michigan Department of State Police v. Sitz* (1990)

Two-parent notification for minors' abortions—*Hodgson v. Minnesota* (1990)

One-parent notification for minors' abortions—*Ohio v. Akron Center for Reproductive Health* (1990)

Race in government decisions—*Metro Broadcasting, Inc. v. FCC* (1990)

Luggage searches for drugs on interstate buses—*Florida v. Bostick* (1991)

Victim testimony at sentencing stage—*Payne v. Tennessee* (1991)

Life sentences for first offenders, drug cases—*Harmelin v. Michigan* (1991)

Racial disparities in death penalty sentences—*McCleskey v. Bowers*, application for stay of execution denied, (1991) and prior cases.

Oliver North conviction—*U.S. v. North* (1991), cert denied

AIDS testing of hospital patients—*Lee v. Baptist Medical Center of Oklahoma*, cert denied (1992)

Informed consent—*Planned Parenthood of Southeastern Pennsylvania v. Casey* (1992)

Twenty-four-hour waiting rule—*Planned Parenthood of Southeastern Pennsylvania v. Casey* (1992)

One-parent consent for minors' abortions—*Planned Parenthood of Southeastern Pennsylvania v. Casey* (1992)

Airport solicitations—*International Society for Krishna v. Lee* (1992)

Airline deregulation prices—*Morales v. TWA* (1992)

Jonathan Pollard spying—*Pollard v. U.S.* (1992), cert denied

Limit on death penalty appeals—*Graham v. Collins, Herrera v. Collins,* and *Lockhart v. Fretwell* (1993)

Hate crimes—*Wisconsin v. Mitchell* (1993)

Deporting Haitians—*Sale v. Haitian Centers Council* (1993)

Property seizures—*Alexander v. U.S.* (1993)

Abortion protest tactics—*NOW v. Scheidler* (1994)

Abortion clinic access—*Madsen v. Women's Health Center* (1994)

One-race college scholarships—*Podberesky v. Kirwan,* and *Greene v. Podberesky* (1994), cert denied

Affirmative action in federal contracts—*Adarand v. Pena* (1995)

Access to holiday displays—*Capitol Square Review and Advisory Board v. Pinette* (1995)

Drug testing for high school students—*Vernonia School District 47J v. Acton* (1995)

Race in college admissions—*Texas v. Hopwood,* cert denied (1996)

Condom distribution in public schools—*Curtis v. School Committee* (1996), cert denied

Motor Voter law—*Wilson v. Voting Rights Coalition* (1996), cert denied

AIDS education in public schools—*Brown v. Hot, Sexy and Safer Productions, Inc.* (1996), cert denied

Gay rights Colorado ballot issue—*Roemer v. Evans* (1996)

One-gender universities—*U.S. v Virginia* (1996)

Business advertising—*44 Liquormart Inc. v. Rhode Island* (1996)

Indian gambling—*Seminole Tribe of Florida v. Florida* (1996)

Paula Jones lawsuit—*Clinton v. Jones* (1997)

Civil commitment of violent sexual predators—*Kansas v. Hendricks* (1997)

Assisted suicide law—*Lee v. Harcleroad* (1997), cert denied

California civil rights initiative—*Coalition for Economic Equity v. Wilson* (1997), cert denied

Sexual harassment—*Oncale v. Sundowner Offshore Services* (1997)

Cable television station must-carry rule—*Turner Broadcasting System v. FCC* (1997)

Abortion protests floating buffer zones—*Schenk v. ProChoice Network of New York* (1997)

Abortion protests fixed buffer zones—*Schenk v. ProChoice Network of New York* (1997)

Karla Faye Tucker death penalty case—*Tucker v. Texas* (1998), and denials of cert or denial of a writ of habeas corpus

Megan's law—*Doe v. Pataki* and *Verniero v. W.P.* (1998), cert denied

Mandatory prison term for using a gun in a crime—*Muscarello v. U.S.* (1998)

Three-strike law—*Monge v. California* (1998)

Executive privilege claims—*Office of the President v. Office of Independent Counsel* (1998), cert denied, and *Rubin v. U.S.* (1998), cert denied

Suspicionless car searches during a routine traffic stop—*Knowles v. Iowa* (1998)

Sexual harassment—*Burlington Industries v. Ellerth* (1998) and related cases

Oklahoma City bombing death penalty appeal—*Timothy Jones McVeigh v. U.S.* (1999)

Additional federal death penalty offenses—*Jones v. U.S.* (1999)

Drivers' license databases—*Reno v. Condon* (2000)

PAC limit of $1,000—*Nixon v. Shrink Missouri Government PAC* (2000)

Elian Gonzalez—In re *Hirschfeld* (2000), cert denied

Welfare cutoff for legal immigrants—*City of Chicago v. Shalala* (2000), cert denied

Grandparent visitation—*Troxel v. Granville* (2000)

Miranda warnings—*Dickerson v. U.S.* (2000)

Gay boy scouts—*Boy Scouts of America v. Dale* (2000)

Specific zone for abortion clinic protests—*Hill v. Colorado* (2000)

Disability status of golfers—*PGA Tour v. Martin* (2001)

Religious groups in public schools—*Good News Club v. Milford Central School* (2001)

Moment of silence—*Brown v. Gilmore* (2001), cert denied

Seat belt law enforcement—*Atwater v. City of Lago* (2001)

Death penalty for mentally retarded killers—*Atkins v. Virginia* (2002)

Independent HMO review—*Rush Prudential HMO v. Moran* (2002)

Student drug testing—*Board of Education of Independent School District 92 of Pottawatomie County v. Earls* (2002)

Any willing provider HMO plan—*Kentucky Association of Health Plans v. Miller* (2003)

Legal status of gay sex—*Lawrence v. Texas* (2003)

Internet filtering in libraries—*U.S. v. American Library Association* (2003)

Soft money—*McConnell v. Federal Election Commission* (2003)

Candidate identification in campaign ads—*McConnell v. Federal Election Commission* (2003)

Copyright extension—*Elred v. Ashcroft* (2003)

Sex offender registries—*Smith v. Doe* (2003)

Pledge of allegiance—*Elk Grove Unified School District v. Newdow* (2004)

Miranda warning and evidence—*Missouri v. Siebert* (2004)

Do-not-call list—*Mainstream Marketing Services v. Federal Trade Commission* (2004), cert denied

Death penalty for juvenile murderers—*Roper v. Simmons* (2005)

Marijuana usage—*Gonzales v. Raich* (2005)

Terri Schiavo case—*Schindler v. Schiavo* (2005), application for a stay denied, and related cases

Ten Commandments on Texas Capitol grounds—*Van Orden v. Perry* (2005)

File sharing—*MGM Studies, Inc. v. Grokster* (2005)

Media ownership limits—*Prometheus Radio Project v. FCC* (2005), cert denied

Partial-birth abortions—*Gonzales v. Carhart* (2007)

Race in school assignments—*Parents Involved in Community Schools v. Seattle School District* (2007)

Pollution standards—*Massachusetts v. EPA* (2007)

Crack cocaine sentencing—*Kimbrough v. U.S.* (2007) and *Gall v. U.S.* (2007)

Lethal injections—*Baze v. Rees* (2008)

Voter ID laws—*Crawford v. Marion County Election Board* (2008)

Affirmative action in promotions tests—*Ricci v. DeStefano* (2009)

Judges' conflicts of interests—*Caperton v. A.T. Massey Coal Co.* (2009)

Gun control—*McDonald v. City of Chicago* (2010)

Tax credit private school scholarships—*Christian School Tuition Organization v. Winn* (2010)

Employee eligibility requirement—*Chamber of Commerce of the U.S. v. Whiting* (2011)

National Day of Prayer—*Freedom from Religion Foundation v. U.S.* (2011), cert denial

Medicaid expansion—*NFIB v. Sebelius* (2012)

Employer mandate—*NFIB v. Sebelius* (2012)

Lifetime coverage, no cancellations—*NFIB v. Sebelius* (2012)

Age 26, parental policies—*NFIB v. Sebelius* (2012)

Small-business tax credits—*NFIB v. Sebelius* (2012)

Credentials checks—*Arizona v. U.S.* (2012)

Recordings of police arrests—*Alvarez v. ACLU of Illinois* (2012), cert denied

Judges and jury decisions—*Southern Union Co. v. U.S.* (2012)

Interim gay marriage rulings—*Hollingsworth v. Perry* (2013) and related cert denials

Preclearance in elections—*Shelby County v. Holder* (2013)

Gay marriage federal benefits—*U.S. v. Windsor* (2013)

NSA surveillance—*Clapper v. Amnesty International* (2013)

Affirmative action ban—*Schuette v. Coalition to Defend Affirmative Action* (2014)

Power plant regulations—*Utility Air Regulatory Group v. EPA* (2014)

Cell phone searches—*Riley v. California* (2014)

Recess appointments—*NLRB v. Canning* (2014)

Union fees—*Harris v. Quinn* (2014)

Gay marriage compliance—*Davis v. Miller* (2015), request for a stay, denied
Health care exchange subsidies—*King v. Burwell* (2015)
Gay marriage—*Obergefell v. Hodges* (2015)
Media threats—*Elonis v. U.S.* (2015)
Birth control coverage—*Zubik v. Burwell* (2016)
Actual harm in class action lawsuits—*Spokeo v. Robins* (2016)
Abortion restrictions—*Whole Woman's Health v. Hellerstedt* (2016)
Union dues—*Janus v. AFSCME* (2018)
Internet sales taxes—*South Dakota v. Wayfair* (2018)
Election polling places—*Minnesota Voters Alliance v. Mansky* (2018)
Cell phone location searches—*Carpenter v. U.S.* (2018)
Sports gambling—*Murphy v. NCAA* (2019)
Deportable aliens—*Nielson v. Preap* (2019)
Gays and lesbians' job status—*Bostock v. Clayton County, Georgia* (2020) and *Altitude Express, Inc. v. Zarda* (2020)
DACA—*Department of Homeland Security v. Regents of the University of California* (2020)
Asylum claims—*Department of Homeland Security v. Thuraissigiam* (2020)
Death penalty—*Bourgeois, et al. v. Barr* (2020), cert denied, and related cases
Parochial and private school scholarships—*Espinoza v. Montana Department of Revenue* (2020)
Faithless electors –*Chiafalo v. Washington* (2020) and *Colorado Department of State v. Baca* (2020)
Transgender employment—*RG and GR Harris Funeral Home v. EEOC* (2020)
Contraception coverage objections—*Little Sisters of the Poor Saints Peter and Paul Home v. Pennsylvania* (2020)
Assault weapons bans—*Worman v. Healey* (2020) and related appeals, denials of certiorari
Trump tax records to New York—*Trump v. Vance* (2020)
Federal death penalty—*Barr v. Lee* (2020) and *Barr v. Purkey* (2020), injunction vacated

SECTION 2—SUPREME COURT DECISIONS INCONSISTENT WITH PUBLIC OPINION

Minimum wages for women—*Morehea, v. New York ex rel. Tipaldo* (1936)
Federal taxation of state and local employee salaries—*Brush v. Commissioner of Internal Revenue* (1937)

Poll tax—*Breedlove v. Suttles* (1937)

Tom Mooney case—*Mooney v. Smith* (1938) and earlier decisions

Communist assemblies—*DeJonge v. Oregon* (1939)

Agricultural Adjustment Act—*Mulford v. Smith* (1939)

Labor picketing –*Thornhill v. Alabama* (1940)

Women on juries—*Glasser v. U.S.* (1942)

Sterilization of criminals—*Skinner v. Oklahoma* (1942)

Production controls—*Wickard v. Filburn* (1942)

Closed shop prior to Taft-Hartley—*U.S. v. American Federation of Musicians* (1943)

Birth control for married persons—*Tileston v. Ullman* (1943)

Texas white primary—*Smith v. Allwright* (1944)

Japanese-Americans' return to the West Coast—*Ex Parte Endo* (1944)

Anti-monopoly regulation of labor unions—*Hunt v. Crumboch* (1945) and *Allen Bradley Co. v. Union* (1945)

Deporting Harry Bridges—*Bridges v. Wixon* (1945)

Portal-to-portal back pay—*Anderson v. Mt. Clemens Pottery Co.* (1946)

Foremen in labor unions—*Packard Motor Co. v. NLRB* (1947)

Aid to parochial schools—*Everson v. Board of Education* (1947)

Tideland oil cases—*U.S. v. California* (1947); *U.S. v. Louisiana* (1950); *U.S. v. Texas* (1950)

Mediation in a strike vote—*UAW v. O'Brien* (1950)

Right to a hearing for a civil service employee accused of being a communist—*Bailey v. Richardson* (1951)

Controversial public speech—*Feiner v. New York* (1951)

Wiretapping evidence in a court—*Schwartz v. State of Texas* (1952)

Anti-communist oath requirement for university professors—*Wieman v. Updegraff* (1952)

Steel seizure case—*Youngstown Sheet & Tube Co. v. Sawyer* (1952)

Blasphemy regulations—*Burstyn v. Wilson* (1952)

Featherbedding—*American Newspaper Publishers Association v. NLRB* and *NLRB v. Gamble Enterprises* (1953)

Firing accused Communists—*Slochower v. Board of Education of New York City* (1956)

Right to work laws—*Railway Employees v. Hanson* (1956)

Communist employment firing—*Cole v. FDA* (1956)

Communist restrictions—*Yates v. U.S.* (1957)

Notice before strikes—*NLRB v. Lion Oil* (1957)

Labor union picketing—*San Diego Building Trades Council v. Garmon* (1959)

Communist jobs in defense factories—*Greene v. McElroy* (1959)

Membership dues in political campaigns—*International Association of Machinists v. Street* (1961) and *Lathop v. Donahue* (1961)

Injunctions in a labor strike—*Sinclair Refinery Co. v. Atkinson* (1962)

School prayer—*Engel v. Vitale* (1962), and *Abington School District v. Schempp* (1963)

Combined decisions on criminal confessions—*Gideon v. Wainwright* (1963), *Escobedo v. Illinois* (1964), and *Miranda v. Arizona* (1966)

Passports for Communists—*Aptheker v. U.S.* (1964)

Required registration for Communist Party members—*Albertson v. Subversive Activities Control Board* (1965)

Censorship practices—*Redrip v. New York* (1967)

Racial real estate practices—*Reitman v. Mulkey* (1967)

Federal fund cutoff to segregated schools—*Green v. New Kent Co. School Board* (1968)

Racial discrimination in housing sales—*Jones v. Mayer* (1968)

Waiting period for welfare—*Shapiro v. Thompson* (1969)

Adam Clayton Powell's seating in Congress—*Powell v. McCormack* (1969)

Miranda warnings and court evidence—*Orozco v. Texas* (1969)

Drug registration requirements—*Leary v. United States* (1969)

State and local voting rights for 18-to-20-year-olds—*Oregon v. Mitchell* (1970)

Naming father of illegitimate welfare children for AFDC—*Shapiro v. Doe* (1970)

Draft board policies—*Gutknecht v. United States* (1970) and *Welsh v. U.S.* (1970)

Same-district school busing for racial integration—*Swann v. Charlotte-Mecklenburg Board of Education* (1971)

Parochial aid—*Lemon v Kurtzman* (1971)

Death penalty—*Furman v. Georgia* (1972)

Reporters' news source confidentiality—*Branzburg v. Hayes* (1972)

Fiscal disparities in educational spending—*San Antonio v. Rodriguez* (1973)

Abortions in clinics or hospitals—*Doe v. Bolton* (1973)

Chicago Seven—*Dellinger v. U.S.* (1973), cert denied

Voting residence of college students—*White v. Whatley* (1974), cert denied

Mandatory death penalty—*Woodson v. North Carolina* (1976)

Spousal consent requirements for abortion—*Planned Parenthood of Central Missouri v. Danforth* (1976)

William Calley conviction—*Calley v. Hoffman, Secretary of the Army* (1976), cert denied

Nazi demonstrators—*National Socialist Party of America v. Village of Skokie* (1977), cert denied

Insanity defense for murder—*Moore v. Duckworth, Warden* (1979)
Pen register telephone taps without a court warrant—*Smith v. Maryland* (1979)
Mandatory retirement age for diplomats—*Vance v. Bradley* (1979)
Laetrile ban for terminally ill patients—*U.S. v. Rutherford* (1979)
Taiwan defense treaty—*Goldwater v. Carter* (1979)
Media access to jury selection—*Gannett Co., Inc. v. DePasquale* (1979)
Attendance at criminal trials—*Richmond Newspapers, Inc. v. Virginia* (1980)
Attendance at criminal trials—*Richmond Newspapers, Inc. v. Virginia* (1980)
Homosexuals in the armed forces—*Beller v. Lehman* (1981), cert denied
Iran settlement agreement—*Dames v. Moore & Regan* (1981)
Police questioning—*Edwards v. Arizona* (1981)
Severance taxes—*Commonwealth Edison v. Montana* (1981)
Independent PAC spending limits—*Common Cause v. Schmitt* (1982) and *Federal Election Commission v. Americans for Change* (1982)
Tuition tax credits for parochial schools—*Mueller v. Allen* (1983)
Handgun ban—*Quilici v. Village of Morton Grove* (1983), cert denied
Minors' abortions—*Akron v. Akron Center for Reproductive Health* (1983)
Nuclear power regulations—*Pacific Gas & Electric v. State Energy Resources* (1983)
Women's retirement benefits—*Arizona Governing Committee v. Norris* (1983)
Bankruptcy and labor contracts—*NLRB v. Bildisco and Bildisco* (1984)
School religious standards—*Wallace v. Jaffree* (1985)
Insanity criminal defenses—*Ake v. Oklahoma* (1985)
Pornography as sexual violence—*American Booksellers Assn., Inc. v. Hudnut* (1986)
Mandatory budget cuts—*Browsher v. Synar* (1986) and companion cases
Affirmative action in jobs—*Local 28 of the Sheet Metal Workers, International Union v. EEOC* (1986)
Asbestos claims—*Raymak Industries v. Bath Iron Works Corp.* (1986)
Affirmative action in hiring and promotion—*Johnson v. Transportation Agency of Santa Clara County* (1987)
Race in promotions—*U.S. v. Paradise* (1987)
Gay employees' firing rights—*Webster v. Doe* (1988)
Victim impact statements at sentencing stage—*Booth v. Maryland* (1987) and *South Carolina v. Gathers* (1989)
Teaching creation science—*Edwards v. Aguillard* (1987)
Teenager criminal punishment—*Thompson v. Oklahoma* (1988)
Phone sex—*Sable Communications v. Federal Communications Commission* (1989)
Death penalty for mentally retarded murderers—*Penry v. Lynaugh* (1989)

Flag burning—*Texas v. Johnson* (1989) and *U.S. v. Eichman* (1990)

Death penalty for teenage murderers—*Stanford v. Kentucky* (1989) and *Wilkins v. Missouri* (1989)

AIDS testing of health care workers—*Eastern Nebraska Community Office of Retardation v. Glover* (1989), cert denied

Withdrawal of life support—*Cruzan v. Missouri* (1990)

Gag rule for abortion providers—*Rust v. Sullivan* (1991)

Nude dancing—*Barnes v. Glen Theatre* (1991)

Crime victim publishing royalty recovery—*Simon & Schuster, Inc. v. Crime Victims Board* (1991)

Libel media standards—*Masson v. New Yorker Magazine* (1991)

Punitive damages limits—*Pacific Mutual v. Haslip* (1991)

Prayers at high school graduations—*Lee v. Weisman* (1992)

Tobacco litigation—*Cipollone v. Liggett Group* (1992)

Husband notification—*Planned Parenthood of Southeastern Pennsylvania v. Casey* (1992)

RU-486 abortion pill—*Benten v. Kessler* (1992), denial of application to vacate a stay

Eating clubs' memberships—*Del Tufo v. Ivy Club* (1992), cert denied

Intrastate trash ban—*Fort Gratiot Sanitary Landfill v. Michigan Dept. of Natural Resources* (1992)

Operation Rescue—*Bray v. Alexandria Women's Health Clinic* (1993)

Racial redistricting—*Shaw v. Reno* (1993) and *Miller v. Johnson* (1995)

Baby Jessica—*DeBoer v. Schmidt* (1993), application for a stay denied

Punitive damages limits—*TXO Production v. Alliance Resources Corp.* (1993)

Interstate trash ban—*C&A Carbone, Inc. v. Town of Clarkstown* (1994)

Term limits—*U.S. Term Limits v. Thornton* (1995)

Racial redistricting—*Miller v. Johnson* (1995)

1990 Census adjustment—*Wisconsin v. City of New York* (1996) and companion cases

Don't ask, don't tell—*Thomasson v. Perry* (1996), cert denied

Political party election spending—*Colorado Republican Federal Campaign Committee v. FEC* (1996)

Racial profiling, traffic stops—*Whren v. U.S.* (1996)

Constitutional right to assisted suicide—*Washington v. Glucksberg* and *Vacco v. Quill* (1997)

Background checks in the Brady bill—*Mack v. U.S.* (1997) and *Printz v. U.S.* (1997)

Internet pornography to minors—*Reno v. ACLU* (1997)

Line-item veto—*Clinton v. City of New York* (1998)

FDA regulation of tobacco as a drug—*FDA v. Brown & Williamson Tobacco Corp.* (2000)

HMO lawsuits for denial of care—*Pegram v. Herdich* (2000)

Student prayers at high school football games—*Santa Fe Independent School District v. Doe* (2000)

Medical marijuana—*U.S. v. Oakland Cannabis Buyers Cooperative* (2000) and related cases

Teaching creationism—*Tangipahoa Parish Bd. of Education v. Freiler* (2000), cert denied

Cable television standards—*U.S. v. Playboy Entertainment Group* (2000)

Judge versus jury sentencing—*Apprendi v. New Jersey* (2000)

Blanket primaries—*California Democratic Party v. Jones* (2000)

Partial birth abortions—*Stenberg v. Carhart* (2000)

Cocaine testing of pregnant women—*Ferguson v. City of Charleston* (2001)

Marijuana as a medical necessity—*U.S. v. Oakland Cannabis Buyers' Cooperative* (2001)

Sentencing in death penalty cases—*Ring v. Arizona* (2002)

Affirmative action in college admissions—*Gratz v. Bollinger* (2003) and *Grutter v. Bollinger* (2003)

Judge suspension in Ten Commandments case—*In re Moore* (2003), petition for writ of mandamus denied

Confidentiality of vice-presidential proceedings—*Cheney v. U.S. District Court* (2004)

Terrorist detention and trial delays—*Rasul v. Bush* (2004) and *Al Odah v. United States* (2004)

American born terrorists—*Padilla v. Rumsfield* (2004)

Naming detainees—*Center for National Security Studies v. U.S.* (2004), cert denied

ERISA regulations—*Aetna Health, Inc. v. Davila* (2004)

Enron liability—*Arthur Anderson v. U.S.* (2005)

Courthouse Ten Commandments display—*McCreary County v. ACLU* (2005)

Reporter confidentiality—*Miller v. U.S.* (2005), cert denied

Property takings—*Kelo v. City of New London* (2005)

Campaign spending limits—*Randall v. Sorrell* (2006)

Holiday displays—*Skoros v. City of New York* (2007), cert denied

Terrorists' habeas corpus—*Boumediene v. Bush* (2008)

Campaign donations—*Citizens United v. FEC* (2010)

Minors' access to violent video games—*Brown v. Entertainment Merchants Assn.* (2011)

Demonstrations at funerals—*Snyder v. Phelps* (2011)

Individual mandate—*NFIB v. Sebelius* (2012)

Insurance company fees—*NFIB v Sebelius* (2012)

Stop and arrest provision—*Arizona v. U.S.* (2012)

Fleeting unscripted material—*FCC v. Fox Television Stations* (2012)

Total limits on campaign donations—*McCutcheon v. FEC* (2014)

License plates—*Walker v. Texas Division, Sons of Confederate Veterans* (2015)

School discipline—*Bell v. Hawanba Co. School Board* (2016), cert denied

Race in college admissions—*Fisher v. Texas* (2016)

Immigration restrictions—*Trump v. Hawaii* (2018)

Census citizenship question—*Department of Commerce v. NY* (2019)

Steel Tariffs—*American Institute for International Steel, Inc. v. U.S.* (2019), cert denied

Partisan gerrymandering—*North Carolina v. Covington* (2019) and *Rucho v. Common Cause* (2019)

Border wall funding—*Trump v. Sierra Club* (2019)

Border wall issues—*Center for Biological Diversity v. Wolf* (2019), cert denied

Indiana abortion law on Downs Syndrome—*Box v. Planned Parenthood of Indiana and Kentucky* (2019), per curiam and denial of certiorari (in part)

Transgender military personnel—*Trump v. Karnoski* (2019) and *Trump v. Stockman* (2019)

Sanctuary cities—*U.S. v. State of California* (2020), cert denied

Vote by mail—*Merrill v. People First of Alabama* (2020) and Wisconsin and Texas cases, certiorari or applications denied

Presidential appointments—*Seila Law LLC v. Consumer Financial Protection Board* (2020)

"Public Charge" immigration rule—*Department of Homeland Security v. New York* (2020)

Trump tax records House committee—*Trump v. Mazars* (2020)

SECTION 3—"UNCLEAR" SUPREME COURT DECISIONS WITH PUBLIC OPINION

National Recovery Act—*A.L.A. Schencter Poultry Corp. v. U.S.* (1935)

Little Rock, Arkansas, school desegregation—*Cooper v. Aaron* (1958)

Sit-ins—*Garner v. Louisiana* (1961)

Right of government employees (policemen) to join a union—*AFSCME v. City of Muskegon* (1963), cert denied

Poll tax—*Harman v. Forssenius* (1965) and *Harper v. Virginia Board of Elections* (1966)

Miscegenation—*Loving v. Virginia* (1967)

Ban on employment discrimination by race—*Griggs v. Duke Power Co.* (1971)

Public employee right-to-strike—*Rogoff v. Anderson* (1971) and *United Federation of Postal Workers v. Blount* (1971)

Labor union campaign funds contributed by members—*Pipefitters Local Union, No. 562 v U.S.* (1972)

First-trimester abortions—*Roe v. Wade* (1973)

Second-trimester abortions—*Roe v. Wade* (1973)

Hatch Act regulations—*U.S. Civil Service Commission v. National Assoc. of Letter Carriers* (1973)

Newspapers printing information regarding criminal cases—*Cox Broadcasting Corp. v. Cohn* (1975), *Nebraska Press Assn. v. Stuart* (1976), and *Smith v. Daily Mail Publishing Co.* (1979)

Private homosexual behavior—*Doe v. Commonwealth's Attorney for the City of Richmond* (1976)

Mandatory death penalty for killing a policeman—*Roberts v. Louisiana* (1977)

Concorde landing—*Port Authority of New York and New Jersey v. British Airways Board* (1977)

Spousal alimony—*Orr v. Orr* (1979)

Federally funded abortions—*Harris v. McRae* (1980)

Military registration for women—*Rostker v. Goldberg* (1981)

Tandem trailers—*Kassel v. Consolidated Freightways Corp.* (1981)

Gay private conduct—*Bowers v. Hardwick* (1986)

Baby Doe case—*Bowen v. American Hospital Assn.* (1986)

Bearer bonds tax treatment—*South Carolina v. Baker* (1988)

Parochial school aid—*Agostini v. Felton* (1997)

Computers to parochial schools—*Mitchell v. Helms* (2000)

Florida presidential election recount—*Bush v. Gore* (2000)

Offensive art—*Hopper v. City of Pasco* (2001), cert denied

School vouchers—*Zelman v. Simmons-Harris* (2002)

Threats to abortion doctors—*American Coalition of Life Activists v. Planned Parenthood of Columbia/Willamette* (2003)

Gay adoptions—*Lofton v. Secretary of Department of Children and Family Services* (2005), cert denied

Seeking work provision—*Arizona v. U.S.* (2012)

Contraceptives in health plans—*Burwell v. Hobby Lobby Stores* (2014)

Police searches of motel registries—*City of Los Angeles v. Patel* (2015)

Gay services denials—*Masterpiece Cakeshop v CCRC* (2018)

Admitting privileges—*June Medical Services v. Russo* (2020)

XL Keystone Pipeline—*U.S. Army Corps of Engineers v. Northern Plains Resources* (2020)

SECTION 4—POLL-MATCHED SUPREME COURT DECISIONS IDENTIFIED AFTER THE COURT'S 2020–2021 TERM AND NOT INCLUDED IN THIS BOOK'S ANALYSIS

Later-Identified "Consistent" Decisions

Death penalty for the mentally ill—*Panetti v. Quarterman* (2006)

Memorial cross on public lands—*Salazar v. Buono* (2010)

Presidential election 2020—*Texas v. Pennsylvania* (2020), application for relief denied, and related cases

Tribal claims in Oklahoma—*McGirt v. Oklahoma* (2020)

Vote counting rule deadline, mail-in ballots—*Republican Party of Pennsylvania v. Degraffenreid* and *Corman v. Pennsylvania Democratic Party* (2020)

Affordable Care Act constitutionality—*California v. Texas* (2021)

Regulations of off-campus student speech—*Mahanoy Area School District v. BL* (2021)

Unions' access to company property—*Cedar Point Nursery v. Hassid* (2021)

Warrantless home entry for criminal suspects—*Lange v. California* (2021)

Centers for Disease Control moratorium on evictions and foreclosures—*Alabama Association of Realtors v. Department of Health and Human Service*, application to vacate a stay denied (June 29, 2021)

Wedding suppliers—*Arlene's Flowers, Inc. v. Washington* (2021), cert denied

Remain in Mexico rule—*Biden v. Texas* (2021), application for a stay denied

Vaccination requirement for college students—*Klassen v. Trustees of Indiana University* (2021), cert denied

Later-Identified "Inconsistent" Decisions

Death penalty appeals—*Oregon v. Guzek* (2006) and *Day v. McDonough* (2006)

Animal crush videos—*U.S. v. Stevens* (2010)

Criminal penalties, improper computer use—*Van Buren v. U.S.* (2021)

Federal Housing Finance Agency appointees—*Collins v. Yellen* (2021)

Life sentence procedures for juveniles—*Jones v. Mississippi* (2021)

COVID church restrictions—*Roman Catholic Diocese of Brooklyn v. Cuomo* (2021)

Public disclosure rules for nonprofit donors—*Americans for Prosperity Foundation v. Bonta* (2021)

Nationwide CDC ban on rent evictions—*Alabama Association of Realtors v. Department of Health and Human Service*, application to vacate a stay granted (August 26, 2021)

Allowing Texas abortion law to remain in place while legal challenges continue—*Whole Woman's Health v. Jackson* (2021)

Later-Identified "Unclear" Decisions

Gay foster care—*Fulton v. City of Philadelphia PA* (2021)

College athletes' compensations—*NCAA* v. Alston (2021)

Transgender student bathroom use—*Grimm v. Gloucester County School Board* (2021), cert denied

Out-of-precinct voting—*Brnovich v. Democratic National Committee* (2021)

Ballot-harvesting—*Brnovich v. Democratic National Committee* (2021)

Bibliography

Abraham, Henry. 2008. *Justices, Presidents, and Senators*. Lanham, MD: Rowman & Littlefield.

Abrajano, Marisa, and Keith T. Poole. 2011. "Assessing the Ethnic and Racial Diversity of American Public Opinion." In *Who Gets Represented?*, edited by Peter K. Enns and Christopher Wlezien, 32–60. New York: Sage.

Ackerman, Bruce. 1991. *We the People: Foundations*. Cambridge, MA: Harvard University Press.

———. 2007. "The Living Constitution." *Harvard Law Review* 120: 1737–1812.

Allan, Herbert. 1948. *John Hancock*. New York: MacMillan.

Amar, Akhil R. 2012. *America's Unwritten Constitution: The Precedents and Principles We Live By*. New York: Basic Books.

Ansolabehere, Stephen, and Ariel White. 2020. "Policy, Politics, and Public Attitudes Toward the Supreme Court." *American Politics Research* 48: 365–376.

Ansolabehere, Stephen, and Nathaniel Persily. 2008. "Vote Fraud in the Eye of the Beholder: The Role of Public Opinion in the Challenge to Voter Identification Requirements." *Harvard Law Review* 121: 1737–1774.

Armaly, Miles T. 2018a. "Politicized Nominations and Public Attitudes Toward the Supreme Court in the Polarization Era." *Justice System Journal* 39: 193–209.

———. 2018b. "Extra-judicial Actor Induced Change in Supreme Court Legitimacy." *Political Research Quarterly* 71: 600–613.

———. 2020a. "Loyalty Over Fairness: Acceptance of Unfair Supreme Court Procedures." *Political Research Quarterly* 72: 1–14.

———. 2020b. "Who Can Impact the Supreme Court's Legitimacy?" *Justice System Journal* 41: 22–36.

Armaly, Miles T., and Adam M. Enders. 2021a. "Affective Polarization and Support for the U.S. Supreme Court." *Political Research Quarterly* 73: 1–16.

———. 2021b. "No Home Court Advantage: The Trump Impeachment Trial and Attitudes toward the U.S. Supreme Court." *Research & Politics* 8: 1–8.

Badas, Alex. 2016. "The Public's Motivated Response to Supreme Court Decision-Making." *Justice System Journal* 37: 318–330.

———. 2019a. "Policy Disagreement and Judicial Legitimacy: Evidence From the 1937 Court-Packing Plan." *Journal of Legal Studies* 48: 377–408.

———. 2019b. "The Applied Legitimacy Index: A New Approach to Measuring Judicial Legitimacy." *Social Science Quarterly* 100: 1848–1861.

———. 2021. "The Chief Justice and Judicial Legitimacy Evidence From the Influence of Public Opinion." *Justice System Journal.* DOI: 10.1080/0098261X.2021.1902439.

Badas, Alex, and Katelyn E. Stauffer. 2017. "Someone Like Me: Descriptive Representation and Support for Supreme Court Nominees." *Political Research Quarterly* 71: 127–142.

Bailey, Michael A. 2013. "Is Today's Court the Most Conservative in Sixty Years? Challenges and Opportunities in Measuring Judicial Preferences." *Journal of Politics* 75: 821–834.

Bailey, Michael A., Brian Kamoie, and Forrest Maltzman. 2005. "Signals From the Tenth Justice: The Political Role of the Solicitor General in Supreme Court Decision Making." *American Journal of Political Science* 49: 72–85.

Bailey, Michael A., and Forrest Maltzman. 2008. "Does Legal Doctrine Matter? Unpacking Law and Policy Preferences on the U.S. Supreme Court?" *American Political Science Review* 102: 369–384.

Bailyn, Bernard. 1974. *The Ordeal of Thomas Hutchinson.* Cambridge, MA: Belknap.

Balkin, Jack M. 2009. "Framework Originalism and the Living Constitution." *Northwestern University Law Review* 103: 549–614.

Ballingrud, Gordon. 2021. "Ideology and Risk Focus: Conservativism and Opinion Writing in the U.S. Supreme Court." *Social Science Quarterly* 102: 281–300.

Bander, Edward J. 1981. *Mr. Dooley & Mr. Dunne: The Literary Life of a Chicago Catholic.* Charlottesville, Virginia: Michie Co.

Barak-Coren, Netta. 2021. "A License to Discriminate? The Market Response to Masterpiece Cakeshop." *Harvard Civil Liberties-Civil Rights Law Review* 56: 315–366.

Barnett, Randy E. 2003. "Justice Kennedy's Libertarian Revolution: *Lawrence v. Texas.*" *Cato Supreme Court Review* 2002–2003: 21–41.

Barnum, David G. 1985. "The Supreme Court and Public Opinion: Judicial Decision Making in the Post-New Deal Period." *Journal of Politics* 47: 652–666.

Barrett, Amy Coney. 2003. "*Stare Decisis* and Due Process." *University of Colorado Law Review* 74: 1011–1074.

———. 2013. "Precedent and Jurisprudential Disagreement." *Texas Law Review* 91: 1711–1737.

———. 2017. "Justice Scalia and the Federal Court: Originalism and *Stare Decisis.*" *Notre Dame Law Review* 92: 1921–1942.

Bartels, Brandon L. 2008. *Unequal Democracy: The Political Economy of the New Gilded Age.* Princeton, NJ: Princeton University Press.

Bartels, Brandon L., and Alyx Mark. 2015. "Lawyers' Perceptions of the U.S. Supreme Court: Is the Court a 'Political' Institution?" *Law & Society Review* 49: 761–794.

Bartels, Brandon L., and Christopher D. Johnston. 2012. "Political Justice? Perceptions of Politicization and Public Preferences Toward the Supreme Court Appointment Process." *Public Opinion Quarterly* 76: 105–116.

———. 2013. "On the Ideological Foundations of Supreme Court Legitimacy in the American Public." *American Journal of Political Science* 57: 184–199.

———. 2020. *Curbing the Court: Why the Public Constrains Judicial Independence.* Cambridge: Cambridge University Press.

Bartels, Brandon L., and Eric Kramon. 2021. "All the President's Justices? The Impact of Presidential Copartisanship on Supreme Court Job Approval." *American Journal of Political Science.* DOI: 10.1111/ajps.12617.

Bartels, Brandon L., and Phillip J. Wininger. 2016. "Genuine Leader or Merely 'First Among Equals'? Probing the Leadership Capacity of the Chief Justice." In *The Chief Justice,* edited by David J. Danelski and Artemus Ward, 251–280. Ann Arbor: University of Michigan Press.

Basinger, Scott J., and Maxwell Mak. 2020. "The 'New Normal' in Supreme Court Confirmation Voting: Hyper-Partisanship in the Trump Era." *Congress & the Presidency* 47: 365–386.

Bassok, Or. 2013. "The Supreme Court's New Source of Legitimacy." *University of Pennsylvania Journal of Constitutional Law* 16: 153–198.

———. 2016. "The Supreme Court at the Bar of Public Opinion Polls." *Constellations* 23: 573–584.

Baum, Lawrence. 1988. "Measuring Policy Change in the U.S. Supreme Court." *American Political Science Review* 82: 905–912.

———. 1989. "Comparing the Policy Positions of Supreme Court Justices From Different Periods." *Western Political Quarterly* 42: 509–522.

———. 2019. *The Supreme Court.* 13th edition. Los Angeles: Sage.

Baumgartner, Frank R., Suzanna L. DeBoef, and Amber E. Boydstun. 2008. *The Decline of the Death Penalty and the Discovery of Innocence.* New York: Cambridge University Press.

Bednar, Jenna. 2010. "The Dialogic Theory of Judicial Review: A New Social Science Research Agenda." *George Washington Law Review* 78: 1178–1190.

Bennett, Thomas R., Barry Friedman, Andrew D. Martin, and Susan Navarro Smelcer. 2018. "Divide & Concur: Separate Opinions & Legal Change." *Cornell Law Review* 103: 817–876.

Berinsky, Adam. 2006. "American Public Opinion in the 1930s and 1940s: The Analysis of Quota-Controlled Sample Survey Data." *Public Opinion Quarterly* 70: 499–529.

Berinsky, Adam, Eleanor Neff Powell, Eric Schickler, and Ian Brett Yohai. 2011. "Revisiting Public Opinion in the 1930s and 1940s." *PS: Political Science and Politics* 44: 515–520.

Bhagwat, Ashutosh, and Matthew Struhar. 2012. "Justice Kennedy's Free Speech Jurisprudence: A Quantitative and Qualitative Analysis." *McGeorge Law Review* 44: 167–199.

Bickel, Alexander. 1962. *The Least Dangerous Branch.* New Haven, CT: Yale University Press.

Bishin, Benjamin G., Justin Freebourn, and Paul Teten. 2021. "The Power of Equality? Polarization and Collective Mis-Representation on Gay Rights in Congress, 1989–2019." *Political Research Quarterly* 74: 1009–1023.

Biskupic, Joan. 2019. *The Chief: The Life and Turbulent Times of Chief Justice John Roberts*. New York: Basic Books.

Black, Ryan C., and Amanda C. Bryan. 2014a. "Explaining the (Non) Occurrence of Equal Divisions on the U.S. Supreme Court." *American Politics Research* 42: 1077–1095.

———. 2014b. "Calling in the Reserves on the U.S. Supreme Court." *Justice System Journal* 35: 4–26.

———. 2016. "The Policy Consequences of Term Limits on the U.S. Supreme Court." *Ohio Northern University Law Review* 42: 821–853.

Black, Ryan C., Justin Wedeking, Ryan J. Owens, and Patrick C. Wohlfarth. 2016a. "The Influence of Public Sentiment on Supreme Court Opinion Clarity." *Law & Society Review* 50: 703–732.

———. 2016b. *U.S. Supreme Court Opinions and Their Audiences*. New York: Cambridge University Press.

Black, Ryan C., and Ryan J. Owens. 2009. "Agenda Setting in the Supreme Court: The Collision of Policy and Jurisprudence." *Journal of Politics* 71: 1062–1075.

Black, Ryan C., Ryan J. Owens, and Justin Wedeking. 2016. "Herding Scorpions: The Chief Justice as Social Leader." In *The Chief Justice*, edited by David J. Danelski and Artemus Ward, 281–305. Ann Arbor: University of Michigan Press.

Black, Ryan C., Ryan J. Owens, Justin Wedeking, and Patrick C. Wohlfarth. 2020. *The Conscientious Justice: How Supreme Court Justices' Personalities Influence the Law, the High Court, and the Constitution*. New York: Cambridge University Press.

———. 2021. "On Estimating Personality Traits of US Supreme Court Justices." *Journal of Law and Courts* 9: 371–396.

Black, Ryan C., Ryan J. Owens, and Miles T. Armaly. 2016. "A Well-Traveled Lot: A Research Note on Judicial Travel by U.S. Supreme Court Justices." *Justice System Journal* 37: 367–384.

Boddery, Scott S., and Jeff Yates. 2014. "Do Policy Messengers Matter? Majority Opinion Writers as Policy Cues in Public Agreement With Supreme Court Decisions." *Political Research Quarterly* 67: 851–863.

Bonica, Adam, Adam Chilton, Jacob Goldin, Kyle Rozema, and Maya Sen. 2017. "Measuring Judicial Ideology Using Law Clerk Hiring." *American Law and Economics Review* 19: 129–161.

———. 2019. "Legal Rasputins? Law Clerk Influence on Voting at the US Supreme Court." *The Journal of Law, Economics, and Organization* 35: 1–36.

Bonica, Adam, and Maya Sen. 2021. "Estimating Judicial Ideology." *Journal of Economic Perspectives* 35: 97–118.

Bonneau, Chris W., Jarrod T. Kelly, Kira Pronin, Shane M. Redman, and Matthew Zarit. 2017. "Evaluating the Effects of Multiple Opinion Rationales on Supreme Court Legitimacy." *American Politics Research* 45: 335–365.

Bosworth, Matthew H. 2017. "Legislative Responses to Unconstitutionality." *Journal of Law and Courts* 5: 243–266.

Boyd, Christina L. 2016. "Representation on the Courts? The Effects of Trial Judges' Sex and Race." *Political Research Quarterly* 69: 788–799.

Boyd, Christina L., and Adam G. Rutkowski. 2020. "Judicial Behavior in Disability Cases: Do Judge Sex and Race Matter?" *Politics, Groups, and Identities* 8: 834–844.

Boyd, Christina L., and Michael J. Nelson. 2017. "The Effects of Trial Judge Gender and Public Opinion on Criminal Sentencing Decisions." *Vanderbilt Law Review* 70: 1818–1843.

Brace, Paul, and Brent D. Boyea. 2008. "State Public Opinion, the Death Penalty, and the Practice of Electing Judges." *American Journal of Political Science* 52: 360–371.

Braden, George D. 1948. "The Search for Objectivity in Constitutional Law." *Yale Law Journal* 57: 571–594.

Bradley, Curtis A., and Neil S. Siegel. 2017. "Historical Gloss, Constitutional Conventions, and the Judicial Separation of Powers." *Georgetown Law Journal* 105: 255–322.

Brenner, Saul, and Harold J. Spaeth. 1995. *Stare Indecisis: The Alteration of Precedent on the U.S. Supreme Court, 1946–1992*. New York: Cambridge University Press.

Breyer, Stephen. 2005. *Active Liberty: Interpreting Our Democratic Constitution*. New York: Alfred A. Knopf.

———. 2011. *Making Our Democracy Work*. New York: Alfred A. Knopf.

———. 2015. *The Court and the World: American Law and the New Global Realities*. New York: Alfred A. Knopf.

———. 2016. *Against the Death Penalty*. Washington, DC. Brookings Institute.

Brookhiser, Richard. 2018. *John Marshall*. New York: Basic Books.

Bryan, Amanda C. 2020. "Public Opinion and Setting the Agenda on the U.S. Supreme Court." *American Politics Research* 48: 377–390.

Bryan, Amanda C., and Christopher D. Kromphardt. 2016. "Public Opinion, Public Support, and Counter-Attitudinal Voting on the U.S. Supreme Court." *Justice System Journal* 37: 298–317.

Bryan, Amanda C., and Ryan J. Owens. 2017. "How Supreme Court Justices Supervise Ideologically Distant States." *American Politics Research* 45: 435–456.

Bryce, James. 1900. *The American Commonwealth*. New York: Macmillan.

Buranelli, Vincent. 1957. *The Trial of Peter Zenger*. New York: New York University Press.

Burstein, Paul. 2003. "The Impact of Public Opinion on Public Policy: A Review and an Agenda." *Political Research Quarterly* 56: 29–40.

Bybee, Keith J. 2010. *All Judges Are Political Except When They Are Not*. Stanford, CA: Stanford University Press.

Calabresi, Steven G., and James Lindgren. 2006. "Term Limits for the Supreme Court: Life Tenure Reconsidered." *Harvard Journal of Law and Public Policy* 29: 769–877.

Caldarone, Richard P., Brandice Canes-Wrone, and Tom S. Clark. 2009. "Partisan Labels and Democratic Accountability: An Analysis of State Supreme Court Abortion Decisions." *Journal of Politics* 71: 560–573.

Caldeira, Gregory A. 1987. "Public Opinion and the U.S. Supreme Court: FDR's Court-Packing Plan." *American Political Science Review* 81: 1139–1153.

Caldeira, Gregory A, and James L. Gibson. 1992. "The Etiology of Public Support for the Supreme Court." *American Journal of Political Science* 36: 635–664.

Calvin, Bryan, Paul M. Collins, Jr., and Matthew Eshbaugh-Soha. 2011. "On the Relationship Between Public Opinion and Decision Making in the US Courts of Appeals." *Political Research Quarterly* 64: 736–748.

Cameron, Charles M., Cody Gray, Jonathan P. Kastellec, and Jee-Kwang Park. 2020. "From Textbook Pluralism to Modern Hyperpluralism." *Journal of Law and Courts* 8: 302–332.

Cameron, Charles M., Jonathan P. Kastellec, and Jee-Kwang Park. 2013. "Voting for Justices: Change and Continuity in Confirmation Voting 1937–2010." *Journal of Politics* 75: 283–299.

Cameron, Charles M., Jonathan P. Kastellec, and Lauren A. Mattioli. 2019. "Presidential Selection of Supreme Court Nominees: The Characteristics Approach." *Quarterly Journal of Political Science* 14: 439–474.

Cameron, Charles M., and Tom Clark. 2016. "The Chief Justice and Procedural Power." In *The Chief Justice*, edited by David J. Danelski and Artemus Ward, 202–234. Ann Arbor: University of Michigan Press.

Canelo, Kayla S. 2020. "State Coalitions, Informational Signals, and Success as Amicus Curiae at the U.S. Supreme Court." *State Politics & Policy Quarterly* 20: 108–130.

Canelo, Kayla S., Thomas G. Hansford, and Stephen P. Nicholson. 2018. "The Paradoxical Effect of Speech-Suppressing Appeals to the First Amendment." *Journal of Politics* 80: 309–313.

Canes-Wrone, Brandice, Tom S. Clark, and Amy Semet. 2018. "Judicial Elections, Public Opinion, and Decisions on Lower-Salience Issues." *Journal of Empirical Legal Studies* 15: 672–707.

Cann, Damon M., and Teena Wilhelm. 2011. "Case Visibility and Electoral Connections in State Supreme Courts." *American Politics Research* 39: 557–581.

Carrington, Nathaniel T., and Colin French. 2021. "One Bad Apple Spoils the Bunch: Kavanaugh and Change in Institutional Support for the Supreme Court." *Social Science Quarterly* 102: 1484–1495.

Casillas, Christopher J., Peter K. Enns, and Patrick C. Wohlfarth. 2011. "How Public Opinion Constrains the U.S. Supreme Court." *American Journal of Political Science* 55: 74–88.

Casper, Jonathan. 1972. *The Politics of Civil Liberties.* New York: Harper & Row.

———. 1976. "The Supreme Court and National Policy-Making." *American Political Science Review* 70: 50–63.

Chabot, Christine K. 2019. "Do Justices Time Their Retirements Politically? An Empirical Analysis of the Timing and Outcomes of Supreme Court Retirements in the Modern Era." *Utah Law Review* 2019: 527–579.

Chemerinsky, Erwin. 2014. *The Case Against the Supreme Court.* New York: Viking.

Chen, Philip G., and Amanda C. Bryan. 2018. "Judging the 'Vapid and Hollow Charade': Citizen Evaluations and the Candor of U.S. Supreme Court Nominees." *Political Behavior* 40: 495–520.

Chilton, Adam, Daniel Epps, Kyle Rozema, and Maya Sen. 2021. "The Endgame of Court-Packing." Working Paper. https://j.mp/32Xhkg8.

Christenson, Dino P., and David M. Glick. 2015a. "Issue-Specific Opinion Change: The Supreme Court and Health Care Reform." *Public Opinion Quarterly* 79: 881–905.

———. 2015b. "Chief Justice Roberts's Health Care Decision Disrobed: The Microfoundations of the Supreme Court's Legitimacy." *American Journal of Political Science* 59: 403–418.

———. 2019. "Reassessing the Supreme Court: How Decisions and Negativity Bias Affect Legitimacy." *Political Research Quarterly* 72: 637–652.

Christenson, Dino P., and Douglas L Kriner. 2017. "The Specter of Supreme Court Criticism: Public Opinion and Unilateral Action." *Presidential Studies Quarterly* 47: 471–494.

Clark, Tom. 2009. "Measuring Ideological Polarization on the U.S. Supreme Court." *Political Research Quarterly* 62: 146–157.

———. 2011. *The Limits of Judicial Independence*. New York: Cambridge University Press.

Clark, Tom, Jeffrey R. Lax, and Douglas Rice. 2015. "Measuring the Political Salience of Supreme Court Cases." *Journal of Law and Courts* 3: 37–65.

Clark, Tom, and Jonathan P. Kastellec. 2015. "Source Cues and Public Support for the Supreme Court." *American Politics Research* 43: 504–535.

Clawson, Rosalee A., Elizabeth Kegler, and Eric N. Waltenberg. 2001. "The Legitimacy-Conferring Authority of the U.S. Supreme Court: An Experimental Design." *American Politics Research* 29: 566–591.

Clayton, Amanda, Diana Z. O'Brien, and Jennifer M. Piscopo. 2019. "All Male Panels? Representation and Democratic Legitimacy." *American Journal of Political Science* 63: 113–129.

Cohen, Adam. 2020. *Supreme Inequality: The Supreme Court's Fifty-Year Battle for a More Unjust America*. New York: Penguin Press.

Colistra, Rita, and Chelsea Betts Johnson. 2021. "Framing the Legalization of Marriage for Same-Sex Couples: An Examination of News Coverage Surrounding the U.S. Supreme Court's Landmark Decision." *Journal of Homosexuality* 68: 88–111.

Collins, Paul M. 2008. *Friends of the Supreme Court: Interest Groups and Judicial Decision Making*. New York: Oxford University Press.

Collins, Paul M., and Matthew Eshbaugh-Soha. 2019. *The President and the Supreme Court*. New York: Cambridge University Press.

Collins, Todd A., and Christopher A. Cooper. 2012. "Case Salience and Media Coverage of Supreme Court Decisions: Toward a New Measure." *Political Research Quarterly* 65: 396–407.

———. 2016. "The Case Salience Index, Public Opinion, and Decision Making on the U.S. Supreme Court." *Justice System Journal* 37: 232–245.

Colucci, Frank J. 2009. *Justice Kennedy's Jurisprudence: The Full and Necessary Meaning of Liberty*. Lawrence: University Press of Kansas.

Comiskey, Michael. 2004. *Seeking Justices – The Judging of Supreme Court Nominees*. Lawrence: University of Kansas Press.

———. 2006. "The Supreme Court Confirmation Process and the Quality of U.S. Supreme Court Justices." *Polity* 38: 295–313.

Converse, Jean M. 1987. *Survey Research in the United States: Roots and Emergence 1890–1960*. Berkeley: University of California Press.

Cook, Beverly B. 1974. "Public Opinion and Federal Judicial Policy." *American Journal of Political Science* 21: 567–600.

Cooke, Jacob Ernest. 1982. *Alexander Hamilton*. New York: Charles Scribner's Sons.

Corley, Pamela. 2010. *Concurring Opinion Writing on the U.S. Supreme Court*. Albany, NY: SUNY Press.

Corley, Pamela, Amy Steigerwalt, and Artemus Ward. 2013. "Revisiting the Roosevelt Court: The Critical Juncture From Consensus to Dissensus." *Journal of Supreme Court History* 38: 20–50.

Corley, Pamela, Udi Sommer, Amy Steigerwalt, and Artemus Ward. 2010. "Extreme Dissensus: Explaining Plurality Decisions on the United States Supreme Court." *Justice System Journal* 31: 180–200.

Costello, Kevin. 2020. "Note: Supreme Court Politics and Life Tenure: A Comparative Inquiry." *Hastings Law Journal* 71: 1153–1180.

Cottrell, David, Charles R. Shipan, and Richard J. Anderson. 2019. "The Power to Appoint: Presidential Nominations and Change on the Supreme Court." *Journal of Politics* 81: 1057–1068.

Coyle, Marcia. 2013. *The Roberts Court*. New York: Simon & Schuster.

Cramton, Roger G. 2007. "Reforming the Supreme Court." *California Law Review* 95: 1313–1334.

Cramton, Roger G., and Paul D. Carrington. 2006. "The Supreme Court Renewal Act: A Return to Basic Principles." In *Reforming the Court: Term Limits for Supreme Court Justices*, edited by Roger C. Cramton and Paul D. Carrington, 467–472. Durham, NC: Carolina Academic Press.

Cushman, Barry. 2002. "Mr. Dooley and Mr. Gallup: Public Opinion and Constitutional Change in the 1930s." *Buffalo Law Review* 50: 7–101.

———. 2015. "Inside the Taft Court: Lessons From the Docket Books." *The Supreme Court Review* 2015: 345–410.

Dahl, Robert. 1957. "Decision-Making in a Democracy: The Supreme Court as a National Policy-Maker." *Journal of Public Law* 6: 279–295.

Danelski, Daniel J. 2016. "The Influence of the Chief Justice in the Decisional Process of the Supreme Court: Personality and Leadership." In *The Chief Justice: Appointment and Influence*, edited by Daniel J. Danelski and Artemus Ward, 64–94. Ann Arbor: University of Michigan Press.

Danelski, Daniel J., and Artemus Ward. 2016. *The Chief Justice: Appointment and Influence*. Ann Arbor: University of Michigan Press.

Devins, Neal. 1996. "Government Lawyers and the New Deal." *Columbia Law Review* 96: 237–268.

———. 1999. "The Democracy-Forcing Constitution." *Michigan Law Review* 97: 1971–1993.

——. 2004. "The Majoritarian Rehnquist Court?" *Law and Contemporary Problems* 67: 63–81.

——. 2017. "Why Congress Does Not Challenge Judicial Supremacy." *William & Mary Law Review* 58: 1495–1548.

Devins, Neal, and Larry Baum. 2017. "Split Definitive: How Party Polarization Turned the Supreme Court into a Partisan Court." *Supreme Court Review* 2017: 301–365.

——. 2019. *The Company They Keep: How Partisan Divisions Came to the Supreme Court.* New York: Oxford University Press.

Devins Neal, and Louis Fisher. 2004. *The Democratic Constitution.* New York: Oxford University Press.

Dorf, Michael C. 2006. *No Litmus Test.* Lanham, MD: Rowman & Littlefield.

——. 2007. "Does Federal Executive Branch Experience Explain Why Some Republican Supreme Court Justices 'Evolve' and Others Don't?" *Cornell Law Faculty Publications.* Paper 77.

Douglas, William O. 1949. "Stare Decisis." *Columbia Law Review* 49: 735–758.

Dovi, Suzanne, and Francy Luna. 2020. "Women 'Doing' the Judiciary: Rethinking the Justice Argument for Descriptive Representation." *Politics, Groups, and Identities* 8: 790–802.

Downs, Donald A. 2021. "Supreme Court Nominations at the Bar of Political Conflict." *Law & Social Inquiry* 46: 540–571.

Driver, Justin. 2021. "The Supreme Court as Bad Teacher." *University of Pennsylvania Law Review* 169: 1365–1428.

Durr, Robert, Andrew Martin, and Christine Wolbrecht. 2000. "Ideological Divergence and Public Support for the Supreme Court." *American Journal of Political Science* 44: 768–776.

Ellis, Christopher R., and James A. Stimson. 2012. *Ideology in America.* New York: Cambridge University Press.

Ellis, Christopher R., and Joseph D. Ura. 2011. "United We Divide? Education, Income, and Heterogeneity in Mass Partisan Polarization." In *Who Gets Represented?*, edited by Peter K. Enns and Christopher Wlezien, 61–92. New York: Sage.

Engel, Stephen M. 2013. "Frame Spillover: Media Framing and Public Opinion of a Multifaceted LGBT Rights Agenda." *Law & Social Inquiry* 38: 403–441.

Enns, Peter K., and Christopher Wlezien. 2011. *Who Gets Represented?* New York: Sage.

Enns, Peter K., and Patrick C. Wohlfarth. 2013. "The Swing Justice." *Journal of Politics* 75: 1089–1107.

Epps, Daniel, and Ganesh Sitaraman. 2019. "How to Save the Supreme Court." *Yale Law Journal* 129: 155–205.

Epstein, Lee, and Andrew D. Martin. 2010. "Does Public Opinion Influence the Supreme Court? Possibly Yes (But We're Not Sure Why)." *University of Pennsylvania Journal of Constitutional Law* 13: 263–280.

Epstein, Lee, Andrew D. Martin, Kevin M. Quinn, and Jeffrey A. Segal. 2007. "Ideological Drift Among Supreme Court Justices: Who, When, and How Important?" *Northwestern University Law Review* 101: 1483–1541.

Epstein, Lee, and Eric Posner. 2018. "If the Supreme Court is Nakedly Political, Can It Be Just?" *New York Times*, July 9.

Epstein, Lee, and Jeffrey A. Segal. 2005. *Advice and Consent*. New York: Oxford University Press.

Epstein, Lee, Jeffrey A. Segal, and Harold J. Spaeth. 2001. "The Norm of Consensus on the U.S. Supreme Court." *American Journal of Political Science* 45: 362–377.

Epstein, Lee, William Landes, and Richard Posner. 2013a. "How Business Fares in the Supreme Court." *Minnesota Law Review* 97: 1431–1472.

———. 2013b. *The Behavior of Federal Judges*. Cambridge, MA: Harvard University Press.

———. 2015. "Revisiting the Ideology Rankings of Supreme Court Justices." *Journal of Legal Studies* 44: 295–317.

———. 2017. "When It Comes to Business, the Right and Left Sides of the Court Agree." *Journal of Law & Policy* 54: 33–55.

Escobar-Lemmon, Maria C., Valerie Hoekstra, Alice J. Kang, and Miki Caul Kittilson. 2016. "Just the Facts? Media Coverage of Female and Male High Court Appointees in Five Democracies." *Politics and Gender* 12: 254–274.

Eskridge, William, Jr., and John Ferejohn. 2001. "Super-Statutes." *Duke Law Journal* 50: 1215–1276.

Fallon, Richard H. 2010. "Jurisdiction-Stripping Reconsidered." *Virginia Law Review* 96: 1043–1135.

———. 2018. *Law and Legitimacy in the Supreme Court*. Cambridge, MA: Belknap Press.

Farganis, Dion. 2012. "Do Reasons Matter? The Impact of Opinion Content on Supreme Court Legitimacy." *Political Research Quarterly* 65: 206–216.

Feldman, Stephen M. 2020. "Court-Packing Time? Supreme Court Legitimacy and Positivity Theory." *Buffalo Law Review* 68: 1519–1559.

Fettig, Shawn C., and Sara C. Benesh. 2016. "Be Careful With My Court: Legitimacy, Public Opinion, and the Chief Justice." In *The Chief Justice: Appointment and Influence*, edited by Daniel J. Danelski and Artemus Ward, 374–394. Ann Arbor: University of Michigan Press.

Fischman, Joshua B. 2019. "Politics and Authority in the US Supreme Court." *Cornell Law Review* 104: 1513–1592.

Fiss, Owen. 2015. *A War Like No Other*. New York: The New Press.

Fitzpatrick, Brian T. 2012. "The Constitutionality of Federal Jurisdiction-Stripping Legislation and the History of State Judicial Selection and Tenure." *Virginia Law Review* 98: 839–895.

Fix, Michael P., and Bailey R. Fairbanks. 2020. "The Effects of Opinion Readability on the Impact of U.S. Supreme Court Precedents in State High Courts." *Social Science Quarterly* 101: 811–824.

Fix, Michael P., and Benjamin Kassow. 2020. *US Supreme Court Doctrine in the State High Courts*. New York: Cambridge.

Fix, Michael P., Justin T. Kingsland, and Matthew D. Montgomery. 2017. "The Complexities of State Court Compliance With U.S. Supreme Court Precedent." *Justice System Journal* 38: 149–163.

Flemming, Roy B., and B. Dan Wood. 1997. "The Public and the Supreme Court: Individual Justice Responsiveness to American Public Moods." *American Journal of Political Science* 41: 468–498.

Fontana, David, and Christopher Krewson. 2020. "Supreme Court Can Do Better When Speaking Up for Itself." *Washington Post*, February 26.

Forbath, William E. 2010. "The Will of the People? Pollsters, Elites, and Other Difficulties." *George Washington Law Review* 78: 1191–1206.

Fowler, William M., Jr. 1980. *The Baron of Beacon Hill – A Biography of John Hancock*. Boston: Houghton Mifflin.

Franklin, Charles H., and Liane C. Kosaki. 1989. "Republican Schoolmaster: The U.S. Supreme Court, Public Opinion, and Abortion." *American Political Science Review* 83: 751–771.

Friedman, Barry. 1993. "Dialogue and Judicial Review." *Michigan Law Review* 91: 577–682.

———. 1998. "The History of the Countermajoritarian Difficulty. Part One: The Road to Judicial Supremacy." *New York University Law Review* 73: 333–433.

———. 2000. "The History of the Countermajoritarian Difficulty, Part Four: Law's Politics." *University of Pennsylvania Law Review* 148: 971–1064.

———. 2001. "The History of the Countermajoritarian Difficulty, Part Three: The Lesson of Lochner." *New York University Law Review* 76: 1383–1455.

———. 2002a. "The History of the Countermajoritarian Difficulty, Part Two: Reconstruction's Political Court." *Georgetown Law Journal* 91: 1–65.

———. 2002b. "The Birth of an Academic Obsession: The History of the Countermajoritarian Difficulty, Part Five." *Yale Law Journal* 112: 153–259.

———. 2010. *The Will of the People: How Public Opinion Has Influenced the Supreme Court and Shaped the Meaning of the Constitution*. New York: Farrar, Straus and Giroux.

———. 2016. "Letter to the Supreme Court." *Vanderbilt Law Review* 69: 995–1018.

———. 2018. "Divide & Concur: Separate Opinions & Legal Change." *Cornell Law Review* 103: 817–876.

Friedman, Barry, and Scott B. Smith. 1998. "The Sedimentary Constitution." *University of Pennsylvania Law Review* 147: 1–90.

Funston, Richard. 1975. "The Supreme Court and Critical Elections." *American Political Science Review* 69: 795–811.

Garrow, David J. 2000. "Mental Decrepitude in the U.S. Supreme Court: The Historical Case for a 28th Amendment." *University of Chicago Law Review* 67: 995–1087.

Gass, Henry. 2019. "Why Chief Justice Roberts is Moving to the Center of the Court." March 26. https://www.csmonitor.com/USA/Justice/2019/0326/Why-Chief-Justice-Roberts-is-moving-to-the-center-of=the-court.

Gelman, Jeremy. 2021. "Partisan Intensity in Congress: Evidence From Brett Kavanaugh's Supreme Court Nomination." *Political Research Quarterly* 74: 450–463.

George, Tracey E., and Chris Guthrie. 2009. "Remaking the United States Supreme Court in the Courts of Appeals Image." *Duke Law Journal* 58: 1439–1475.

Gerber, Scott. 2011. *A Distinct Judicial Power*. New York: Oxford University Press.

Gerhardt, Michael J. 2002. "Supreme Court Selection as War." *Drake Law Review* 50: 393–410.

———. 2006. "Super Precedent." *Minnesota Law Review* 90: 1204–1231.

Gibson, James L. 1980. "Environmental Constraints on the Behavior of Judges: A Representational Model of Judicial Decision Making." *Law & Society Review* 14: 343–370.

———. 2007. "The Legitimacy of the U.S. Supreme Court in a Polarized Polity." *Journal of Empirical Legal Studies* 4: 507–538.

———. 2012. *Electing Judges: The Surprising Effects of Campaigning on Judicial Legitimacy*. Chicago: University of Chicago Press.

———. 2017. "Performance Evaluations Are Not Legitimacy Judgments: A Caution About Interpreting Public Opinion Toward the United States Supreme Court." *Washington University Journal of Law & Policy* 54: 71–88.

Gibson, James L., and Gregory A. Caldeira. 2011. "Has Legal Realism Damaged the Legitimacy of the U.S. Supreme Court?" *Law & Society Review* 45: 195–219.

Gibson, James L., Gregory A. Caldeira, and Lester Kenyatta Spence. 2003a. "The Supreme Court and the U.S. Presidential Election of 2000: Wounds, Self-Inflicted, or Otherwise?" *British Journal of Political Science* 33: 535–556.

———. 2003b. "Measuring Attitudes Toward the United States Supreme Court." *American Journal of Political Science* 47: 354–367.

———. 2005. "Why Do People Accept Public Policies They Oppose? Testing Legitimacy Theory With a Survey Based Experiment." *Political Research Quarterly* 58: 187–201.

Gibson, James L., Gregory A. Caldeira, and Vanessa A. Baird. 1998. "On the Legitimacy of National High Courts." *American Political Science Review* 92: 343–358.

Gibson, James L., and Michael J. Nelson. 2014. "The Legitimacy of the US Supreme Court: Conventional Wisdoms and Recent Challenges Thereto." *Annual Review of Law and Social Science* 10: 201–219.

———. 2015. "Is the U.S. Supreme Court's Legitimacy Grounded in Performance Satisfaction and Ideology?" *American Journal of Political Science* 59: 162–174.

———. 2016. "Changes in Institutional Support for the US Supreme Court." *Public Opinion Quarterly* 80: 622–641.

———. 2017. "Reconsidering Positivity Theory: What Roles Do Politicization, Ideological Disagreement, and Legal Realism Play in Shaping U.S. Supreme Court Legitimacy?" *Journal of Empirical Legal Studies* 14: 592–617.

Gibson, James L., Miguel M. Pereira, and Jeffrey Ziegler. 2017. "Updating Supreme Court Legitimacy: Testing the 'Rule, Learn, Update' Model of Political Communication." *American Politics Research* 45: 980–1002.

Gibson, James L., Milton Lodge, and Benjamin Woodson. 2014. "Losing, But Accepting: Legitimacy, Positivity Theory, and the Symbols of Judicial Authority." *Law & Society Review* 48: 837–866.

Gilens, Martin. 2005. "Inequality and Democratic Representation." *Public Opinion Quarterly* 65: 778–796.

———. 2011. "Policy Consequences of Representational Inequality." In *Who Gets Represented?*, edited by Peter K. Enns and Christopher Wlezien, 247–284. New York: Sage.

———. 2012. *Affluence and Influence: Economic Inequality and Political Power in America.* Princeton, NJ: Princeton University Press.

Gilens, Martin, and Benjamin I. Page. 2014. "Testing Theories of American Politics: Elites, Interest Groups, and Average Citizens." *Perspectives on Politics* 12: 564–581.

Giles, Micheal W., Bethany Blackstone, and Richard L. Vining, Jr. 2008. "The Supreme Court in American Democracy: Unraveling the Linkages between Public Opinion and Judicial Decision Making." *Journal of Politics* 70: 293–306.

Glennon, Colin, and Logan Strother. 2019. "The Maintenance of Institutional Legitimacy in Supreme Court Justices' Public Rhetoric." *Journal of Law and Courts* 7: 241–261.

Glock, Judge. 2020. "The Politics of Disabled Supreme Court Justices." *Journal of Supreme Court History* 45: 151–166.

Gooch, Donald M. 2015. "Ideological Polarization on the Supreme Court: Trends in the Court's Institutional Environment and Across Regimes, 1937–2008." *American Politics Research* 43: 999–1040.

Gorsuch, Neil. 2019. *A Republic, If You Can Keep It.* New York: Crown Forum.

Graber, Mark. 1993. "The Non-Majoritarian Difficulty: Legislative Deference to the Judiciary." *Studies in American Political Development* 7: 35–73.

———. 2006. *Dred Scott and the Problem of Constitutional Evil.* New York: Cambridge.

———. 2017. "Judicial Supremacy Revisited: Independent Constitutional Authority in American Constitutional Law and Practice." *William & Mary Law Review* 58: 1549–1607.

Greenhouse, Linda. 2012. "Public Opinion & the Supreme Court: The Puzzling Case of Abortion." *Daedalus* 141: 69–82.

Grove, Tara. 2018. "The Origins (and Fragility) of Judicial Independence." *Vanderbilt Law Review* 71: 465–545.

Haglin, Kathryn, Soren Jordan, Alison Higgins Merrill, and Joseph Daniel Ura. 2020. "Ideology and Specific Support for the Supreme Court." *Political Research Quarterly* 73: 1–15.

Hall, Melinda Gann. 1992. "Electoral Politics and Strategic Voting in State Supreme Courts." *Journal of Politics* 54: 427–446.

———. 1995. "Justices as Representatives – Elections and Judicial Politics in the American States." *American Politics Quarterly* 23: 485–503.

———. 2014. "Representation in State Supreme Courts: Evidence From the Terminal Term." *Political Research Quarterly* 67: 335–346.

Hall, Matthew E. K. 2013. *The Nature of Supreme Court Power.* New York: Cambridge University Press.

———. 2014. "The Semiconstrained Court: Public Opinion, the Separation of Powers, and the U.S. Supreme Court's Fear of Nonimplementation." *American Journal of Political Science* 58: 352–366.

———. 2018. *What Justices Want.* New York: Cambridge University Press.

Hall, Matthew E. K., Justin H. Kirkland, and Jason Harold Windett. 2015. "Holding Steady on Shifting Sands: Countermajoritarian Decision Making in the US Courts of Appeals." *Public Opinion Quarterly* 79: 504–523.

Hammond, Thomas H., Chris W. Bonneau, and Reginald S. Sheehan. 2005. *Strategic Behavior and Policy Choice on the US Supreme Court.* Stanford, CA: Stanford University Press.

Hanley, John, Michael Salamone, and Matthew Wright. 2012. "Revising the Schoolmaster: Reevaluating Public Opinion in the Wake of *Roe v. Wade.*" *Political Research Quarterly* 65: 408–421.

Hansford, Thomas G., Chanita Intawan, and Stephen P. Nicholson. 2018. "Snap Judgment: Implicit Perceptions of a (Political) Court." *Political Behavior* 40: 127–147.

Hansford, Thomas G., and Chelsea Coe. 2019. "Linguistic Complexity, Information Processing, and Public Acceptance of Supreme Court Decisions." *Political Psychology* 40: 395–412.

Hansford, Thomas G., and James F. Spriggs, II. 2006. *The Politics of Precedent on the U.S. Supreme Court.* Princeton, NJ: Princeton University Press.

Harvey, Anna, and Barry Friedman. 2006. "Pulling Punches: Congressional Constraints on the Supreme Court's Constitutional Rulings, 1987–2000." *Legislative Studies Quarterly* 31: 533–562.

Hasen, Richard L. 2016. "Celebrity Justice: Supreme Court Edition." *Green Bag* 19: 157–170.

Hazelton, Morgan L. W. 2021. "Strategy and Supreme Court Decision Announcements." Paper Presented at the Midwest Political Science Association Annual Conference, Chicago, IL. April 4–7.

Heise, Michael, Martin T. Wells, and Dawn M. Chutkow. 2020. "Does Docket Size Matter? Revisiting Empirical Accounts of the Supreme Court's Incredibly Shrinking Docket." *Notre Dame Law Review* 95: 1565–1592.

Hemel, Daniel. 2021. "Can Structural Changes Fix the Supreme Court?" *Journal of Economic Perspectives* 35: 119–142.

Hendershot, Marcus E., Mark S. Hurwitz, Drew Noble Lanier, and Richard L. Pacelle, Jr. 2012. "Dissensual Decision Making: Revisiting the Demise of Consensual Norms Within the U.S. Supreme Court." *Political Research Quarterly* 66: 467–481.

Henderson, M. Todd. 2007. "From Seriatim to Consensus and Back Again: A Theory of Dissent." *The Supreme Court Review* 2007: 283–344.

Hitt, Matthew P. 2013. "Presidential Success in Supreme Court Appointments: Informational Effects and Institutional Constraints." *Presidential Studies Quarterly* 43: 792–813.

Hitt, Matthew P., and Kathleen Searles. 2018. "Media Coverage and Public Approval of the U.S. Supreme Court." *Political Communication* 35: 566–586.

Hoekstra, Valerie. 1995. "The Supreme Court and Local Public Opinion." *American Political Science Review* 94: 89–100.

———. 2005. "Competing Constraints: State Court Responses to Supreme Court Decisions and Legislation on Wages and Hours." *Political Research Quarterly* 58: 317–328.

———. 2009. "The Pendulum of Precedent: U.S. State Legislative Response to Supreme Court Decisions on Minimum Wage Legislation for Women." *State Politics and Policy Quarterly* 9: 257–283.

Hoffer, Peter Charles, William James Hull Hoffer, and N. E. H. Hull. 2018. *The Supreme Court.* Lawrence: University of Kansas Press.

Holden, Richard, Michael Keane, and Matthew Lilly. 2021. "Peer Effects on the United States Supreme Court." *Qualitative Economics* 12: 981–1019.

Holmes, Oliver Wendell, Jr. 1882. *The Common Law.* London: MacMillan.

Hopkins, David A., and Laura Stoker. 2011. "The Political Geography of Party Resurgence." In *Who Gets Represented?*, edited by Peter K. Enns and Christopher Wlezien, 93–128. New York: Sage.

Howard, A. E. Dick. 2015. "The Changing Face of the Supreme Court." *Virginia Law Review* 101: 231–316.

Howe, Amy. 2021. "In Harvard Speech, Breyer Speaks Out Against 'Court Packing'." *Scotusblog*, April 7.

Hulse, Carl. 2019. *Confirmation Bias.* New York: HarperCollins.

Igo, Sarah E. 2007. *The Averaged American: Surveys, Citizens, and the Makings of a Mass Public.* Cambridge, MA: Harvard University Press.

Illing, Sean. 2020. "The Case for Stripping the Supreme Court of its Power." *Vox*, October 27.

Jaclyn Kaslovsky, Jaclyn, Jon C Rogowski, and Andrew R Stone. 2021. "Descriptive Representation and Support for Supreme Court Nominees." *Political Science Research and Methods* 9: 583–598.

Jacobs, Lawrence R., and Theda Skocpol. 2005. *Inequality and American Democracy: What We Know and What We Need to Learn.* New York: Sage.

Jamieson, Kathleen Hall, and Michael Hennessy. 2007. "Public Understanding of and Support for the Courts: Survey Results." *Georgetown Law Journal* 95: 899–902.

Jessee, Stephen, and Neil Malhotra. 2013. "Public (Mis)perceptions of Supreme Court Ideology." *Public Opinion Quarterly* 77: 619–634.

Johnson, Ben, and Logan Strother. 2021. "The Supreme Court's (Surprising?) Indifference to Public Opinion." *Political Research Quarterly* 74: 18–34.

Johnson, Benjamin, and Keith E. Whittington. 2018. "Why Does the Supreme Court Uphold So Many Laws?" *University of Illinois Law Review* 118: 1001–1047.

Johnson, Timothy R., and Andrew D. Martin. 1998. "The Public's Conditional Response to Supreme Court Decisions." *American Political Science Review* 92: 299–309.

Johnston, Christopher D., and Brandon L. Bartels. 2010. "Sensationalism and Sobriety: Differential Media Exposure and Attitudes Toward American Courts." *Public Opinion Quarterly* 74: 260–285.

Johnston, Christopher D., D. Sunshine Hillygus, and Brandon Bartels. 2014. "Ideology, the Affordable Care Act Ruling, and Supreme Court Legitimacy." *Public Opinion Quarterly* 78: 963–973.

Karol, David. 2007. "Has Polling Enhanced Representation? Unearthing Evidence From the Literary Digest Issue Polls." *Studies in American Political Development* 21: 16–29.

Kastellec, Jonathan P. 2016. "Empirically Evaluating the Countermajoritarian Difficulty." *Journal of Law and Courts* 4: 1–42.

———. 2018. "Judicial Federalism and Representation." *Journal of Law and Courts* 6: 51–92.

Kastellec, Jonathan P., Jeffrey R. Lax, and Justin H. Phillips. 2010. "Public Opinion and Senate Confirmation of Supreme Court Nominees." *Journal of Politics* 72: 767–784.

Kastellec, Jonathan P., Jeffrey R. Lax, Michael Malecki, and Justin H. Phillips. 2015. "Polarizing the Electoral Connection: Partisan Representation in Supreme Court Confirmation Politics." *Journal of Politics* 77: 767–784.

Kelsh, John P. 1999. "The Opinion Delivery Practices of the United States Supreme Court, 1790–1945." *Washington University Law Quarterly* 77: 137–182.

Kernell, Samuel. 2000. "Life Before Polls: Ohio Politicians Predict the 1828 Presidential Vote." *PS* 33: 569–574.

Kirkpatrick, Jennet. 2020. "Fairness Has a Face: Neutrality and Descriptive Representation on Courts." *Politics, Groups, and Identities* 8: 803–811.

Klarman, Michael. 1995. "*Brown*, Originalism, and Constitutional Theory: A Response to Professor McConnell." *Virginia Law Review* 81: 1881–1936.

———. 1996. "Rethinking the Civil Rights and Civil Liberties Revolutions." *Virginia Law Review* 82: 1–67.

———. 1998. "What's So Great About Constitutionalism?" *Northwestern University Law Review* 93: 145–259.

Knowles, Helen J. 2008. "The Supreme Court as Civic Educator: Free Speech According to Justice Kennedy." *First Amendment Law Review* 6: 252–284.

———. 2009. *The Tie Goes To Freedom: Justice Anthony M. Kennedy on Liberty.* Lanham, MD: Rowman & Littlefield.

———. 2021. *Making Minimum Wage.* Norman: University of Oklahoma Press.

Knowles, Helen J., and Julianne A. Toia. 2014. "Defining 'Popular Constitutionalism': The Kramer Versus Kramer Problem." *Southern University Law Review* 42: 31–56.

Kramer, Larry D. 2004. *The People Themselves: Popular Constitutionalism and Judicial Review.* New York: Oxford University Press.

———. 2012. "Judicial Supremacy and the End of Judicial Restraint." *California Law Review* 100: 621–634.

Krewson, Christopher N. 2019. "Save this Honorable Court: Shaping Public Perceptions of the Supreme Court Off the Bench." *Political Research Quarterly* 72: 686–699.

Krewson, Christopher N., David Lassen, and Ryan J. Owens. 2018. "Research Note: Twitter and the Supreme Court: An Examination of Congressional Tweets about the Supreme Court." *Justice System Journal* 39: 322–330.

Krewson, Christopher N., and Jean R. Schroedel. 2020. "Public Views of the U.S. Supreme Court in the Aftermath of the Kavanaugh Confirmation." *Social Science Quarterly* 101: 1430–1441.

Krewson, Christopher N., and Ryan J. Owens. 2021. "Public Support for Judicial Philosophies: Evidence From a Conjoint Experiment." *Journal of Law and Courts* 9: 89–110.

Kritzer, Herbert M. 1979. "Federal Judges and Their Political Environment: The Influence of Public Opinion." *American Journal of Political Science* 23: 194–207.

Kromphardt, Christopher D., and Michael F. Salamone. 2021. "Unpresidented! What Happens When the President Attacks the Federal Judiciary on Twitter." *Journal of Information Technology & Politics* 18: 84–100.

Kugler, Matthew B., and Lior Jacob Strahilevitz. 2016. "Actual Expectations of Privacy. Fourth Amendment Doctrine and the Mosaic Theory." *Supreme Court Review* 2015: 205–263.

———. 2017. "The Myth of Fourth Amendment Circularity." *University of Chicago Law Review* 84: 1747–1812.

Lain, Corinna Barrett. 2004. "Countermajoritarian Hero or Zero? Rethinking the Warren Court's Role in the Criminal Procedure Revolution." *University of Pennsylvania Law Review* 152: 1361–1452.

———. 2012. "Upside-Down Judicial Review." *Georgetown Law Journal* 101: 113–183.

———. 2015. "God, Civic Virtue, and the American Way: Reconstructing *Engel*." *Stanford Law Review* 67: 479–555.

———. 2016. "Three Supreme Court 'Failures' and a Story of Supreme Court Success." *Vanderbilt Law Review* 69: 1019–1074.

Landes, William M., and Richard Posner. 1976. "Legal Precedent: A Theoretical and Empirical Analysis." *Journal of Law & Economics* 19: 249–307.

Lauderdale, Benjamin E., and Tom S. Clark. 2012. "The Supreme Court's Many Median Justices." *American Political Science Review* 106: 847–866.

Lerner, Craig S., and Nelson Lund. 2010. "Judicial Duty and the Supreme Court's Cult of Celebrity." *George Washington Law Review* 78: 1255–1259.

Leuchtenburg, William E. 2005. "Symposium: Locating the Constitutional Center Judges and Mainstream Values: A Multidisciplinary Exploration: Charles Evans Hughes – The Center Holds." *North Carolina Law Review* 84: 1187–1202.

Levendusky, Matthew W. 2010. *The Partisan Sort: How Liberals Became Democrats and Conservatives Became Republicans.* Chicago: University of Chicago Press.

Levinson, Sanford. 1988. *Constitutional Faith.* Princeton, NJ: Princeton University Press.

Lindgren, James, and Steven G. Calabresi. 2001. "Ranking the Presidents of the United States 1789–2000." *Constitutional Commentary* 18: 583–603.

Lindquist, Stefanie A., and Pamela C. Corley. 2013. "National Policy Preferences and Judicial Review of State Statutes at the United States Supreme Court." *Publius* 43: 151–178.

Linos, Katerina, and Kimberly Twist. 2016. "The Supreme Court, the Media, and Public Opinion: Comparing Experimental and Observational Methods." *Journal of Legal Studies* 45: 223–254.

Lippmann, Walter. 1922. *Public Opinion.* New York: Harcourt.

———. 1925. *The Phantom Public.* New York: Harcourt.

Liptak, Adam. 2019. "Supreme Court Lets Trump Proceed on Border Wall." July 26.

———. 2021. "Justice Barrett Says the Supreme Court's Work is Not Affected by Politics." *New York Times*, September 13.

Lizotte, Mary-Kate. 2020. *Gender Differences in Public Opinion: Values and Political Consequences.* Philadelphia: Temple University Press.

Lofgren, Charles A. 1987. *The Plessy Case: A Legal-Historical Interpretation.* New York: Oxford University Press.

Lu, Fan, and Bradford Jones. 2019. "Effects of Belief Versus Experiential Discrimination on Race-Based Linked Fate." *Politics, Groups, and Identities* 7: 615–624.

Main, Jackson Turner. 1961. *The Antifederalists: Critics of the Constitution.* Chapel Hill: University of North Carolina Press.

Malhotra, Neil, and Stephen A. Jessee. 2014. "Ideological Proximity and Support for the Supreme Court." *Political Behavior* 36: 817–846.

Mansbridge, Jane. 1999. "Should Blacks Represent Blacks and Women Represent Women? A Contingent 'Yes.'" *Journal of Politics* 61: 628–657.

Mark, Alyx, and Michael A. Zilis. 2018. "The Conditional Effectiveness of Legislative Threats: How Court Curbing Alters the Behavior of (Some) Supreme Court Justices." *Political Research Quarterly* 73: 570–583.

Marshall, Thomas R. 1989. *Public Opinion and the Supreme Court.* London: Allen-Unwin.

———. 2008. *Public Opinion and the Rehnquist Court.* Albany: SUNY Press.

———. 2015. "The Debate Over Health Care." In *Polarized Politics: The Impact of Divisiveness in the US Political System,* edited by William Crotty, 309–326. Boulder, CO: Lynne Rienner.

———. 2016. *Public Opinion, Public Policy, and Smoking.* Lanham, MD: Lexington Press.

Marshall, Thomas R., and John Connolly. 2021. "The Triumph of Legal Realism: Americans' Changing Perceptions of the United States Supreme Court." Paper Presented at the 2021 Annual Meeting of the Midwest Political Science Association, Chicago, IL, April 4–7.

Martens, Allison. 2007. "Reconsidering Judicial Supremacy: From the Counter-Majoritarian Difficulty to Constitutional Transformations." *Perspectives on Politics* 5: 447–459.

Martin, Andrew D., and Kevin M. Quinn. 2002. "Dynamic Ideal Point Estimation via Markov Chain Monte Carlo for the U.S. Supreme Court, 1953–1999." *Political Analysis* 10: 134–153.

———. 2007. "Assessing Preference Change on the US Supreme Court." *Journal of Law, Economics, & Organization* 23: 365–385.

Mason, Alpheus T. 1956. *Harlan Fiske Stone: Pillar of the Law.* New York: Viking.

———. 1964. *The States Rights Debate: Antifederalists and the Constitution.* Englewood Cliffs, NJ: Prentice-Hall.

Masood, Ali S., Benjamin J. Kassow, and Donald R. Songer. 2019. "The Aggregate Dynamics of Lower Court Responses to the US Supreme Court." *Journal of Law and Courts* 80: 159–186.

Maveety, Nancy. 2008. *Queen's Court: Judicial Power in the Rehnquist Era.* Lawrence: University of Kansas Press.

McClain, Paula D., Jessica D. Johnson Carew, Eugene Walton, Jr., and Candis S. Watts. 2009. "Group Membership, Group Identity, and Group Consciousness:

Measures of Racial Identity in American Politics?" *Annual Review of Political Science* 12: 471–485.

McFadden, Trevor N., and Vetan Kapoor. 2021. "The Precedential Effects of the Supreme Court's Emergency Stays." *Harvard Journal of Law and Public Policy* 44: 827–915.

McGinnis, John O. 1999. "Justice Without Justices." *Constitutional Commentary* 16: 541–548.

McGuire, Kevin T. 2015. "Birth Order, Preferences, and Norms on the U.S. Supreme Court." *Law & Society Review* 49: 945–972.

McGuire, Kevin T., and James A. Stimson. 2004. "The Least Dangerous Branch Revisited: New Evidence on Supreme Court Responsiveness to Public Preferences." *Journal of Politics* 66: 1018–1035.

Meiklejohn, Alexander. 1961. "The First Amendment is an Absolute." *Supreme Court Review* 1961: 245–266.

Metroka, Brandon. 2018. "Rethinking the Assignment of Ideological Direction." *Justice System Journal* 38: 331–377.

Middlekauff, Robert. 1982. *The Glorious Cause: The American Revolution 1763–1789*. New York: Oxford University Press.

Miller, John C. 1959. *Alexander Hamilton: Portrait in Paradox*. New York: H.B. Harper & Brothers.

Minor, Benjamin Stuart, and Georg Vanberg. 2016. "Judicial Retirements and the Staying Power of U.S. Supreme Court Decisions." *Journal of Empirical Legal Studies* 13: 5–26.

Mischler, William, and Reginald S. Sheehan. 1993. "The Supreme Court as a Countermajoritarian Institution? The Impact of Public Opinion on Supreme Court Decisions." *American Political Science Review* 87: 87–101.

Mondak, Jeffrey J., and Shannon Smithey. 1997. "The Dynamics of Public Support for the Supreme Court." *Journal of Politics* 59: 1114–1142.

———. 1994. "Response: Popular Influence on Supreme Court Decisions." *American Political Science Review* 88: 716–724.

Moyer, Laura P., John Szmer, Susan Haire, and Robert K. Christensen. 2020. "Diversity, Consensus, and Decision Making: Evidence From the U.S. Courts of Appeals." *Politics, Groups, and Identities* 8: 822–833.

Murphy, Walter F. 1964. *Elements of Judicial Strategy*. Chicago: University of Chicago Press.

Nash, Gary. 2005. *The Unknown American Revolution*. London: Viking.

Nelson, Michael J., and Alicia Uribe-McGuire. 2017. "Opportunity and Overrides: The Effect of Institutional Public Support on Congressional Overrides of Supreme Court Decisions." *Political Research Quarterly* 70: 632–643.

Nelson, Michael J., and James L. Gibson. 2019. "How Does Hyperpoliticized Rhetoric Affect the US Supreme Court's Legitimacy?" *Journal of Politics* 81: 1512–1516.

Nelson, Michael J., and Patrick D. Tucker. 2021. "The Stability and Durability of the US Supreme Court's Legitimacy." *Journal of Politics* 83: 767–771.

Nemacheck, Christine. 2021. "Trump's Lasting Impact on the Federal Judiciary." *Policy Studies* 42: 544–562.

Neumann, Elizabeth Noelle. 1977. "Public Opinion and the Classical Tradition: A Reevaluation." *Public Opinion Quarterly* 43: 143–156.

Nicholson, Stephen P., and Thomas G. Hansford. 2014. "Partisans in Robes: Party Cues and Public Acceptance of Supreme Court Decisions." *American Journal of Political Science* 58: 620–636.

Norpoth, Helmut, and Jeffrey A. Segal. 1994. "Comment: Popular Influence on Supreme Court Decisions." *American Political Science Review* 88: 711–716.

O'Brien, David M. 2020. *Storm Center: The Supreme Court in American Politics.* 9th edition. New York: W.W. Norton & Company.

Overby, L. Marvin, Beth Henschen, Michael H. Walsh, and Julie Strauss. 1992. "Courting Constituents? An Analysis of the Senate Confirmation Vote on Justice Clarence Thomas." *American Political Science Review* 86: 997–1003.

Owens, Mark E. 2018. "Changing Senate Norms: Judicial Confirmations in a Nuclear Age." *PS* 51: 119–123.

Owens, Ryan J., and David A. Simon. 2012. "Explaining the Supreme Court's Shrinking Docket." *William & Mary Law Review* 53: 1219–1285.

Owens, Ryan J., and Justin Wedeking. 2012. "Predicting Drift on Politically Insulated Institutions: A Study of Ideological Drift on the United States Supreme Court." *Journal of Politics* 74: 487–500.

Owens, Ryan J., and Patrick C. Wohlfarth. 2017. "Public Mood, Previous Electoral Experience, and Responsiveness Among Federal Circuit Court Judges." *American Politics Research* 45: 1003–1031.

———. 2019. "The Influence of Home-State Reputation and Public Opinion on Federal Circuit Court Judges." *Journal of Law and Courts* 80: 187–214.

Pacelle, Richard L., Jr. 2002. *The Role of the Supreme Court in American Politics.* Boulder, CO: Westview.

Page, Benjamin I., and Robert Y. Shapiro. 1982. "Changes in Americans' Policy Preferences, 1935–1979." *Public Opinion Quarterly* 46: 24–42.

———. 1983. "Effects of Public Opinion on Policy." *American Political Science Review* 77: 175–190.

———. 1992. *The Rational Public.* Chicago: University of Chicago Press.

Palmer, Paul A. 1936. "The Concept of Public Opinion in Political Theory." In *Essays in History and Political Theory in Honor of Charles H. McIlwain,* edited by Carl F. Wittke, 230–257. Cambridge, MA: Harvard University Press.

Parker, Christopher M. 2018. "Federalism and Historical Voting on the U.S. Supreme Court." *Justice System Journal* 39: 228–252.

Parker, Christopher M., and Benjamin W. Woodson. 2020. "Normative Preferences and Responses to Dissension on the U.S. Supreme Court." *Justice System Journal* 41: 220–243.

Parmet, Wendy. 2021. "Roman Catholic Diocese of Brooklyn v. Cuomo – The Supreme Court and Pandemic Controls." *New England Journal of Medicine* 384: 199–201.

Pasley, James. 2019. "45 Landmark Supreme Court Cases That Changed American Life As We Knew It." *Business Insider,* August 29. https://www.businessinsider.com/landmark-us-supreme-court-cases-2019-8.

Paulson, Michael S. 2016. "Checking the Court." *New York University Journal of Law & Liberty* 10: 18–115.

Pederson, William D., and Norman W. Provizer. 1993. *Great Justices of the U.S. Supreme Court: Ratings & Case Studies.* New York: Peter Lang.

Peltason, Jack. 1955. *Federal Courts in the Political Process.* Garden City, NY: Doubleday & Co.

Perry, Barbara A. 1989. "The Life and Death of the 'Catholic Seat' on the United States Supreme Court." *Journal of Law & Politics* 55: 55–92.

———. 1991. *A "Representative" Supreme Court? The Impact of Race, Religion, and Gender on Appointments.* Westport, CT: Greenwood Press.

Perry, Barbara A., and Henry J. Abraham. 1998. "A 'Representative' Supreme Court? The Thomas, Ginsburg, and Breyer Appointments." *Judicature* 81: 158–165.

Perry, H. W. 1991. *Deciding to Decide: Agenda Setting in the United States Supreme Court.* Cambridge, MA: Harvard University Press.

Persily, Nathaniel, Jack Citrin, and Patrick J. Egan, eds. 2008. *Public Opinion and Constitutional Controversy.* New York: Oxford University Press.

Persily, Nathaniel and Kelli Lammie. 2004. "Perceptions of Corruption and Campaign Finance: When Public Opinion Determines Constitutional Law." *University of Pennsylvania Law Review* 153: 119–180.

Phillips, Michael J. 2000. *The Lochner Court, Myth and Reality: Substantive Due Process From the 1890s to the 1930s.* Westport, CT: Praeger.

Pildes, Richard H. 2011a. "Is the Supreme Court a 'Majoritarian' Institution?" *The Supreme Court Review* 2010: 103–158.

———. 2011b. "Why the Center Does Not Hold: The Causes of Hyperpolarized Democracy in America." *California Law Review* 99: 273–333.

Pohlman, Zachary B. 2020. "*Stare Decisis* and the Supreme Court(s): What States Can Learn From *Gamble.*" *Notre Dame Law Review* 95: 1731–1762.

Posner, Eric A., and Cass R. Sunstein. 2016. "Institutional Flip-Flops." *Texas Law Review* 94: 485–536.

Posner, Richard A. 2008. *How Judges Think.* Cambridge, MA: Harvard University Press.

———. 2013. "The Supreme Court and Celebrity Culture." *Chicago-Kent Law Review* 88: 299–305.

Post, Robert C. 2001. "The Supreme Court Opinion as Institutional Practice: Dissent, Legal Scholarship, and Decision-Making in the Taft Court." *Minnesota Law Review* 85: 1267–1390.

———. 2011. "Participatory Democracy and Free Speech." *Virginia Law Review* 97: 477–489.

Powell, Thomas Reed. 1924. "The Judiciality of Minimum-Wage Legislation." *Harvard Law Review* 37: 545–573.

Primus, Richard. 2010. "Public Consensus as Constitutional Authority." *George Washington Law Review* 78: 1207–1231.

Pritchett, C. Herman. 1941. "Divisions of Opinions Among Justices of the U.S. Supreme Court, 1939–1941." *American Political Science Review* 35: 890–898.

———. 1948. *The Roosevelt Court: A Study in Judicial Politics and Values, 1937–1947.* New York: Macmillan.

Putnam, William L. 1997. *John Peter Zenger and the Fundamental Freedom.* Jefferson, NC: McFarland & Company.

Racek, Scott A. 2014. *Public Opinion and the Roberts Court.* Ph.D. Dissertation. College Park, MD: University of Maryland.

Ramirez, Mark D. 2008. "Procedural Perceptions and Support for the U.S. Supreme Court." *Political Psychology* 29: 675–698.

Randall, Willard S. 2003. *Alexander Hamilton: A Life.* New York: Harper Collins.

Rehnquist, William H. 1986. "Constitutional Law and Public Opinion." *Suffolk University Law Review* 20: 751–769.

———. 1987. *The Supreme Court: How It Was, How It Is.* New York: Morrow.

Rice, Douglas. 2014. "The Impact of Supreme Court Activity on the Judicial Agenda." *Law & Society Review* 48: 63–90.

Robinson, Claude. 1932. *Straw Polls: A Study of Political Prediction.* New York: Columbia University Press.

———. 1937. "Recent Developments in the Straw Poll Field." *Public Opinion Quarterly* 1: 45–56.

Rogol, Natalie C., Matthew D. Montgomery, and Justin T. Kingsland. 2018. "Going Public: Presidential Impact on Supreme Court Decision-Making." *Justice System Journal* 39: 210–227.

Rogowski, Jon C., and Andrew R. Stone. 2019. "How Political Contestation Over Judicial Nominations Polarizes Americans' Attitudes Toward the Supreme Court." *British Journal of Political Science* 51: 1–19.

Rosen, Jeffrey. 2006. *The Most Democratic Branch: How the Courts Serve America.* New York: Oxford University Press.

Rosenberg, Gerald. 1991. *The Hollow Hope: Can Courts Bring About Social Change?* Chicago: University of Chicago Press.

Rosenblum, Victor. 1955. *Law as a Political Instrument.* Garden City, NY: Doubleday & Co.

Rossiter, Clinton. 1964. *Alexander Hamilton and the Constitution.* New York: Harcourt, Brace & World.

Ruiz, Rebecca R., Robert Gebeloff, Steve Eder, and Ben Protess. 2020. "Trump Stamps G.O.P. Imprint on the Courts." *New York Times*, March 19.

Sachs, Stephen E. 2015. "Originalism as a Theory of Legal Change." *Harvard Journal of Law & Public Policy* 38: 817–888.

Salamone, Michael F. 2018. *Perceptions of a Polarized Court: How Division Among Justices Shapes the Supreme Court's Public Image.* Philadelphia: Temple University Press.

Salzberger, Eli M. 1993. "A Positive Analysis of the Doctrine of Separation of Powers, or Why Do We Have an Independent Judiciary?" *International Review of Law and Economics* 13: 349–379.

Scalia, Antonin. 1989. "Originalism: The Lesser Evil." *University of Cincinnati Law Review* 57: 849–865.

Schauer, Frederick. 2019. *"Stare Decisis* – Rhetoric and Reality in the Supreme Court." *Supreme Court Review* 2018: 121–143.

Scheb, John M., II, and William Lyons. 2000. "The Myth of Legality and Public Evaluations of the Supreme Court." *Social Science Quarterly* 81: 928–940.

———. 2001. "Judicial Behavior and Public Opinion: Popular Expectations Regarding the Factors That Influence Supreme Court Decisions." *Political Behavior* 23: 181–194.

Scherer, Nancy. 2005. *Scoring Points: Politics, Activists, and the Lower Federal Court Appointment Process.* Palo Alto, CA: Stanford University Press.

Schmidt, Christopher W. 2013. "Beyond the Opinion: Supreme Court Justices and Extrajudicial Speech." *Chicago-Kent Law Review* 88: 487–509.

Schoenherr, Jessica A., Elizabet A. Lane, and Miles T. Armaly. 2020. "The Purpose of Senatorial Grandstanding During Supreme Court Confirmation Hearings." *Journal of Law and Courts* 8: 333–358.

Schwartz, Bernard. 2000. "Supreme Court Superstars: The Ten Greatest Justices." In *The Supreme Court in American Society*, edited by Kermit Hall, 315–359. New York: Garland.

Segal, Jeffrey A., and Harold J. Spaeth. 1993. *The Supreme Court and the Attitudinal Model.* New York: Cambridge University Press.

———. 1996. "The Influence of *Stare Decisis* on the Votes of United States Supreme Court Justices." *American Journal of Political Science* 40: 971–1003.

———. 2002. *The Supreme Court and the Attitudinal Model Revisited.* New York: Cambridge University Press.

Segal, Jeffrey A., Harold J. Spaeth, and Sara C. Benesh. 2005. *The Supreme Court in the American Legal System.* New York: Cambridge University Press.

Segall, Eric J. 2018. "Eight Justices Are Enough: A Proposal to Improve the United States Supreme Court." *Pepperdine Law Review* 45: 547–573.

Sen, Maya. 2017. "How Political Signals Affect Public Support for Judicial Nominations: Evidence from a Conjoint Experiment." *Political Research Quarterly* 70: 374–393.

Shapiro, Ilya. November 13, 2016. "Justice Kennedy: The Once and Future Swing Vote." https://www.cato.org/commentary/justice-kennedy-once-future-swing -vote.

———. 2020. *Supreme Disorder: Judicial Nominations and the Politics of America's Highest Court.* Washington, DC: Regnery.

Shapiro, Robert. 2011. "Public Opinion and American Democracy." *Public Opinion Quarterly* 75: 982–1017.

Sharma, Hemant, and Colin Glennon. 2013. "A Case for Supreme Court Term Limits? The Changing Ideological Relationship Between Appointing Presidents and Supreme Court Justices." *Politics & Policy* 41: 267–297.

Sheldon, Charles H. 1967. "Public Opinion and High Courts: Communist Party Cases in Four Constitutional Systems." *Western Political Quarterly* 15: 341–360.

Sherry, Suzanna. 2016. "Is the Supreme Court Failing at Its Job, or Are We Failing at Ours?" *Vanderbilt Law Review* 69: 909–917.

————. 2020. "Our Kardashian Court (And How to Fix It)." *Iowa Law Review* 106: 181–228.

Siegel, Neil. 2005. "A Theory in Search of a Court, and Itself: Judicial Minimalism at the Supreme Court." *Michigan Law Review* 103: 1951–2019.

Sill, Kaitlyn L., Emily T. Metzgar, and Stella M. Rouse. 2013. "Media Coverage of the U.S. Supreme Court: How Do Journalists Assess the Importance of Court Decisions?" *Political Communications* 30: 58–80.

Silverstein, Gordon, and John Haley. 2010. "The Supreme Court and Public Opinion in Times of War and Crisis." *Hastings Law Journal* 61: 1453–1501.

Sinozich, Sofi. 2016. "Public Opinion on the US Supreme Court, 1973–2015." *Public Opinion Quarterly* 81: 173–195.

Smith, Joseph H. 1976. "An Independent Judiciary: The Colonial Background." *University of Pennsylvania Law Review* 124: 1104–1156.

Smith, Rogers M. 1997. *Civic Ideals: Conflicting Visions of Citizenship in U.S. History*. New Haven, CT: Yale University Press.

Smith, Tom W. 1990. "The First Straw? A Study of the Origins of Election Polls." *Public Opinion Quarterly* 54: 21–36.

Solberg, Rorie Spill, and Jennifer Segal Diascro. 2020. "A Retrospective on Obama's Judges: Diversity, Intersectionality, and Symbolic Representation." *Politics, Groups, and Identities* 8: 471–487.

Solomine, Michael E., and James L. Walker. 1994. "The Supreme Court, Judicial Review, and the Public: Leadership Versus Dialogue." *Constitutional Commentary* 11: 1–6.

Sonnert, Gerhard. 2020. "Give Chance a Chance: An Alternative Process for Selecting U.S. Supreme Court Justices." *Alternatives: Global, Local Political* 45: 33–49.

Spier, Hans. 1950. "Historical Development of Public Opinion." *American Journal of Sociology* 55: 378–388.

Spriggs, James F., II, and Paul J. Wahlbeck. 1997. "Amicus Curiae and the Role of Information at the Supreme Court." *Political Research Quarterly* 50: 365–386.

Spriggs, James F., II, and Thomas G. Hansford. 2001. "Explaining the Overruling of U.S. Supreme Court Precedent." *Journal of Politics* 63: 1091–1111.

Sternberg, Sebastian, Sylvain Brouard, and Christoph Honnige. 2021. "The Legitimacy-Conferring Capacity of Constitutional Courts: Evidence From a Comparative Survey Experiment." *European Journal of Political Research*. DOI: 10.1111/1475-6765.12480.

Stimson, James A. 1991, 1999. *Public Opinion in America – Moods, Cycles, and Swings*. Boulder, CO: Westview.

————. 2012. "On the Meaning & Measurement of Mood." *Daedalus* 141: 23–34.

Stone, Geoffrey. 2010. "Understanding Supreme Court Confirmations." *The Supreme Court Review* 2010: 381–467.

Strayhorn, Joshua A. 2020. "Ideological Competition and Conflict in the Judicial Hierarchy." *American Journal of Political Science* 64: 371–384.

Strother, Logan. 2019. "Case Salience and the Influence of External Constraints on the Supreme Court." *Journal of Law and Courts* 7: 121–147.

Strother, Logan, and Colin Glennon. 2021. "An Experimental Investigation of the Effect of Supreme Court Justices' Public Rhetoric on Perceptions of Judicial Legitimacy." *Law & Social Inquiry* 46: 435–454.

Sunstein, Cass R. 1999. *One Case at a Time: Judicial Minimalism on the Supreme Court.* Cambridge, MA: Harvard University Press.

———. 2005. *Radicals in Robes.* New York: Basic Books.

———. 2006. "Problems With Minimalism." *Stanford Law Review* 58: 1899–1918.

———. 2007. "If People Would Be Outraged by Their Rulings, Should Judges Care?" *Stanford Law Review* 60: 155–212.

———. 2015. "Unanimity and Disagreement on the Supreme Court." *Cornell Law Review* 100: 769–823.

Thayer, James Bradley. 1893. "The Origin and Scope of the American Doctrine of Constitutional Law." *Harvard Law Review* 7: 129–156.

Tocqueville, Alexis de. 1848, 1966. *Democracy in America.* Edited by J. P. Mayer and Max Lerner. New York: Harper.

Truman, David. 1951. *The Governmental Process: Political Interests and Public Opinion.* New York: Alfred A. Knopf.

Tushnet, Mark. 1999. *Taking the Constitution Away From the Courts.* Princeton, NJ: Princeton University Press.

———. 2020. *Taking Back the Constitution: Activist Judges and the Next Age of American Law.* New Haven, CT: Yale University Press.

Tushnet, Mark, Alan L. Chen, and Joseph Blocher. 2017. *Free Speech Beyond Words.* New York: New York University Press.

Unah, Isaac, and Ange-Marie Hancock. 2006. "U.S. Supreme Court Decision Making: Case Salience, and the Attitudinal Model." *Law & Policy* 28: 295–320.

Unah, Isaac, Kristen Rosano, and K. Dawn Milam. 2015. "U.S. Supreme Court Justices and Public Mood." *Journal of Law & Politics* 30: 293–339.

Unger, Michael A. 2008. "After the Supreme Word: The Effect of *McCreary County v. ACLU* (2005) and *Van Orden v. Perry* (2005) on Support for Public Displays of the Ten Commandments." *American Politics Research* 36: 750–775.

Ura, Joseph Daniel. 2014. "Backlash and Legitimation: Macro Political Responses to Supreme Court Decisions." *American Journal of Political Science* 58: 110–126.

Ura, Joseph Daniel, and Patrick C. Wohlfarth. 2010. "'An Appeal to the People': Public Opinion and Congressional Support for the Supreme Court." *Journal of Politics* 72: 939–956.

Vidmar, Neil, and Phoebe Ellsworth. 1974. "Public Opinion and the Death Penalty." *Stanford Law Review* 26: 1245–1270.

Vining, Richard L., and Teena Wilhelm. 2012. "The Chief Justice as Advocate-in-Chief." *Judicature* 95: 267–274.

———. 2016. "The Chief Justice as Administrative Leader: Explaining Agenda Size." In *The Chief Justice,* edited by David J. Danelski and Artemus Ward, 357–373. Ann Arbor: University of Michigan Press.

Vladeck, Stephen I. 2019. "The Solicitor General and the Shadow Docket." *Harvard Law Review* 133: 123–162.

Waldron, Jeremy. 2014. "Five to Four: Why Do Bare Majorities Rule on Courts?" *Yale Law Journal* 123: 1692–1731.

Walker, Thomas G., Lee Epstein, and William J. Dixon. 1988. "On the Mysterious Demise of Consensual Norms in the United States Supreme Court." *Journal of Politics* 50: 361–389.

Ward, Artemus. 2003. *Deciding to Leave: The Politics of Retirement From the United States Supreme Court.* Albany: SUNY Press.

Warren, Earl. 1955. "The Law and the Future." *Fortune* 52: 106–108.

Wedeking, Justin, and Michael Z. Zillis. 2018. "Disagreeable Rhetoric and the Prospect of Public Opposition: Opinion Moderation on the U.S. Supreme Court." *Political Research Quarterly* 71: 381–394.

Weissberg, Robert. *Public Opinion and Popular Government.* Englewood Cliffs, NJ: Prentice-Hall.

Wells, Lloyd M. 1957. "The Supreme Court and Public Opinion 1937–1957." In *The Politics of Judicial Review 1937–1957*, edited by John M. Claunch, 33–46. Dallas: Southern Methodist University Press.

Whittington, Keith E. 2005. "'Interpose Your Friendly Hand': Political Support for the Exercise of Judicial Review by the United States Supreme Court." *American Political Science Review* 99: 583–596.

———. 2006. "Presidents, Senates, and Failed Supreme Court Nominations." *The Supreme Court Review* 2006: 401–438.

———. 2014. "The Least Activist Supreme Court in History: The Roberts Court and the Exercise of Judicial Review." *Notre Dame Law Review* 89: 2219–2252.

Williams, Ryan J., and Jacob F. H. Smith. 2019. "Keeping Up Appearances: Non-Policy Court Responses to Public Opinion." *Justice System Journal* 39: 54–74.

Wilson, James G. 1993. "The Role of Public Opinion in Constitutional Interpretation." *Brigham Young University Law Review* 1994: 1039–1138.

Winter, Steven L. 1991. "An Upside/Down View of the Countermajoritarian Difficulty." *Texas Law Review* 69: 1881–1927.

Wlezien, Christopher, and Stuart N. Soroka. 2011. "Inequality in Policy Responsiveness?" In *Who Gets Represented?*, edited by Peter K. Enns and Christopher Wlezien, 285–310. New York: Sage.

Wolkins, George G. 1922. "The Seizure of John Hancock's Sloop *Liberty.*" *Proceedings of the Massachusetts Historical Society* 55: 239–284.

Woodson, Benjamin. 2015. "Politicization and the Two Modes of Evaluating Judicial Decisions." *Journal of Law and Courts* 3: 193–221.

———. 2018. "The Dynamics of Legitimacy Change for the U.S. Supreme Court." *Justice System Journal* 39: 79–94.

———. 2019. "The Causes of the Legitimacy-Conferring and Republican Schoolmaster Capabilities of Courts." *Journal of Law and Courts* 7: 281–303.

Yamomoto, Eric K. 2018. *In the Shadow of Korematsu: Democratic Liberties and National Security.* New York: Oxford University Press.

Zigerell, L. J. 2013. "Justice Has Served: U.S. Supreme Court Justice Retirement Strategies." *Justice System Journal* 34: 208–227.

Zilis, Michael A. 2015. *The Limits of Legitimacy*. Ann Arbor: University of Michigan Press.

———. 2017. "The Political Consequences of Supreme Court Consensus: Media Coverage, Public Opinion, and Unanimity as a Public-Facing Strategy." *Washington University Journal of Law and Policy* 54: 229–241.

———. 2020. "How Identity Politics Polarizes Rule of Law Opinions." *Political Behavior* 43: 1–21.

———. 2021. "Cognitive Heuristics, Inter-Institutional Politics, and Public Perceptions of Insulated Institutions: The Case of the U.S. Supreme Court." *International Journal of Public Opinion Research* 33: 76–98.

Zilis, Michael A., and Xander Borne. 2021. "Defying the Supreme Court: The Impact of Overt Resistance to Landmark Legal Rulings." *Social Science Quarterly* 102: 920–938.

Zink, James R., James F. Spriggs, II, and John T. Scott. 2009. "Courting the Public: The Influence of Decision Attributes on Individuals' Views of Court Opinions." *Journal of Politics* 71: 909–925.

Index

ideological and representative drift, 89–91, 124; ideologically balanced Courts and representation, 97–99, 128–30, 135
interest groups, 3, 16, 28

Jefferson, Thomas, 12–13
jurisdiction stripping, 14, 130–31, 135
justices, Supreme Court: as issues in presidential elections, 27; life tenure and term limits, 2, 10, 31–32, 92, 128–29; "most dangerous" justice, 48, 80; nominations, 21–22, 38n23, 131–35; popularity of, 68; retirements and replacements of, 22, 78, 89–92, 128; speeches and appearances by, 23

legitimacy, 18–19, 134–35, 137n13
liberty of contract, theory of, 13
Literary Digest poll, 15
living constitution, theory of, 33, 88–89

Madison, James, 12–13
marriage equality, 1–4
Marshall, John, 75
mechanistic jurisprudence, theory of, 32
media coverage, 20–21, 46
minimalism, theory of, 35, 88–89, 132
Monroe, James, 12–13

New Deal era, 16–17, 131
normative versus empirical arguments, 35
norms: defined, 75–76, 78n22; examples of, 75–76. *See also* representation

Obergefell v. Hodges (2015), 1–4, 53, 105
originalism, theory of, 32, 88, 132

partisanship: in justices' voting patterns, 109–10, 112, 116–18, 119nn15–17, 125, 131–32; public perceptions of, 22–28, 118, 125; on Supreme Court nominations, 21–22, 28–29, 132–33

poll correction, 68–71, 73–75, 122–23, 132
poll-matching: advantages and limitations of, 45–49; classification scheme, 52–54; defined, 3–5, 45–55; list of poll-matched decisions, 139–58; reweighting procedures, 47, 54–55, 77n2
poll updating, 71–73, 122–23, 132
popular constitutionalism, 19–20
precedents and super-precedents, 32–33, 63, 71–73
preferred position. *See* counter-majoritarianism
public mood measure, 44–45
public opinion: approval ratings for the Supreme Court and justices, 26, 68, 133; impact on Supreme Court behavior, 17–19, 43, 66, 100; meanings of, 11–12; measurement of, 4, 11, 15–16; "most important problem" poll question, 62; perceptions of and preferences for Supreme Court decision-making, 24–32, 121, 126–27; public knowledge of Supreme Court, 48–49; settled expectations, 63–65, 76; Supreme Court's impact on, 19, 67–68, 122
public opinion polls: modern polls, 4, 15–16, 105–6; straw polls, 15

racial cases, 13–14, 61, 115–16
Rehnquist, William, 34, 95
representation: colonial era courts, 9–11; patterns in, 60–76, 79–101, 105–18, 122–26, 132, 135; proposed reforms, impact of, 127–33, 135; specific groups, 6, 13–14, 32, 105–18, 121, 123–25; Supreme Court compared to other policymakers, 5, 68–71, 73–75, 123, 130. *See also* academic views of the Supreme Court; decisional impact; great and near-great justices;

About the Author

Thomas R. Marshall is professor of political science at the University of Texas at Arlington where he teaches classes in American government, public opinion, and campaigns and elections. He received his BA from Miami University and his PhD from the University of Minnesota. He has authored four prior books and numerous articles and book chapters focusing on public opinion, elections, health care, and the Supreme Court.

www.ingramcontent.com/pod-product-compliance
Lightning Source LLC
Chambersburg PA
CBHW050651280326
41932CB00015B/2865